WHAT WARS LEAVE BEHIND

WHAT WARS LEAVE BEHIND

The Faceless and the Forgotten

J. Malcolm Garcia

University of Missouri Press
Columbia

University of Missouri Press, Columbia, Missouri 65211
Printed and bound in the United States of America

First paperback printing, 2022

Cataloging-in-Publication data is available from the Library of Congress
ISBN 978-0-8262-2021-9 (hardcover : alk. paper)
ISBN 978-0-8262-2275-6 (paperback : alk. paper)

∞ This paper meets the requirements of the
American National Standard for Permanence of Paper
for Printed Library Materials, Z39.48, 1984.

Typefaces: Alia JY, Myriad Pro

Contents

Acknowledgments

My deepest thanks to the editors of *Ascent Magazine, Guernica: A Magazine of Art & Politics, McSweeney's, New Letters, Southampton Review, Superstition Review, Vice Magazine, and Virginia Quarterly Review* for first publishing these stories.

Jesse Barker, Scott Canon, Heather World, Doug Worgul, Chuck Murphy, Leonore Dvorkin, and Lucian Truscott IV all read early drafts of these stories and often read them more times than any one person should. I cannot thank all of you enough for your critiques. And no, I'm sorry to say, my spelling and punctuation has not improved despite your best efforts.

Everyone at University of Missouri Press has made this a wonderful writing experience, especially Clair Willcox, Sara Davis, Kristi Henson, and others whose names I do not know but who also put their time into the making of this book.

I especially want to thank Polly Kummel for her insightful copy edits line by line, paragraph by paragraph, page by page. I learned from you and am a better writer for it.

As always, thanks to Stella Ferrer, David Littlejohn, Dale Maharidge, and Scott Olsen for their encouragement and Molly Giles for her patience with my first strained efforts at storytelling.

Finally, I want to thank my former colleagues at the Ozanam Center and Hospitality House in San Francisco and the homeless men and women I once worked with there. All of you supported my first hesitant steps toward journalism. I won't forget you.

WHAT WARS
LEAVE BEHIND

Introduction

I slipped, fell, and started sliding off the rock ledge. I reached for a sapling, roots, anything, waving my arms until finally I seized the prosthetic leg of the man behind me as I passed him. He clung to the arm of a man ahead of him, and together they pulled me up. Shaken, I sat beside him on the ledge fronting the entrance to his cave.

"You don't look too good, but your leg is strong," an old man said to the man who helped me.

The three of us laughed. The year was 2002. July. I was filing a story from the Afghan city of Bamiyan, about a ten-hour drive north of Kabul and known best for the Buddha statues that had been carved into the cliffs in the sixth century. They were destroyed in March 2001 after the Taliban government declared they were idols and therefore sacrilegious.

Those cliffs then housed about 200 mostly ethnic Hazara families. Desperation drove them there. It was windy. It was boiling hot in the summer, frigid in the winter. It was hard to reach. It was easy to slip on the loose gravel and narrow footpaths. A man's prosthetic leg had just saved me from tumbling down a mountain. I was alive, sitting outside a remote cave with destitute war survivors and dying for an ice-cold glass of water. Instead I got what I came for: a story.

The man with the prosthetic leg told me that in 1994 he had stood here and watched the Taliban battle their way into Bamiyan. He saw men and women killed by machine guns and mortar fire. He left and walked to Kabul. He stepped on a mine and lost his leg. He had only recently returned. Before, he said, he had a home. Now he had a cave.

The Hazara are the dominant ethnic group in Bamiyan and date to Genghis Khan's warriors. In the late 1990s reports of Taliban fighters' massacring Hazara men, women, and children in northern and central Afghanistan were common. The Taliban ransacked and destroyed homes.

After the Taliban were routed by the American-led international military coalition that invaded Afghanistan a little more than a month after the World Trade Center fell, Hazara families returned to villages that had been reduced to rubble. So they resorted to the caves, an uneven patchwork of openings across wind-chiseled rock. The caves interconnect like a beehive above the ruined city.

When I arrived in Kabul in November 2001 on my first overseas assignment, I knew little about Bamiyan and the slaughter of the Hazara and even less about Afghanistan. I knew social work because that's what I did until I was forty, when I decided to break into journalism. At the time, 1997, I was more than a little worried that, to follow a new calling, that of the wandering scribe, I had just thrown away a successful fourteen-year career helping homeless people.

Four years later I got my first glimpse of the consequences of war. Kabul's downtown was a giant rock pile of bomb-blasted buildings destroyed during decades of wars. Men with turbans and thick beards wandered the streets in frayed sandals. Donkeys pulled carts. Women drifted by in billowing body-length veils. Boys pushed wheelbarrows filled with grinning goat heads. Older boys shouldered Kalashnikovs. The broken streets teemed with commotion and dust and the shouts of vendors and the supplications of beggars. Makeshift camps without water or plumbing overflowed with refugees.

I returned to the States three months later and felt lost. I couldn't stop thinking about Afghanistan and the vacant stares I had absorbed from people who had lost everything. So I put them out of my mind by returning to Kabul again and again to be among them. No longer were they memories trapped inside my head but real people I lived with and who told me their stories. I also became acquainted with photographers from Europe, Asia, and South America. They pitched editors story ideas they had for Pakistan, the Middle East, and Africa. We hooked up, and I began writing about the poor and forgotten families I encountered along the way.

The people I have met and continue to meet in my travels across the globe move me, and I am angry that their suffering so easily falls beneath the radar of news coverage. I write about them because their anguish is what wars leave behind, what corruption and ineptitude and sheer meanness leave behind. I am drawn by the detritus of human upheaval—the prosthetic leg that may have saved my life—not the thrill of the kill.

I wrote the stories in this collection between 2004 and 2013. They take place in Kosovo, Chad, Egypt, Syria, and Afghanistan and Pakistan; the last two countries are where I have spent most of my time overseas and where American policy has played a large role. The stories reflect my interest in people who face problems I find hard to imagine: a mother seeking the release of her imprisoned son in Cairo, American soldiers on patrol in Kabul, Syrian children surviving as refugees. These people and others live in a universe parallel to the one the rest of us take for granted, with a roof over our heads, meals on our tables, the noise of children playing, the humdrum security of our lives. Yet we are not that far removed from the forgotten and overlooked. An unanticipated event such as the recent recession can devastate our lives in a flash and turn a comfortable dinner at home into a trip to the soup kitchen and a soiled mat on a gymnasium floor.

Reporting helps keep the world real for me, making it a tangible place where people live, breathe, survive, and occasionally triumph in ways that may seem dwarfed by their circumstances. I thrive by going to places I've never been and relying on instinct to ferret out the "people stories" lurking below the surface of the news.

I pack light: two pairs of pants, underwear, and socks, two shirts, and basic hygiene supplies. I carry my pack and laptop on the plane. I research and make plans, but I allow plenty of room for the serendipitous chance encounter, for the curve in the road that takes me somewhere I had not anticipated.

Which brings me back to Bamiyan.

I stayed on the mountain to interview the cave dwellers until late afternoon. Then I walked down the mountain, followed by the man with the prosthetic leg, who worried I might fall again. When I reached the city, I caught a taxi. The driver took me to a building that had once housed

Taliban government officials but now provided rooms for the staff of the Belgian humanitarian aid organization Solidarités, which was putting me up.

When I arrived, an Afghan man working for Solidarités was sweeping the hall outside my room. He saw me and pointed to what I had dismissed as meaningless graffiti-like squiggles scrawled across my door. He explained that the thick black loops and scattered dots scrawled with a marker spelled the name of a Taliban leader, Mullah Mohammad Hassan, who had lived in my room. He too had lost a leg in the fighting.

"The Taliban arrested 300 Hazara people in Bamiyan," the Afghan said. "We were not fed. At night we were whipped on our backs with metal cables."

He held out his arms, palms up, to show me where Taliban soldiers had held his wrists against a boiling tub of water. He could no longer bend them. He moved down the hall to another door.

"Mullah Gul Mohammad Akhund," he read. (The Taliban will always be together.)

I heard someone yell something in French. In a minute music started to play. Several members of the Solidarités staff stepped out of a room and began dancing in the hall. The Afghan watched them. Then he took my hands and pressed my fingers against the scarred wrist of his right arm until I felt the rough ridges of dead skin that were like petrified wood. He looked at me as if he expected me to say something.

As if now I could understand.

PART I

Conflict Zones

I

Securing District 4

Kabul, Afghanistan: April 2004

I arrive at the base toward evening for a night patrol in the rain.

The captain, however, must pick up an Afghan police officer. On paper the American, Canadian, Icelandic, and western and eastern European soldiers of the international security assistance forces play only a supportive role for the central Afghan government. The captain explains that protocol requires an Afghan police officer to lead patrols. The captain calls me by my last name, as he does his soldiers, and tells me I will ride with him. I am an embedded reporter.

An hour later we leave the base in southern Kabul in a convoy of four Humvees, six soldiers in each vic, for the District 4 police station. The rain has stopped and the late afternoon light washes the sky and a few remaining clouds pink; as we proceed, it fades almost instantly to an impenetrable depth without stars.

Kids wave to us from the shadows, as they always do when we go out on a night patrol, but it seems to me they also have one hand behind their back—and then I'll hear their rocks ding our doors.

Our dirt road climbs a hill. Birds swarm the broken towers of a stone castle that overlooks our progress. A soldier seated behind me tells me he served in Bosnia. There he knew who was hostile and who was not. In Afghanistan he doesn't. Every Afghan, he says, is suspect. "We're all scared. This is not our country, not our culture. Going out at night in town with all these people with weapons, it's very different for us. My gun is nothing compared to their cache of rocket-propelled grenades. The minute we stop being scared is the time something will happen."

We drive until we reach the ruins of a square cinder-block building. An oil lamp lights one small window. We get out, stones crunching beneath our boots. We hear someone approaching, and then a man in a green uniform, illuminated by our headlights, materializes before us.

"Who are you?" he asks our translator.

The captain shows him a paper.

"What do you need?" he asks, glancing at the document.

"We need a police officer on our patrol," our captain says through the translator.

"Which spot is yours to patrol?"

"District 4. Your station is part of District 4. We're here because we are mandated to bring a police officer along with us."

"We'll get you a guy."

He turns and disappears into the dark. He returns a short time later—first the sound of his boots and then he again materializes in the headlights—accompanied by a short thin man in a green jacket much too large for his narrow body. His pants form pools of cloth around his ankles, and mud has turned his sandals to boots. Patchy stubble mars his face like a burn. He introduces himself: Saif Ali.

Without another word he gets into the front seat of my vehicle and sits beside the captain, next to the passenger door. Saif turns around to shake hands. He does not distinguish me, the American reporter in the backseat wearing a helmet and Kevlar, from the soldiers in the Humvee.

We start up again and follow a narrow stone road that takes us behind the police station and into some woods. The opaque shapes of leafless trees loom above us. Dogs bark in a disjointed chorus. Mud huts stand stark and mute in the sweep of our headlights. We cross a bridge and listen to water rushing invisibly beneath us until we reach a checkpoint. A man on a cot outside a shack kicks out from some blankets and waves us through.

The captain tells me we have entered a bad area. Lots of robberies. But we should be fine, because we won't be stopping to do foot patrols. Don't need to. We're on a presence patrol only. We're not to do anything.

People just need to see us drive through and know we're here, nothing more.

The captain turns on the headlamp to illuminate Saif so the locals can see him. Saif stares out the windshield and raises a hand and smiles as if to reassure anyone watching us. Veiled women appear fleetingly on the side of the road, revealed by the sweep of our headlights. Stooped old men hold the hands of boys and watch us without expression, turning their heads slowly, as if pressured by a heavy wind. Dogs with sharply defined ribs snap at things in the rushing gutters.

The crackling of the radio pulls our attention away from the road. A static-filled voice shouts that unexploded ordnance has been found outside the Canadian Embassy in downtown Kabul. We're needed to assist in cordoning off streets around the embassy while engineers from a Canadian security detail detonate the ordnance.

The captain orders the driver to stop. We slow to a halt. Dust swirls, enveloping us as if we have been consumed by a gray cloud. The radio makes sporadic hissing sounds, and then the hissing stops altogether. The captain looks at Saif. No unauthorized national is allowed to enter a security cordon staffed by international forces. Saif's police station is in the opposite direction from the embassy. "We don't have time to drop him off," the captain says.

"Where's the translator?"

"In the vic behind us, sir," a soldier says.

The captain shrugs.

"Thank you," he says, reaching over Saif and opening his door. "Thank you." Saif doesn't move. He looks at the captain, head cocked to one side. *What?* is written all over his face.

"Thank you," the captain says again and shoves him. Saif shifts away, moves one leg out the door, looks at the captain, and says something that sounds like a question, but none of us can understand him.

"Thank you!" the captain snaps, pushing Saif the rest of the way out the door. Saif waves his arms to keep his balance but collapses in the dirt. A soldier beside me gets out, steps over Saif, sits in his seat, and slams the door shut.

Twenty minutes later we arrive at the Canadian Embassy and take positions at two intersections. An electrical storm quakes the sky, and the ground appears to shudder beneath our feet. We wait for the engineers from the security detail to disarm and remove the ordnance.

To break the monotony we shout, "Thank you!" back and forth to each other, because, really, there was something hilarious about the captain's dumping Saif off like that.

After a while we stop shouting, "Thank you!" having wrung the joke of all its humor. In the tedium of waiting we become quiet and irritable, and we shrug off the begging children clutching at our pants. In the silence I think of Saif, the look on his face.

We were out of there so fast. Did Saif make it back to the police station? I don't know. I do know we left him in our dust, and he scrambled backward, crab-like, as our Humvees spewed stones and raced past him. I turned and watched Saif staring after us, staring through me, the confused look on his face changed to fury. Then the night swallowed him whole, as in a movie, when the camera pulls back and the image left behind shrinks in an ever-tightening circle of dimming light.

I mill around the perimeter of the Canadian Embassy in what feels like an endless night. A dirty moon holds the sky. The silence fills spaces. That look of Saif's. It still bores into me more an hour later, a presence demanding to be addressed. *The captain decided to toss you out, Saif, not me. What could I have done? I am not a soldier.*

I close my eyes, but Saif stays with me. His expression does not change. He bides his time. The captain could not wait. He had his duty. But he will need Saif tomorrow and the day after that and the day after that and the day after that.

2

Beneath Us the Ground Still Moves

Pakistan: April 2006

In the hazy afternoon light I walk past row after row of tan Pakistan army tents, taut and erect and aligned, past row after row of aluminum toilet stalls and water dispensers on parched ground. My translator, Tahir, shoos children away, stops them from clutching my hands, but they follow us anyway, churning dust around their sore-covered feet.

"Fifty rupees," a girl begs, hand cupped out to me.

Ahead of us, older kids kick a soccer ball but don't chase it. We proceed toward them and they part in the still air.

Open mouthed and squinting, men and women and more children peer out of their tents in silent confusion, puzzled by the commotion of my passing, and then they too follow us, revived by something that is breaking the humid monotony of the afternoon, suddenly so different from the stagnation of their waiting lives. Waiting for what? Certainly not for me, but for now I will do.

"Where you from?"

"Who are you?"

"What do you want?"

A man stops me and shows me a petition. "Help us," he says.

"Sir," Tahir says, reading it to me, "we are earthquake victims of Azad Kashmir. Sir, we are staying at H-11 tent village in Islamabad. Sir, the governments of Pakistan and Azad Kashmir tell us to go back. Sir, our houses and lands are totally destroyed in the earthquake. We don't want to go there because we are afraid of living there. Sir, after 31 March the government stopped the work of relief in H-11 tent village [in] Islamabad. Sir, that is why we are signing this petition to you of the United Nations for you to help us."

"I am not with the United Nations," I say and hand the petition back.

The man stares at the worn creased paper and its uncertain signatures of people unaccustomed to writing. He watches me, mouth slowly going slack, eyes turned dull. He walks back to his tent, where a woman and some children wait. Together they sit by the open flap and stare out at nothing, eyes immobile and unblinking, the sweat-dampened petition still in his hand.

"Who gives these people the darkness? They are not Muslim. They turned away from Islam," Tahir says. "That's why they are here."

This is a constant refrain with Tahir, a moralizing drumbeat that gives me a headache: the people have turned from Allah to pursue lives of sin, and for this they are being punished, just as some fundamentalist Christians claimed that Hurricane Katrina was the result of the sinful lives of the people of New Orleans.

"Bullshit," I say.

"The Holy Koran says there is a beginning and an end. I think the earthquake was the start of the end of time."

I continue through the dust and the desultory heat toward the administration tent and swat at flies. No breeze.

I had not visited Pakistan since the spring of 2004, when President Pervez Musharraf said in a CNN interview that a high-level Qaeda leader was cornered in the tribal territories bordering Afghanistan. Perhaps Osama bin Laden himself. It turned out to be no one of significance, a local criminal at best, but not before I—and dozens of other journalists—descended on Pakistan and chased phantoms for weeks until, exhausted and discouraged and empty-handed, we abandoned our dreams of the story of the century and left for home and tamer fare.

When a 7.6-magnitude earthquake struck Pakistan and Kashmir a year and a half later, on October 8, 2005, I saw BBC news reports of the dust and the blood, broken homes and broken bones, landslides and buried villages, wailing mothers and dead children. I frantically e-mailed Yassin, my driver in Pakistan.

In the two months we had worked together, I had found Yassin to be a soft-spoken man who adhered to the old school of the British Raj. His graying hair was slicked cleanly to one side, his mustache clipped and dead even over his lip. He called me sir, opened the car door for me, carried my backpack, and refused to state a specific salary but accepted whatever I paid him without counting it in my presence. At first I mistakenly called him "Yeltsin," which drove him to distraction.

"My name is Yassin, sir," he would remind me, the shell of his austere professionalism cracking with frustration.

In contrast Yassin's brother-in-law Tahir had liked to indulge in conspiracy theories I considered nonsensical. He questioned the existence of Osama bin Laden—a figment of the American government to explain September 11, which was really the result of an Israeli conspiracy to pit Americans against Muslims, he asserted.

"Just translate," I would say.

He laughed, his long black hair bouncing about his shoulders. He was a smooth-faced naive young man who lived with his parents and didn't know jack shit outside the anti-American propaganda all around him. Yet, when I covered an anti-American protest following the Abu Ghraib prison scandal and was shoved to the ground and kicked and punched by angry demonstrators, Tahir pulled me to safety.

Neither he nor Yassin was harmed in the quake. I stopped watching the BBC reports. Knowing they were safe put the catastrophe out of my mind. Although the earthquake was the strongest on record for Pakistan and left thousands of people dead, it created little buzz in the United States. The devastation of Hurricane Katrina was little more than a month old, and no Americans had died in Pakistan.

But the earthquake was on par with Katrina—both in terms of its human toll and its show of nature's sheer power. The quake began as a wave undulating the ground, but the convulsions quickly grew wilder, shaking walls, rooftops, and floors. Within seconds mud-brick homes collapsed, larger buildings imploded, and landslides buried entire villages. The epicenter was just six miles south of Muzaffarabad, the river-valley capital of Pakistani Kashmir—known here as Azad Kashmir, or Free Kashmir—and close enough to the surface to jolt that city of

750,000 people down to its foundations in seconds. Buildings rocked a hundred miles away in Islamabad and even in Kabul and New Delhi. In less than half a minute more than 87,000 people were dead, at least 17,000 of whom were in Pakistani Kashmir. Muzaffarabad and scores of other towns and villages didn't vanish, but they looked as if a giant had trampled them. And it wasn't over. The first shock was followed by twenty-two aftershocks, including one temblor with a magnitude of 6.2—strong enough to move houses off their foundations.

Given the quake's catastrophic impact, Pakistan's role in the U.S.-led war on terror, and the destabilizing effect thousands of displaced people could have on the government, Yassin expected more interest from me. He would call periodically, asking why I hadn't visited, why I wasn't active on behalf of "poor Pakistan."

"But you are OK," I told him.

"Excuse me, sir," he said. "This is not about Mr. Yassin. The people have no homes. We are afraid. Don't forget us. Beneath us the ground still moves."

The ground has moved for centuries. As the Indian subcontinent continues to creep about 1.6 inches farther north every year, earthquakes are the inevitable consequence of Earth's internal belching, which is still causing uplift and forming mountains in the Himalayan, Karakoram, Pamir, and Hindu Kush ranges. A severe earthquake rocked central Asia as far back as 962. In 1555 a quake in northern Pakistan is said to have created gaping holes in the ground that rerouted rivers and swallowed houses whole. On May 31, 1935, the southern city of Quetta was awakened by what many thought was thunder until the noise roared up from beneath their feet. Calling to various gods, people ran from their houses. At least 36,000 people perished. Next door, in the Indian province of Gujarat on the morning of January 26, 2001, one of the deadliest earthquakes in Indian history killed nearly 20,000 people.

The impact was similar to the legendary 1906 San Francisco earthquake. Back then wooden buildings collapsed within seconds. The ground opened and closed. Buildings fell to ruins. Fires devastated the city, consuming nearly 29,000 buildings in a 4.7-square-mile area. About 3,000 people died, and thousands were left homeless. I was living in San Francisco eighty-three years later when, on October 17, 1989, an earthquake with a magnitude of 7.1 struck the San Francisco Bay Area again just before the third game of the World Series at Candlestick Park. The tremor collapsed a section of the San Francisco–Oakland Bay Bridge. Power was knocked out, and the city was dark for the first time since 1906. The quake killed 62 people throughout central California, injured 3,757, and left more than 12,000 homeless. I was in my Mission District house when the floor started moving. I planted myself in a doorway as the floor continued to roll. I tipped left and right, then tilted more deeply as the house swayed and rattled. I knew that if the shaking did not stop soon, the house would come crashing down on top of me.

Mohammed Norin Qajia, the camp administrator, sits beneath a large burlap overhang waving a fistful of wilted flowers near his face. Around him silent men sort through papers without interest. No one moves except to push his turban off his hot forehead. I smell their perspiration, the stink of their heat-laden boredom.

Qajia raises his eyes at the sight of me, mildly surprised. Considering me, he strokes his brown-stained, chest-length beard. He looks at my curious followers standing a few feet away and sighs.

"You are?"

"Journalist."

"Why are you here?"

"I want to know about the relief effort."

"The relief is over. We are into reconstruction. A few people have gone. Some have returned to their villages, others just moved on."

He waves the flowers and lets out a long breath.

"Tea?"

"No, thank you."

He watches a boy try to fly a paper kite. It falls and rips on the stony ground.

"The rest stay," Qajia says, the worn flowers drooping in his hand. "They will all go back one day, whether they want to or not. I just don't know when."

In February, when Yassin's appeals finally convinced me to prepare for a trip to Islamabad, the Pakistani government announced that all 170 earthquake-relief camps sheltering 200,000 people would be closed on March 31. The government and aid officials declared that emergency assistance was finished. It was time for displaced families to rebuild their villages. But government officials privately conceded it would take at least three years to construct 600,000 new housing units and restore 6,000 schools, 400 hospitals, and dozens of government buildings.

International aid had also fallen short. The United Nations received about $352 million in quake aid instead of the urgently requested $550 million. The lack of funds forced the U.N. to reduce, and sometimes ground, flights to remote villages that needed emergency food supplies. After a hesitant start the Pakistani military and outside relief organizations coordinated their efforts to clear roads and airlift tons of blankets and tents to stranded survivors. Unusually warm winter temperatures eased the suffering of the nearly 400,000 people that the U.N. estimated were living in the mountains.

Shortly after the earthquake the government promised affected families a one-time payment of 25,000 rupees ($417) to meet basic needs. These same families were to receive another one-time payment of 75,000 rupees ($1,250), as well as up to 175,000 rupees ($2,917) to repair or rebuild their houses. Families with at least three children younger than eighteen would be eligible for an additional cash grant of 3,000 rupees ($50) per month for six months, according to Nadeem Ahmed, a general in the Pakistani army and deputy chair of the Earthquake Reconstruction and Rehabilitation Authority.

"We encourage the people to return and do some work in their villages and rehabilitate themselves," Ahmed said. "We have categorically insisted that this be voluntary."

Officials with aid organizations, however, said that families in relief camps received much less assistance than promised. Just a tent, some food, and a free lift home. No cash. And they questioned the voluntary nature of the families' departure from the camps.

The U.N. High Commissioner for Refugees cited evidence of the application of intense psychological pressure to move people out, whether they had a village to return to or not. Some camp managers, the UNHCR found, were telling families to leave on a specific date and that this would be the only time free transportation would be available to them.

"There was an element, a push factor, being exercised by people eager to see the camps empty earlier," acknowledged Jan Vandemoortele, the U.N.'s resident humanitarian coordinator in Islamabad. "We have contacted locals and gone to these areas and clarified the situation."

Yassin waits for us in the car, protecting it from thieves. He trims his mustache. Tahir stoops to pick up a coin.

"Fifty rupees the girl asked for, but I find," he says, pocketing the coin.

"Lucky you."

"You don't approve, sir?"

"It's less than a dollar, man. What does it mean to you? Give it to the girl."

"Allah says worship me. They do not, and the earth swallowed them, and they suffer. That is what I think."

A man gestures to us from his tent, and he pulls the flap back. I duck my head, enter the cramped quarters, and sit on a straw mat between a stack of malodorous blankets and dirty pots, pans, and plastic tubs. The people who have been following me crowd inside. Others remain outside, sealing the open flap with their bodies. The stifling air fills my lungs with cotton.

The man hands me a cup of tea and a plate of chicken. I put the tin plate by my feet to draw away the flies and so I can sip the tepid tea without distraction. Outside the tent I see the lurking elongated shadows of bearded men who are wondering who we are and what we are doing. Everyone around me talks at once.

"The earth shook as much as it was possible for it to shake. I have lost everything."

"I saw buildings fall, people crushed."

"I thought India had attacked us."

"The earth made dreadful noises like *gloom, gloom, gloom.*"

"I have been here six months."

"Four months."

"Five."

"How long can we stay here?"

I raise my hands, imploring them to stop. But they keep shouting above one another for my attention, and I turn away from their distorted faces, which are so close to mine that the stench of their frustration clouds my mind. A girl opens the back of the tent, and the rest quiet down, as if their breath has been drawn out with the hot air. A baby with a swollen bug bite on the back of her leg makes the only noise, wailing in discomfort. Her mother, a woman in her midtwenties, Shahkeel Ahmad, holds her, rocking back and forth. The straw mat crackles beneath her legs.

"Our homes are lost in Kashmir," Shahkeel says. "Five children died here in this camp in the winter. The government says it will provide everything but you see nothing. Now we face summer. What will the results be from the heat?"

She stares at me, a white veil slipping back from her face. I shake my head.

"I don't know."

"I was asleep. It was very difficult. The house was falling all around me. It was like a blast. The earth made dreadful noises. We have been here six months. We don't have a home anywhere. How long can we stay?"

"I don't know."

"No one does. We are alone. All around us are people like you—people we don't know, who know nothing."

Women throw water on the makeshift clinic's brick floor to wash away the dust, but the water turns it into muddy pools. Behind a counter men stand next to shelves stuffed with bottles and sacks of pills. Dr. Bababar Bilal examines Shahkeel's baby, squeezing the bite gently with his fingers. He gives Shahkeel some ointment. She leaves, head bowed, not even a backward glance in my direction.

"I see a lot of that, bug bites," Dr. Bilal says, wiping his hands on a washcloth. "Mostly I see acute diarrhea. With blood, without blood. Water is the problem. Old adults and babies. I see 40 to 50 people a day, 25 to 30 with diarrhea. We also see chicken pox, measles, acute respiratory problems due to overcrowding."

He introduces me to Mohammed Younis, a man in his fifties who is stretched on a cot with an intravenous drip in his arm. The blazingly white walls reflect the bare lightbulbs that illuminate the hall. Flies dart back and forth. Mohammed, who is surrounded by twenty-five neatly made beds, squints at us. Acute diarrhea. He has been in the camp four months. A Kashmiri. Everything gone.

In his Muzaffarabad clinic Dr. Bilal was examining a patient when the patient said, “Doctor, it’s an earthquake,” and then the roof collapsed on the man, and he died where he lay. Dr. Bilal tried to reach the door but was thrown backward into his chair and buried in debris. He remained conscious. His only thoughts were “Get me out. Someone needs to find me.”

He called from beneath the broken cinder blocks covering his body, and his coworkers dragged him free. That night his feet hurt but nothing more. Yes, yes, people tell him he talks very fast now, but nothing is wrong. His nerves are fine. He just has a lot on his mind, a lot to do. “They say rehabilitation and all that stuff comes now. I’ll decide what to do when I see what happens. My house still stands, but it is not habitable, so I came here to work.”

On a piece of paper he scribbles an address as fast as he talks and thrusts it at me. “Here, here, here. My house in Muzaffarabad. Go. See for yourself what happened there.”

Dr. Bilal looks at Mohammed, who stares at the ceiling. Even after we leave the room, Mohammed doesn’t stir; he is alive but vacant. His only connection to reality is the needle in his arm.

Yassin drives me to the ten-story Margalla Towers in Islamabad, a posh apartment complex for the well-to-do that was destroyed in the earthquake. I stare up at the collapsed rooms. Exterior stairways hang off the walls like broken jaws. Jagged hills of concrete lie in piles. Stray dogs pick their way through the mountainous rubble. Shredded bits of clothing cling to crushed cars.

“Sir,” Yassin says, “afterward we had too much little shaking.”

“Aftershocks, you mean.”

“Yes. Everyone was afraid. No one wanted to be inside. I see rich people sleeping on the ground. No AC, no fans. Just themselves.”

I nod. I show Yassin the slip of paper from Dr. Bilal and ask, “How far is Muzaffarabad?”

“Three-, four-hour drive.”

“Can you take us tomorrow?”

"No problem, sir. Why not?"

I fold the paper and stuff it back into my pocket. Traffic races by us just feet away, but it sounds distant. Cars honk, trucks spew black clouds of diesel exhaust. Vendors push jangling ice-cream carts and wagons filled with cheap tourist knickknacks, and I hear the day's cricket scores announced on a radio somewhere nearby yet far from the tomb-like quiet sheathing me in the ruins of the Margalla Towers.

"Sir?"

"Yes?"

"It is OK. Not so many died here."

He points to a shattered first-floor apartment; there, standing yet, is a cracked table that holds a teacup and teaspoon on a saucer and a small pitcher for cream.

"It was morning time. I was in the bed. That night my family and I also slept outside. The earthquake made us all equals."

For days after the San Francisco earthquake in 1989, I would wake in the middle of the night, jump out from under the sheets, and stand in a doorway, braced against what I thought was another shock wave. This happened night after night until eventually I realized that my knees were knocking together, shaking the bed while I slept, and that when I felt the bed move, I was the one quaking.

At the guesthouse in Islamabad I put a pillow between my knees and try to sleep despite this lonely memory of my fears.

A gray drizzly morning, low skies. Driving to Muzaffarabad four hours north. We climb steep looping roads through densely green, tree-covered mountains, past closed shops and restaurants. We stop for water served in oilcans at roadside stalls, sit on crates stuffed with live chickens for market, and wrap ourselves in shawls against the cold and rain. I listen to water spill out of gutters and, using my fingers, eat beef kebab and rice. The rain forges trenches in the hills around us, pouring onto the road where boulders from landslides create an obstacle course for traffic.

We reach Muzaffarabad by late afternoon. The twisting streets, gouged with potholes, bustle with donkey-drawn carts that are stacked with firewood and jockey for position next to a jam-up of cars and garishly decorated buses. Herding water buffalo and goats, boys with sticks saunter along the side of the road. Men converse, squatting flat-footed at the side of the road. I hear hammers pounding steel. It looks to me like Muzaffarabad has recovered from the quake.

Then I see the tents, hundreds of them, lining the hills amid the rubble where houses once stood, on the rooftops of shops—a combination of squatters' huts and organized government-financed shelters. Road crews with pickaxes, shovels, and wheelbarrows are still clearing the streets. Flapping in the air above them are the flags of dozens of nongovernmental aid organizations.

We stop by the World Food Programme to arrange a ride on a relief flight, but the government has grounded the WFP until further notice. "They say relief is over. We have all this food but can't get off the ground," Abdul Qadir, a flight coordinator, tells us.

At Mercy Corps, an American aid agency, Saqib Awan, an engineer, tells us the same thing. He also mentions a Muzaffarabad relief camp where, he says, families have been asked to leave. "The chief of police told everyone they must go from there."

"Don't rely on rumor," his director tells him.

"This is happening," Saqib insists.

He walks us to the door.

"It is called Camp Narul."

Toward evening I sit in a restaurant drinking tea with Hagi Javed-ul-Hassan. He explains that he is in charge of the Jamaat-ud-Dawa relief camps in Muzaffarabad and gives me his business card. Jamaat-ud-Dawa epitomizes the complexities of Kashmir. The group took the lead in earthquake aid efforts, operating clinics and seventeen camps, even working alongside U.S. soldiers in October, but on April 28 (while I was in the country), the State Department announced it was freezing the U.S. assets of Jamaat-ud-Dawa and its sister organization, Idara Khidmat-e-Khalq, on the ground that both groups merely served as fronts for Lashkar-e-Taiba, a Kashmiri organization of Islamist terrorists opposing the Indian government. According to the State Department, Lashkar-e-Taiba simply changed its named to Jamaat-ud-Dawa in 2001 after Lashkar was targeted by the U.N. for its ties to al-Qaeda and created IKK "as a public welfare organization that it utilizes to collect funds and undertake other activities." Some of its actions do indeed seem dubious, such as taking donations through its website for the purchase of livestock to sacrifice in prayers for earthquake victims—donations that must be wired directly to Jamaat-ud-Dawa bank accounts in Lahore. But no one questions that the organization has helped UNICEF, the U.N. High Commissioner for Refugees, World Food Programme, and World Health Organization. The question is its motive. Jamaat-ud-Dawa says it is helping earthquake victims ignored by the West because they are Muslims. The U.S. State Department says Jamaat-ud-Dawa is recruiting.

"We welcome you, we share in relief work together," Hagi says, smiling. "The American soldier without a gun is very sweet. The government and religious organizations cannot face alone this destruction. It's a good opportunity to normalize relations between ideologies and communities. What do you think?"

I had heard a similar sentiment that morning at our hotel when a bearded young man who claimed to be a Taliban fighter and a member of Jamaat-ud-Dawa pulled Tahir aside and asked to speak to me. Later, in his room, he offered to share his breakfast of fried eggs and toast and told me his name was Hamza. He had been fighting in Indian-controlled Kashmir; a battered Kalashnikov rifle stood in one corner. He pointed out the window at a truckload of squatting shawl-cloaked men.

"Mujahideen," he said. "Freedom fighters."

"Coming from the Indian side?"

"Yes."

He appraised me from head to foot and then asked to snap my picture with his cell phone. "Don't worry, American," he said, focusing his shot. "I won't kill you."

He laughed at my startled expression. "You see," Hamza said, "I know you are here to help."

But to help with what? To raise awareness for earthquake victims or to give good press to Jamaat-ud-Dawa? For people here who believe that the earthquake signaled the beginning of the end of time, Jamaat-ud-Dawa becomes attractive as a chance to practice a form of Islam as supposedly pure as the Taliban had in Afghanistan—a last-ditch effort to purge themselves of their sins. Of course, if the world does not end—as thankfully it hasn't yet—through guys like Hamza, Jamaat-ud-Dawa still increases its membership, its political clout, and the reach of its militant philosophy and anti-Western rhetoric.

For tonight it doesn't matter. I'm grateful for this temporary halt in hostilities. In the damp restaurant I smile at Hagi Javed-ul-Hassan and warm myself with tea. He smiles too, then says, "United States aggression is another thing from the relief effort. Relief work cannot remove the real evil of American foreign policy. This we will always resist. More tea?"

The announcer's box above the ruins of a mossy weed-filled soccer stadium serves as the administrative office of Camp Narul, known officially as Camp Management Organization. Empty for years, it was being rebuilt when the earthquakes struck. Now, cracked and broken from neglect and the massive temblor, it will probably never be repaired.

Rain has turned the camp into a swamp. Tahir and I slog toward the announcer's box through ankle-deep mud around dozens of tents. Tahir wipes his new brown loafers with every step. People emerge from their tents, walking on their toes in the mud, and call to us, pleading for information.

Tahir and I walk up a broken stairwell on the back side of the stadium. Blankets and sheets and boxes of food fill spaces in walls left vacant by fallen cinder blocks. At the top of the stairwell is the door to the announcer's box. I open it. Men, all shouting on cell phones, crowd around the one desk in the otherwise empty room. They need supplies. They need a truck. They need someone who's not in the building. But they haven't forgotten their manners. When we enter, they offer us chairs, and an elderly man scurries into the hall to make tea.

"This camp will not close by force," says the budget manager, Fazal Urrehman, speaking above the mad ringing of his cell phone. "People go voluntarily. If only one family stays, this camp will remain open."

Every one of the 14,673 families still in the camp will be helped, he assures me, but they must remain flexible. He points out the window to a mountain dotted with tents, many between undamaged homes. "Most of the land where people have tents belongs to someone else. There is a conflict with people returning to their property and people camped on their property. This land does not belong to the government. So we may move this camp to another tent village on government land."

He shows me a press release announcing national cricket and soccer games: national entertainment to reduce the trauma of the earthquake.

He laughs. "There is no trauma among these people. The trauma is here among us working in these facilities for the last six months with people unwilling to leave here."

Tahir and I walk outside into an upheaval of activity. Jeeps spraying jets of brown water from deep puddles jounce up the rocky roads snaking through the camp. The drivers park beside tents where families have already stacked their belongings under the searing blaze of the sun: *blankets, pots, pans—*

Everyone is shouting. A camp manager speaks into a microphone: "The government of Pakistan is helping you move back. We provide only transportation. Everything you want to keep, you can keep. The government will provide you with farm equipment."

—a door, a bed, bags of flour, boxes filled to bursting, sheets wrapped around more pots and pans—

"What are we to do now?" asks a man.

"The government will tell you, not me," says the camp manager. "If you don't want to go back to your village, see who is in charge of your section of the camp, and they will tell you your options."

—chairs, tents, trunks, tin plates, tubs, shoes, firewood—

"They said I must go."

"Then you go. Don't give money to the police to let you live here."

—tarps, stacks of bread wrapped in scarves.

They shout and shove and throw things into the jeep.

"We've established tent villages for the disabled and those who don't want to go," the camp official assures the crowd through the microphone. "But you have to leave this place. The government will give you money."

The jeeps pull away, carrying families squeezed into spaces in the chaos of their packing. Behind them are barren plots of withered ground where their tents once stood. Strewn scraps of clothing, a red shirt, a black shoe, torn scarves, bricks, nothing worth picking through by those who remain, staring after the jeeps, which are gone now but for the fading sound of strained engines passing through the trees. Gone too: the noise and commotion here just seconds ago, leaving behind the gaping hole of sudden departure. Those here now will also soon be gone, their lives at a moment's notice a whirlwind of activity and flight followed by all this empty silence, with still others, staring and alone, left behind them. This is the transition from aid to rebuilding.

We follow the convoy out of the camp but lose it temporarily when a demonstration by Jamaat-ud-Dawa blocks the road. It takes us an hour to maneuver through the congestion of the crowd and continue out of Muzaffarabad, trailing the convoy toward the village of Punein. We stop at a roadside stall for water. A bridge spans the churning waters of the Jhelum River, and I walk over it to five fresh graves decorated with ribbons. A barefoot man, Mohammed Nazir, sweeps the graves and adjusts vases of plastic flowers.

"Earthquake?"

Mohammed nods, points.

"Here is my brother, daughter, wife, mother, father."

Mohammed tells me he has received only 25,000 rupees from the government—enough to bury his family and buy food but not enough to rebuild his house. He sleeps under the sky. He continues sweeping and starts to weep. He puts aside the fistful of twigs he uses as a broom and holds my hands, crying silently, head bowed. Unable to think of anything adequate, I say nothing.

"I was in Muzaffarabad at the time of the earthquake. I walked here [in] five hours," he tells me. "All the roads were blocked by landslides. I find the way myself. I was scared about my house and family. I just wanted to see one person who could give me news of my family. When I did, they told me they were dead."

The Jhelum boils past us in its rush downstream toward Muzaffarabad, where it courses through the city center, a torrent of mud and froth roiling beneath the bridge we just crossed. A strand of ribbon blows away from one of the graves. The wind carries it over rippling rice fields and the channels of cold clear water flowing through them.

"I always pray for them now," Mohammed says, still holding my hands. "I am waiting for my family to come back to me. It would be a sign of love if they come back. What do you think?"

We shadow the Jhelum through dense green fields and tree-lined mountains and an immense blue sky, the air refreshingly cool, and I am lulled almost to sleep, except for the memory of the grieving man that pricks me awake each time my eyes close. Then Yassin stops the car.

"What's wrong?"

"Look," he says.

Giant boulders from a recent landslide block the road. Construction crews remove the smaller rocks by hand and in wheelbarrows. Around us people move onto a steep narrow trail that leads from the road and into the mountains and around the landslide to the other side. They carry trunks heaved onto their shoulders, fat bundles of clothing slung over their backs. Small children and adults tramping a pedestrian thoroughfare into the woods. Some jeeps I saw earlier in Camp Narul turn around and return to Muzaffarabad.

"No more than a thirty-minute walk," a police officer tells Tahir.

Yassin lights a cigarette. "I'll stay here and watch the car, sir."

He drops the back of his seat, closes his eyes, and tells me, "I will pray for your safe return."

Within minutes I am out of breath from the climb. My legs ache and my heart pounds through my rib cage. None of the people burdened with their possessions seems fatigued. "They are mountain people," Tahir gasps. "Be strong, sir."

The fresh air and exercise inspire Tahir to philosophical musings after we bump past several men with long black beards. "You see them? These men with beards are jihadists. They hate America. They don't like your President Bush. But if one person is corrupt does not mean the whole country is corrupt? People don't know how to see the difference. What do you think?"

An informal traffic pattern exists. Outbound travelers use the trail below us, while my trail serves incoming hikers. Men stand on steep inclines and hold out their hands to help us maintain our balance and not give in to the pull of gravity. In return we tip them 25 cents.

No one talks except Tahir. "The Danish cartoonists made a mistake and we had protests. This is not good. What do you think?"

We follow the rough contours of the trail, slipping repeatedly on the pebble-strewn ground. Cracks from the earthquake fissure the soil, and I peer into one's black depths. We all freeze when someone dislodges a rock, afraid it may trigger a landslide, and we listen to it tumble downward until it fades into nothing. Then we proceed once again, climbing, gripping low-hanging tree limbs, sliding forward on our asses, getting back up, walking. Through it all Tahir continues undeterred. "If the Holy Koran is a book, and you read it and recite from it and don't understand it, are you Muslim? What do you think?"

After an hour we emerge into a clearing. Far below me I see the road and the Jhelum splashing over fallen rocks, taxi drivers out-hustling one another for those of us emerging from the mountain.

Our taxi vibrates violently and fills with gas fumes. The windows don't roll down. My head swims and Tahir's eyes bug out of his head. The driver lights a cigarette, and I cringe against the expected explosion, but nothing happens. We proceed down the pitted road and through shattered villages where flattened roofs look like rafts coasting off the sides of buildings clawed in half.

The driver follows the road around the Jhelum and into mountains. We chug and shake upward until we level out in a meadow and brake beside a shop. Tahir and I fall out of the taxi gasping.

"Are you not fine?" the shopkeeper asks us.

When I clear my lungs of gas fumes, I ask about Punein village. He points toward some tents. Beside the tents stand huts patched together with broken doors, strips of aluminum siding, and stacked chairs.

"This is Punein village," he says.

"Yes, I was in Narul camp," Parveen Akhtar tells me after a long moment.

She stares at the ground. When she entered the tent, she bowed her head and pulled a scarf below her eyes. Now as I speak to her, I notice how long it takes her to respond. Tahir repeats my questions several times. "She is too simple," he whispers.

"We were thrown out by the man in charge of camp," she says finally. "He said, 'We can't provide for you anymore.' He said, 'The aid of the world is not so much. If they can't give, how can we?' For six days he told us this. We left today."

Parveen was cleaning dishes when the earthquake started. The ground shifted beneath her feet and the roof collapsed on her. Her mother pulled her out, and together with Parveen's eight-year-old son and ten-year-old daughter they walked to Muzaffarabad.

I ask her how it feels to be back in Punein. She stares at her feet. I wait, Tahir translates, asks her again and again. Still nothing. "She is so simple. She can't answer your question," Tahir says.

Slowly Parveen turns to me. "What can I feel? My brother, sister, nephew died. My husband is in the army. I have two children. I am back here with nothing."

"I'm sorry."

"You are sorry—"

She looks at her feet, and I know she won't speak to me again.

I watch Parveen leave the tent, the flap scraping the hard ground as it closes behind her, sealing us in the stale air with her sadness until it presses down on me with the weight of a crowded room. I have seen too many people like her, not simple but lost, their lives suspended by grief and abandonment.

I don't get it. In its push to empty the relief camps the Pakistani government has turned thousands of displaced people into homeless refugees, in a country already facing strong internal antagonism from jihadist factions opposed to President Musharraf's close alliance with the United States. But American and Pakistani officials have all but abdicated the relief effort to Jamaat-ud-Dawa, despite their suspicion of its ties to terrorists, despite the hundreds of thousands of earthquake survivors who are likely to feel deep gratitude to people bent on our destruction. Instead the Pakistani government has withdrawn to the comfort of its flowcharts, which neatly delineate the relief phase from the reconstruction effort. It all works on paper. And that's good enough for us.

"You are sorry—"

I am sorry, Parveen, I truly am. I feel complicit in these empty plans because I accepted them, believed they were enough. As your sorrow, the sorrow around me here, simmers to a boil in the days, weeks, and months ahead, I will know my guilt is not enough. And I'm sorry for that, too.

Tahir and I leave Punein with our impervious taxi driver and are nearly asphyxiated by the time he drops us off at the trail. We begin the long painful uphill climb and gradually work our way back to the car, relieved to stumble off the mountain for good. Hands on our knees, we collect our breath. We have been gone four hours. I see Yassin's head tipped back in his seat. Asleep. Bastard.

"Come on," I tell Tahir. We creep toward the car. Shopkeepers in dilapidated roadside stalls watch us. At the count of three we push up and down on the trunk.

"Zalzala!" Tahir shouts in Urdu. "Earthquake!"

Yassin explodes, all legs and arms, bursts out of the car, and bolts down the road.

"Ai!"

I double over, convulsed with laughter. The shopkeepers cover their mouths, but I can see the smile in their eyes. Tahir howls and pounds on the car. I hear Yassin cursing and I laugh harder.

It is evening, and I sit on the third-floor deck of the Al-Habib Hotel, avoiding our room. The toilet—a porcelain shit hole in the floor—stinks like hell. A bare lightbulb above our three beds casts a hepatitis-yellow pall across the walls, further diminishing the room's appeal.

The mountains form dark lumps behind the Muzaffarabad skyline, and dozens of tents stand like beacons, reflecting the glow of moonlight. I see campfires and the flicker of oil-burning lamps. A truck rumbles down the road below us, and I feel its vibrations shudder through the walls.

In the room next to ours are Ishtiaq Ahmad, his wife, and their three boys; they have just returned from Karachi where they took refuge with his parents after the earthquake. Hours from now, as Tahir and I helicopter out with a team from the International Committee of the Red Cross to Talgran, a mountaintop village inaccessible by road, Ishtiaq and his family will return to their home in Hattian Bala village, not far from Punein.

"I am very lucky. No one in our family was hurt. I will help my brother in Hattian Bala prepare to be wed."

"Congratulations."

"It is life," he says, considering the mountains and the deepening night.

I watch his boys climb over trunks and mounds of clothes his wife tries to sort. One boy lurches against the bed. The balcony shakes. I assume another truck has passed below, but I see no traffic on the street.

"Zalzala," Ishtiaq gasps.

The shaking increases. I hear screams. Plaster chips off the walls and I grip my chair. I am not laughing now.

Then it stops.

"Aftershock," Ishtiaq says in a whisper. I let go of my chair, my fingers still clenched. Ishtiaq checks on his family. No one is hurt. Beneath us, as Yassin warned me, the ground still moves.

Midnight. Yassin snores like a bull. Tahir sleeps buried under blankets. I stare at the rotating ceiling fan and the cracks running around it.

"Yassin!" I shout.

He sleeps on. Through my window I see storm clouds seethe in the mountains, flashes of lightning. Scavenging dogs bark. I add the numbers locked in my head like counting sheep.

"Fifteen in my family die."

"Seven die in my family."

"My wife, my mother, they are gone."

Fifteen and seven and two. Twenty-four.

"Three in my family die. All are nephews."

"Ten in my family die. All are children and were in school."

Thirteen more. Fifty. The drone of still more voices keeps me counting.

"Six . . . four . . . eight . . ."

Yassin snores to wake the dawn. Tahir sleeps. I listen to an approaching thunderstorm. Counting into the night, I watch the fan spin. Counting into the night, I wait for our morning flight to Talgran.

I sit with Massimiliano Cartura of the International Committee of the Red Cross (ICRC) on the second floor of a concrete building surrounded by the collapsed mud huts of Talgran. The tents stand near plowed ground, and I smell damp earth and cow manure. A deep valley spreads below Talgran; melting mountain snow fills cold streams, and I can hear the water below the tops of trees.

I want to stay here longer than the few hours we have, so I can sleep in the grass under the stars, listen to the water. I have to remind myself that in this pastoral Eden of 1,700 souls, more than 300 men, women, and children died in the earthquake.

Massimiliano and I watch the villagers unload the helicopter that carried us here. They remove tools, vegetable seeds, and clothing. He checks off boxes on his clipboard. The villagers shout instructions to one another.

"Come! Take the bags!"

"Seeds over there!"

"Drop the tools there!"

Massimiliano's partner, Rashad Akhundov, talks to a man below our window who has not seen his nephew since the earthquake.

"When did you last see him?"

"That morning. He was going to his job in the clinic."

"Where?"

"Muzaffarabad."

"Do you know the name of the clinic?"

Massimiliano listens. Minutes ago he told the village elders that the ICRC could not provide for the people who had left the village and were now returning. All calculations of relief supplies, he explained, were based on the number of people in the village, without considering those who had left. The villagers would have to share with the returnees whatever they could spare.

"I'm sorry," Massimiliano said. "They say it's reconstruction, but people still need shelter and food, I know. But there is only so much we can do."

The men left muttering.

"How was he getting to Muzaffarabad?" Rashad asks the man with the missing nephew.

"By car."

Massimiliano arrived in Muzaffarabad in December. Three months later he was in Natajan when a tractor driver clearing a landslide discovered a body. From its shoes children recognized the corpse as that of a local fifteen-year-old boy.

"For me that moment was fundamental," Massimiliano says. "It was my first contact with death. Not by media reports or the stories of survivors but with my own eyes. Do you understand what I mean?"

I nod, but I have not seen any dead bodies here. I have walked through the remains of houses that presumably had bodies beneath them. Tahir and Yassin always wait for me by the car. They refuse to walk on the dead. I have never seen whomever might be under my feet.

"Was the car found?" Rashad asks.

"Yes."

"Was anyone in it?"

"Yes but not my nephew."

"Where was the car?"

"In landslide."

Massimiliano's translator, eighteen-year-old Amer Malik, joins us, passing around a bottle of water.

The day of the earthquake he saw many dead bodies but felt nothing in his heart. Then he heard girls calling from beneath a collapsed dormitory building. "Save us," they pleaded. He called to his neighbors, "Please, we have to help them," but they said no: "We have our own family problems. We don't know where our children are." "I'll do my best to save you," he told the girls and brought them water that he slid down a hole to them.

He returned in the morning. No one answered his calls. A bad smell rose out of the ground.

"They all died, I think. Now every day I feel those girls with me." His eyes redden and he looks away. Below us I hear a man complain that the shovels that arrived today have no handles.

"Were other bodies found in the car?" Rashad asks.

"Yes but not my nephew."

"Did you call the clinic?"

"Yes."

"Did he make it in that morning?"

"They had not seen him."

"This doesn't sound good."

Rashad rubs his eyes. Massimiliano, listening, shakes his head. Amer frowns. All this shared loss, and a helicopter full of supplies, and still we cannot find this man's nephew.

Today we leave Muzaffarabad for Islamabad, where I will catch a flight back to the States, but I want to find Dr. Bilal's house before we go. Yassin asks a clerk at our hotel for directions, but we instantly get lost in the maze of narrow congested streets that converge around jammed marketplaces of sagging shops fashioned out of broken buildings.

We stop often and show shopkeepers Dr. Bilal's address, until Yassin turns down a street he thinks is the right one. A two-story house stands alone next to empty lots filled with chunks of shattered concrete, fallen pillars, collapsed roofs, rotted doors. We ask a man if he knows Dr. Bilal. Was that his house? The man, Mohammed Masken, cannot say. He points at the rubble.

"Over there was a school. There a clinic. There a barn for my goats. There my son's house."

I know without asking that his son died.

"Twenty-two years of age," Mohammed says, reading my mind. "Six of my daughters died and my wife. I tried to save them. I have no one around me now. I'm alive because Allah gave me a chance to redeem my sins."

We consider this. We watch crows land in the destroyed lots, peck around the concrete for food, and fly away. Cows graze in a trash pile nearby on what was once a patio and where now dogs sleep. Clouds block the sun, and shadows consume boys picking through the garbage for plastic bottles. In the midst of the wreckage, tied to a broken tree branch, hangs one of the green-and-white bandannas worn by members of Jamaat-ud-Dawa.

"This is much too difficult a way to find forgiveness," Yassin says finally. I nod and so does Tahir. Mohammed sighs and closes his eyes.

On this point we all agree.

3

African Promise

Chad: August–September 2006

The throbbing music emanating from Le Carnivore Restaurant behind our hotel grows tinnier with each tortured beat, the voices rising to ever-higher levels of screeching. Although Darren and I feel exhausted from the twenty-four-hour flight from Boston to here, N'Djamena, the corrupt capital of the ruined African country of Chad, the merciless pulse of distortion refuses us sleep. We have no choice but to immerse ourselves until we are inured to the shrill bombardment and find, if not sleep, at least an accommodation with the noise.

We seat ourselves at a round table that tips beneath the weight of our elbows and sinks into the soft dirt floor. Ravenous cats dart about, devouring meat scraps. We squint in the pale candlelight at murals of pink camels advancing ponderously through purple sand dunes. Dwarfing the murals are the jagged lunging shadows of the singers. Players of trumpet, saxophone, banjo, and guitar sit in a ring beneath a plastic Valentine's heart of colored lights and a blinking neon wreath.

U.S. oil workers shout over their sauce-smeared plates on which a few French fries lie untouched. Their shadows bob, entwined with those of the singers in a crazed copulation. The singers themselves gyrate without expression, as if they have lost all connection to the stage. To me the singers seem to exist only as a manifestation of the dead weight overwhelming me that in time might pass for sleep. Suddenly trails of exploding static dim their voices to broken barks.

Women in bright orange and yellow dresses strut past the stage—unbidden and not the least distracted by this failure of the sound system—to troll the oil workers. One by one they escort the men into the street, where the night absorbs them just beyond a fringe of blinking lights.

A young woman asks to join us and sits down without waiting for an answer. She orders a beer. Our dime. She introduces herself. Princess. A hairdresser and, she adds, a great soccer player. Perhaps she will leave for London and turn professional. What do we think?

Of course. Makes perfect sense.

"Do you want to go to a club?"

"No."

She strokes little swirls through the sweat-dampened hairs on my arm. I shake my head no.

She asks Darren to take her to our room for a back rub.

"No."

Princess shrugs and finishes her beer.

"Where will you go from here?" she asks.

"Abeche."

"And then?"

"The border."

"With Sudan."

"Yes."

"We think of the Sudan border as people trying to solve an ethnic problem. It's a private problem."

She stands, peels the plastic tablecloth from her hot arms, then kisses me on both cheeks, turns, and dissolves into the crowd. Her thin scent hovers about my face until it too passes.

I ask a server where the bathroom is and she points outside. Soldiers and security guards lounging on the backs of pickup trucks watch where I go. The cave darkness of the overcast August sky has not a star and deepens ever blacker with storm clouds. It is the last month of the rainy season. Disoriented in the gloom, I slosh through puddles. I recognize an oil worker from the restaurant and ask him for directions to the bathroom before I realize that he stands naked from the waist down, pants pooled at his ankles before a kneeling woman. She pauses in her ministrations, bloodshot eyes barely discernible in the depthless shadows, and pleasantly points the way toward the toilet.

"Thank you," I say.

I retreat toward a dimly lit hall, abandoning her to her transaction in the secluded corner of a broken cinder-block wall.

"What do you do?" a man on our flight to N'Djamena had asked Darren.

A freelance photographer, Darren had answered only "journalist."

"Oh. I do something counterproductive. I'm in oil."

Back in Le Carnivore, I watch an oil worker prance on stage, exposing his buttocks to us bleary-eyed pilgrims, the boards quaking beneath the heavy clomp of his boots. Darfur and Chad and the plight of thousands of people lie lost somewhere beneath the abundance of money dispensed for drinks and whores and whatever other tawdry commerce might come available this night. Darren and I wave off the servers, mutely mesmerized by the obscenity of that jiggling white ass blurring before us as, slumped in our chairs, our eyes closing, sleep finally comes.

Since 2003 millions of dollars' worth of oil has been pumped out of Chad and neighboring Sudan, putting huge profits into a few well-connected hands.

Little, if any, of that revenue has benefited Chad. The Berlin-based organization Transparency International conducts an annual survey of the abuse of public office for private gain and measures the degree to which corruption is perceived to exist among a country's public officials and politicians. Chad is tied with Bangladesh for most corrupt in the world.

In January 2006 the corruption became so apparent that the World Bank, which helped finance Chad's oil boom, suspended $124 million in loans and grants and stopped payment of an additional $125 million in oil royalties after the government resisted pressure to invest its oil profits in projects to aid its impoverished people, who survive on an average income of $30 a month. Chad's president, Idriss Deby, threatened to shut down the country's oil production unless the World Bank released the funds. The World Bank stood firm. Deby then demanded that Chad's oil consortium, led by the U.S. oil giant ExxonMobil, pay at least $100 million to tide the country over until the World Bank released Chad's royalties. U.S. diplomats acted on behalf of American oil companies. Deby received his money, thank you very much, and the roads, hospitals, running water, and schools remain little more than dusty dreams.

There could be no better symbol of his corruption than the one Deby himself has chosen for his political party, the so-called Patriotic Salvation Movement. The logo features an AK-47 assault rifle (the weapon that has ensured Deby's power) crossed with a hoe (what better emblem of the poverty of those scratching out existence in rural villages?). Above it all floats an eternal flame, fueled by the oil that virtually assures that the strong-arm tactics and fiscal dishonesty will never end.

Making matters worse is the tide of refugees from Sudan. Divided between its Arab heritage in the north and its African heritage to the east and south, Sudan is cleaved along linguistic, religious, racial, and economic lines, resulting in civil war and ethnic cleansing in the Darfur region. More than 250,000 people, the majority of them civilians, are believed to have died in Darfur, and the United Nations estimates that one million people more have been displaced. Already ranked the world's fifth-poorest country, Chad absorbed about 235,000 Sudanese refugees between 2003 and 2006.

In April 2006 a new twist came in the bloody, three-year-old conflict in Darfur. Sudan announced that its ABCO corporation—37 percent of which is owned by the Swiss company Cliveden—had begun drilling in Darfur, where preliminary studies showed vast quantities of oil. A China-owned consortium already pumps more than 300,000 barrels of oil a day from Sudanese wells. What might Darfur yield? Washington and the European Union had all but ignored the atrocities taking place there for three years, but now that the crisis threatened to disrupt the opening of Sudan's lucrative oil fields to Western companies, the United States started waving the threat of U.N. sanctions against Sudan.

As it is, there is no love lost in Chad for the government of Sudan. At the start of the Darfur war in 2003, Sudan-armed Arab militiamen called the Janjaweed, many of whom came from Chadian Arab tribes, to quash a political uprising by Darfur's black villagers who wanted increased autonomy—but the Janjaweed heeded no borders and occasionally led raids into eastern Chad. About 8,000 Chadian rebels maintain a camp in Darfur; earlier this year they fought with Chadian government forces sixty miles south of the strategic border town of Adre.

To head off further fighting after the discovery of oil, the Sudanese government signed a peace agreement with the strongest of the rebel groups, but since the agreement was reached, Darfur has grown more chaotic and violent. Meanwhile Darfur rebel groups that did not sign the peace agreement have splintered and realigned, creating new ties and divisions that have made the conflict more complex and dangerous. Most important, a faction of the Sudan Liberation Army (SLA) and the Justice and Equality Movement, an Islamist group, have joined to form the National Redemption Front (NRF), which claims to have gunned down Sudanese military aircraft. Some humanitarian aid organizations worry that oil will only increase Khartoum's resolve against the NRF in Darfur and encourage its scorched-earth policy against rebels' communities.

"No one doesn't see oil as not a big element in all this," a Western diplomat told me, his words twisting into a careful knot of negatives. "Chad broke relations with Taiwan and sided with China. China has oil markets in Sudan. Is Chad trying to get China on their side so that Sudan will stop supporting Chadian rebels? What we do know is that the Chadian people are not seeing any benefit from oil."

In the morning Darren and I wander out, following rolling breaks of daylight in a desperate search for coffee. Mud clings to our boots. Women with their children sit on the ground and hawk trays of cigarettes. Men fan mobile-phone cards in our faces, exhorting us to buy. Clouds gather. The air turns gray, cool, then still. Boys selling corn hold out their hands, look skyward, and run.

Curtains of rain sweep down upon us. The soft ground explodes beneath our feet, and dirt paths suck in the rain until the ground can absorb no more, and the water rises back up through the saturated earth and stands in pools, spreading, consuming whatever patches of dust remain. The rising pools become streams, rage into torrents, sweeping up piles of garbage, sending it spinning past us. Harder and harder it rains, and the water rises and rises. Women with bundles of clothes strapped to their backs hold onto parked cars against the pull of the thick water. We stand on railings and watch, our weak coffee splashed by rain, clumps of curdled cream like bobbing islands.

After half an hour the rain falters, then stops. We emerge from beneath a tin overhang and make our way back to the hotel past sodden vendors, who peer with doubt at the still sky. Boys mince through the water holding their shoes above their heads. Mosquitoes spin madly in the gauzy sunlight. Almost immediately the sun begins to burn the water off.

I call Djimte Salomon, a spokesman for the aid organization World Vision. He offers to drive us to the ministry for public security and immigration. We need permits to travel within Chad, a bit of red tape begun after an April coup attempt prompted an already paranoid dictatorial government to track all foreigners within its borders. The failed overthrow followed months of rising tensions between Chad and Sudan over the Darfur war. Chad's President Deby comes from the same Zaghawa tribe as many Darfurians, and Khartoum has accused him of secretly backing rebels opposed to the Sudanese government by allowing them sanctuary in Chad.

"I am from the Sara tribe," Solomon tells us, his car swerving on the slick mud streets. "If I killed a man, I would have to pay a fine. But if I was Zaghawa, I would pay nothing. Deby would protect me."

Someone, however, wanted Deby to pay for interfering with Darfur. Chadian rebels attacked N'Djamena on April 13 but were defeated. On national radio Deby declared the situation under control, but residents, diplomats, and journalists reportedly heard shots for days afterward. Chad accused Sudan of backing the eastern-based rebels, some of whom appear to have been joining in Janjaweed attacks.

"They came early morning," Solomon recalls of the rebels. "It was nothing planned. They had never seen N'Djamena. They had been too long hiding in Sudan. They got lost and asked directions for the presidential palace. The people were excited. Fed up with Deby. The rebels got confused and attacked the parliament. At one point the rebels' truck died. They ran away and left mines and other ordnance in the truck. People came out to loot the truck and blew themselves up.

"Rebels, we don't know what's in their minds. I think if they get in power they will think, 'Now it is our time to get rich.' Just another cycle. The best thing, keep Deby and ask him to help all the people."

He turns down a narrow street. Burlap stalls, drooling with rainwater, stand beside flooded fields, where shacks slant in the unstable ground.

Solomon says his job does not pay well enough for him to live like Deby and his henchmen, but at least he does not have to live underwater like the families outside our windows. He drives off the road to make room for a shiny Hummer barreling toward us.

"Stupid World Bank," he mutters. "Can they not see? How does a man who earns less than $500 a month afford a Hummer?"

He rubs his fingers together, kisses them, and gestures toward a billboard of a grinning Deby, beside Muammar al-Gadhafi, promoting oil development.

"That's how."

At the ministry a drab cinder-block building where women sweep ankle-deep water out the door and into a flooded courtyard, a clerk tells us our papers won't be ready until the afternoon—if then—unless of course we pay additional fees. We refuse. The clerk shrugs. Chickens run down the hall past the clerk's supervisor, a large woman with a pendulum walk who thrusts herself into the office and spills folders onto the desk. She asks our business and we tell her.

"What is the problem?" she asks.

"Nothing," the clerk says. He gives us our papers. We walk back to the car.

"When do you leave for Abeche?" Solomon asks.

"Tomorrow."

He starts the car. Rain begins falling.

"Don't cross into Sudan. Journalists used to do that. Now they are arrested."

Darren and I arrive in Abeche aboard a fourteen-seat propeller plane, courtesy of the United Nations. We wait outside the empty airport for our ride. Dusty streets. A few mud-brick buildings where dogs pant and soldiers in T-shirts and khaki pants sit with AK-47s balanced against their legs. Turbaned nomads with scarves across their faces ride their snorting horses like characters broken free from some myth to wreak havoc. A U.N. Land Rover maneuvers around the riders and stops beside us. We get in.

Our driver, Matt Conway, has been the U.N. flack in Abeche since February. The rain has kept things quiet, he says, but we can expect the fighting in Darfur and skirmishes between the Chad army and Chadian rebels to resume when the rains stop.

We turn down a rutted street toward the U.N. compound. Nothing on either side of us but aid organizations. A circling of the wagons against what lies beyond this alley.

"Journalists from *National Geographic* were jailed for crossing into Sudan from Chad earlier this month," Matt says. "They probably went in with the faction of the Sudanese Liberation Army that signed the peace agreement."

"And were betrayed by them?"

"Yeah."

"To score points with Khartoum?"

Outside a pair of towering spiked gates, Matt brakes the Land Rover and honks. A guard opens a panel and looks at us. Then the doors open and Matt drives through. All that's missing is the moat.

"Everyone is just out for themselves, man," Matt says. "It's all about survival."

Matt's office. Paper-strewn desks. Computers humming off generators. Maps on the walls. Circles that indicate "areas of concern" in eastern Chad.

Abeche, where we are: "Degradation of the security situation in town ongoing."

Bahai: "Presumption of recruitment by Sudanese rebels in the camps."

Guereda: "Permanent Sudanese and Chadian rebels' or bandits' threats."

Farchana: "Permanent risk of military confrontation."

With my fingers I trace the arrows and circles and small dots for towns. Tomorrow we leave for the Farchana refugee camp. Mustafa Mohammad, a thirty-five-year-old man whom Matt recommended as an interpreter, stands beside me, his shaved head tipped back as he contemplates the map. He was born in Abeche, speaks English, studied in Khartoum, and knows Arabic. He worked for the Chinese-owned Great Wall Drilling Company in the oil fields of southern Chad. A radio operator. He still has his ID tags, shows them with pride.

"Bad?" I ask.

"No, nice map."

"I mean going out to the camps. Too dangerous?"

"No, not too dangerous. Not for me."

"And me?"

"For you little bit dangerous."

I tell Mustafa to meet us at eight o'clock in the morning.

"I give you African promise."

"What is that?"

"You tell me to meet you at eight o'clock, African promise means I will see you no later than nine o'clock."

"Meet me at seven."

We can't leave, however, until we register our travel permits with the local chief of police, still referred to, in this former French colony, as the *commissar*. His secretary sits behind a wobbly wooden desk. A broken dust-covered typewriter and an ink-cartridge box take up a corner. He looks at our papers, mutters, reads them a dozen times, asks when we arrived. He takes a stamp from a drawer, presses it into an ink pad. He grinds our papers with the stamp so thoroughly that he leaves a stain on the desk, examines his handiwork, blows on the ink. Satisfied, he advises us to wait for the commissar.

We stand outside on the windblown road where beggars lie in ditches and raise wrinkled arms to all who pass them. Empty oil cans collect rainwater. The commissar pulls up in a Suzuki jeep. We follow him into his office. Dank white walls, dirt floor grimed with chicken droppings. He tears into his secretary for not having our papers numbered correctly. He reviews the stamps and signs his initials. He points out the Louisiana flag he has on his desk. He studied at the Baton Rouge police academy. He gives us our papers, on which the ink is still damp. He warns us against going out at night. Bandits. He asks if we like jazz.

"Yes."

He smiles and nods and follows us to the door. Through the rear window of the Land Rover I watch him. He grows smaller, waving the Louisiana flag.

We begin the three-hour drive to Farchana with Claude, a retired Canadian marine in charge of overseeing the gendarmes—Chadians hired to provide security for refugee camps. The U.N. pays the gendarmes a monthly incentive fee of $150 to offset their paltry $64-a-month government salary. This arrangement was intended to motivate the gendarmes and provide a firewall against bribes from rebel forces. Unfortunately the plan has backfired. The gendarmes effectively hold the U.N. hostage for ever-increasing incentives, and the U.N. has little choice but to pay up if it wants to maintain camp security and ensure the safety of its personnel. The Deby government happily encourages this lopsided relationship, as it allows the government to avoid spending oil profits on maintaining the cronyism that passes for loyalty within its ranks.

Meanwhile the gendarmes do little more than escort U.N. personnel—without raising a finger to actually protect them or the refugees in their camps. Before Darren and I arrived in N'Djamena, Chadian rebels kidnapped 4,000 men and children from a U.N.-run refugee camp near Goz Beida in the south. The gendarmes did nothing. Thirty-five NGO vehicles were stolen in eight months; U.N. personnel also were assaulted in carjackings and burglaries. Again, the gendarmes did nothing. So all travel, even under supposed guard, is understandably tense.

We follow a dirt road out of Abeche and into the brush toward Farchana. Our driver stops at checkpoints, where our papers are inspected and laboriously stamped again, our names recorded on curled sheets of paper dusted with the ancient import of the old men writing on them. Scavengers had passed this way before us and dug up the bones of cattle and goats and camels and other animals whose shiny skulls leer at us in the glare. We turn north onto a narrow dirt road, crushing scrub brush under our wheels.

Claude talks without end, his voice amazingly steady despite our being tossed about by the deep ruts we hit and our driver's insistent speeding. "The camps are better organized than the towns around them," Claude says. He raises his hands against the roof for balance against the bumps. "They are jealous, these towns, but they don't understand. This is not home for the refugees. They can't work. They have small living quarters. I'm going to see how the police are doing. Sometimes there are small problems. Like they beat people."

We stop at a soupy brown wadi—Arabic for a dry riverbed—filled with roiling rainwater. Boys whip donkeys with switches, and the donkeys bellow their protest and refuse to cross the frothing waters. Nomads on camels pause at the edge of the water and let their mounts drink. Toll keepers ask us for money to grow grass to keep the shoreline stable. I look at the crumbled ground without a hint of greenery.

OK.

Boys shovel dirt into the sandy craters swallowing the wheels of another Land Rover ahead of us. Our driver drops a franc from the Central African Republic, worth about 25 cents, out his window to them. The boys scamper after the limp paper bill, swinging their shovels at one another. The wind teases the bill just out of reach until it vanishes in the mottled dusty air and drops invisibly into the water.

The toll takers advise us to drive straight, don't stop. Our driver backs up, guns the engine, and, picking up speed, takes a running start toward the wadi. Water explodes in all directions and we're thrown against our seats. The Land Rover plows forward, and we feel the resistance of the water against the grill and our tires spinning madly. The muddy slough rises to the doors as we sink, brown geysers jetting outward like wings of a bird, and we pass another Rover roped to complaining mules in the middle of the wadi. We pass naked men lined up chest deep in the water, encouraging us, and we grind on, humping up the opposite bank, sluicing water and mud, emerging triumphant onto land.

"We don't have much time," Claude says, inspecting the sky. "See those clouds? They are nothing now. But tomorrow. We have until tomorrow afternoon or we'll be stuck for days by rains, because the wadi will be too deep."

Five-year-old Mukhatar Ahmad stares at me from his parents' hut in Farchana refugee camp. His right eye protrudes white and glassy from its socket. He does not talk. He will not tell Mustafa how his eye was damaged. Perhaps playing with other boys, one woman suggests. Perhaps he was born like that. Flies suck at the eye. Mukhatar does not blink. Faces balloon and shrink, huts curve, reflected grotesquely in his eye.

Three years he has been in this place. The weight of time, the slow drain. He pours water from a heat-swelled oil jug.

"I am here because of war. I saw fighting, killing by helicopter, by guns. Militia of Janjaweed. I saw dead. I can't describe it. Because of this problem we left Darfur."

Mukhatar moves his head and I follow his dead eye, the world turning in its silent orbit. Mountains green from rain. Women carrying buckets of water on their heads. Goats kicking at the dirt.

"They shoot people in the head. I stayed in my village. Hid in my room. Saw through window. Many killed. I hope I return. The situation is worse here. No money. Not enough food."

A child takes my pen, tries to suck the ink from it. Boys drag toy trucks made from the rusted tin of sardine cans. Toothpicks as axles. Tires of mud. Putrid heat within the tents, where they play despite their parents' apathy. Pallets of dirty blankets. The boys hold their toys for me to see.

"War came in three ways. Some by helicopter. Some by the Janjaweed on camels. Some by soldier in trucks. They attacked in the morning. Many times come with guns and shoot. We were in school. Some escape, not all."

"We must go," Claude says.

The U.N. has rules. All its people must be inside by 4 p.m. He stands to leave, and I step out of Mukhatar's compass, leaving the globe of his eye to the flies. He watches me go, his hand raised, outstretched fingers ready to clasp my hand if I offer it to him. "Take me with you," he seems to say, but his lips do not move. Just that eye in its blindness following me. "Take me with you."

We make the three-hour drive back to Abeche the following afternoon and beat the rains by just under an hour.

"This would have stranded us at the wadi," Claude says.

We sit in a screened-in building that serves as a cafeteria. I nod, pick at my plate of rice and beef liver.

"Oh, that would have been awful," tut-tuts Rodolphe, another security man who monitors the gendarmes in northern Chad. He served more than twenty years in the French Foreign Legion. He looks to be well into his sixties. Shaved head, trim and taut as a wire.

Rain slashes through the screen. I wipe the water off a map Darren and I are consulting. We want to drive north to Guereda, spend the night, and continue to Iriba and then Bahai in the Sahara Desert. Then drive south to the border town of Adre.

"Impossible," Claude says. "No roads from Iriba to Adre. And what about water, what would you do about water?"

"Carry it."

"You'd have to carry a well. That's the Sahara, man."

He traces a dirty fingernail from Abeche to Guereda. The road is bad, he explains. It will take us at least five to six hours. He cannot say that it is safe. In the past few days more than one hundred Chadian soldiers were deployed in Guereda. The drive from Guereda to Iriba would be very bad. Even U.N. convoys do not follow that route.

"Bandits, man, when you pack your gear they know where you're going," Claude says. "Why do you think you fill out all that paperwork? Information is passed along."

"At first," Rodolphe adds, "they won't know when you leave here. But when you check in at Guereda, then they'll know. Travel with others. Don't discuss plans with your driver or translator. What's their tribe?"

We shrug.

"My God, you don't know? Always know people's tribes. The president is Zaghawa. If your men are Zaghawa, nothing will happen to you, because they are part of the president's tribe. But if they are Tama, don't go. A Sudanese tribe. No one likes them."

"Why?"

"They were strong once, like Zaghawa."

"Any other tribes that would be bad?"

"No. Just Tama. Give me your names."

I write them down. He scowls at my handwriting.

"I will notify the *préfet* in Guereda you are coming. Villages are still run on the French administrative system. The préfet is the administrative leader. He will protect you once he knows you are there."

He examines our map.

"Bahai is a hot spot. The main road from Sudan to Guereda goes through Bahai. A rebel route. At night many things happen. Four people on camels shot up Kounougo camp in Guereda two nights ago."

"Why?"

"Why not? It's a war, man."

In the morning we sit outside the cafeteria and wait for Mustafa and Abdullah, the driver we hired. Rodolphe stops in for bread and cheese. He flies to Guereda in a few days to organize security for a visit from U.S. Senator Barack Obama.

"That senator must be an expert on Chad," he says. "Two hours in Guereda, and he will know everything. I wish I could work for him. Maybe I will see you, eh?"

He stuffs bread in his mouth, interrupting his laughter.

Mustafa waves to us from the gate. I call him over.

"What is your tribe?"

"Masalit."

"Abdullah's?"

"Masalit."

"Not Tama?"

"No. Why?"

"No reason."

We drive through the rain-cooled desert. A thin layer of green scrub grass stretches across the sand. The seething, clay-colored waters of wadis carve the land into an irregular patchwork of dunes and bare trees.

Men and women pause to watch our passage, moving between their morning cook fires. We wave, and they raise their arms, and the children chase our dust, shouting for candy.

"Is that a baboon?" I ask Mustafa and point to a red monkey squatting below a tree.

"No."

"What kind is it?"

"We have three kinds of monkey. Small, bigger, biggest. That one is small."

"Thank you."

A flock of gray African quail crosses the cattle trail that serves as our road. Abdullah accelerates. The quail scurry and begin squawking, and I hear one thump beneath our Land Rover. Abdullah takes a knife off the dashboard and runs back a few yards, looking at the side of the trail. He pauses at a clump of weeds, knife raised, then makes a slashing motion. He looks up smiling and carries the dead quail by its feet.

"Dinner," Darren says.

The administrator of the Guereda compound is out, a guard informs us, so we decide to check in with the chief of the gendarmes. We ask directions of some men on the street. They look inside the Land Rover without answering. They look at us, reach with their hands, but decide against touching our clothes. Finally one points down the road to a clot of square mud buildings.

The security chief paces behind a desk, above which hang pendulum-shaped hives. Black wasps circle our heads. An aide sleeps on a cot. The security chief examines our papers upside down, lips moving. He stamps them with heavy deliberation, applying his whole body as he leans over the stamp. He blows on the ink, signs his initials, holds it out as if determining its suitability for framing. He tells us to return to the U.N. compound. He will bring the préfet to us momentarily.

Emmanuel, the compound administrator, meets us at the gate. His red-rimmed eyes speak of sleepless nights, of nerves on edge.

"How did you get here? Drive?"

He doesn't let us answer.

"How long will you be here? My God, you came through the jungle. Since January rebels have been attacking Guereda. Since April NGOs have lost six vehicles to road bandits. We have had attempted carjackings on two cars. A policeman was killed, another injured."

He pauses, breathing hard. A Rwandan, he survived the genocide there by escaping into the compound of an aid organization. All his family was killed. He survived only to be kidnapped here in February by rebels. They held him for forty-five minutes before he was released. Looking at him, I realize he lost more than just forty-five minutes. He must have thought Rwanda had finally caught up with him.

"We don't talk of curfew, but after four o'clock we enter our no-movement phase. We don't leave the compound. Six hundred soldiers arrived two days ago. They were promised since April. Maybe they are here because of the U.S. senator. I don't know."

He fusses with paper on his desk. A fan scatters the papers, and his hands scramble after the fleeing memos and lists of protocols.

We step outside the compound, look at our watches. Where's the security chief?

Two men lounging on the ground beside a blanket buried under pots and pans tell Mustafa that rebels came through yesterday but did not bother them. They were after soldiers.

We walk away, but I feel the two men watching us.

"They won't tell you, but there is much violence here," Mustafa says.

"How do you know?"

"They are Tama tribe. This was Tama territory. Before, each family of Tama have 200 to 300 cows. They were destroyed by Zaghawa. Before, you would see hundreds of camels and cows on the road to market. Now, nothing."

We tire of waiting for the security chief and decide to see the préfet ourselves. The two Tama men point us down a rock-strewn road toward a building that resembles a mosque. Giant vultures perch in vast nests that consume the tops of the trees. They stare down at us with their red faces and featherless necks.

The brown-robed préfet sits alone in a room equipped with only a rug.

"Go back to the U.N. and make your plans," the préfet tells us in a voice somehow disconnected from his jowly face.

Outside the vultures have roused themselves and circle overhead.

"The préfet knows nothing," Mustafa says under his breath. "He is a stupid man. He can't read, can't write, but he is of Deby's tribe."

An hour later Mustafa comes to our room. The security chief came by. Pissed off. We should not have seen the préfet without him. Now, he informs Mustafa, we cannot visit the camps.

Middle of the night. Lights out. Breathing in the dark. Darren complains the pheasant was tough. Mosquito net heavy on my face. I hear the little fuckers buzzing, wanting me. I need to piss but dread the outhouse. The fetid stink. The flies. The lumbering black beetles.

Pop, pop, pop.

"You hear that?"

"Gunfire."

"AKs."

"Maybe."

Pop, pop, pop.

"More."

"Yeah."

"I have to piss."

"Can't help you."

The security chief meets with Emmanuel in the morning. Darren and I sit with Mustafa and Abdullah. We wait to see if he will relent on grounding us. I understand we bruised his ego. By meeting with the préfet without him, we effectively said he doesn't matter. The préfet too was insulted. We violated protocol, cut around the chain of command, and strode without escort into his inner sanctum.

"You should not have seen the préfet," Emmanuel scolds us. "I have spoken with the chief of security. He understands you are new so you won't be punished."

"Punished?"

"Jailed, thrown out. It doesn't matter. He will escort you to Mile camp."

An armed convoy of Toyota pickups filled with gendarmes holding rocket-propelled grenade launchers and machine guns waits outside the compound.

We reached Mile camp by midmorning. I see women and children swarming to a hospital tent for free milk. Most young men were either killed in the flight from Darfur and Chad border towns or have joined a rebel militia.

A boy with "sla" printed on his sandals stops me. Slung over his shoulder is a butchered goat. Blood runs down his back. He looks at the soldier-filled pickup just feet away and laughs.

"We have no security in the camp. Sometimes at night the Janjaweed attack doctors. Sometimes shoot guns. In all of Chad there is no security."

He points to the letters on his sandals.

"Before we are refugee we are Sudanese. We support the opposition to the government. After the rains, there will be fighting. We wait for fight."

He walks away, the head of the goat flopping. I tell Mustafa we should leave. We need to return to Abeche for the night and then in the morning drive to Adre, an hour east of Farchana, where we will spend the night. No roads run from Guereda to Adre, so we must backtrack. No hurry. Leave in about an hour. African promise. I laugh, slap him on the shoulders. Mustafa nods but doesn't smile. His eyes follow the goat's blood trail.

"There is no promise," he says. "Especially in Africa."

"Mustafa, tell Abdullah to slow down."

"What is the problem?"

"Those are goats."

"It is good."

"I can handle birds, no goats."

"Maybe one."

"We are close to Abeche. We'll eat there."

"Abdullah, drive slowly."

After a night in Abeche we return to Farchana on the way to Adre. We stop for bread and sardines. Mustafa and I drink tea. I lean against the wall of the tea shop. Suddenly my back burns. The pain increases. I take off my shirt and my back has exploded with welts and red slashes as if I'd been whipped. No one knows what has bitten me. I fight panic, feel my heart race. I want to spin in circles and slap at my back. Mustafa applies across my back a mud poultice mixed with wet tea leaves. It helps. The welts recede. We need to continue to Adre. My back itches. I swallow a fistful of Benadryl tablets.

In Adre road signs fallen in the soft sand point the way to Sudan. Across a wadi where children splash in the water, we see the rough hills burned brown in the sun, and cattle spot the hills close enough that I can see their bent heads scouring the ground for grass.

"El Geneina," Mustafa says. "Sudan."

"We can't cross over," I remind him. "Always know where the border is. We'll get arrested."

Abdullah drives into the town center. Armed soldiers, expressionless behind their sunglasses, monitor the roads. People stop what they are doing to watch us. The vendors selling car tires. The women washing clothes in buckets. The boys chasing one another down the narrow streets. Sheep stand behind a butcher stall and the butcher watches us too, sharpening his knives.

We drive past walls cluttered with faded oil company advertisements. Children and goats stand by mud stoops, and vultures observe the commotion from the branches hanging over vendor stalls. Rap music carries faintly from cassette players. We pass a herder of goats, the animals wide-eyed from the clanging of metal coming from one of the huts;

there an old man beats shapes out of metal that is orange from the light of a forge fire.

We stop at Adre Hospital. Guards lounging within the crevices of broken walls rouse themselves and lead us to the main office, where we meet Dr. Autid Adam.

"Patients live under trees. Many injured. Many refugees. No medicine, no doctors. Shooting injuries. Situation not good. It is too difficult. All is lost."

He calls an orderly to escort us through the halls. The soles of my boots stick to the floor. Flies collect on discarded bandages. Women sit outside dimly lit rooms, impassive to the flies scrambling across their faces. One woman grabs my hand. Her boy. There. On the brown plastic mat where dirty sheets peek out from beneath a mosquito net. That boy. He fell from a tree, fractured his left leg. The cast won't dry in the humidity.

Across from him lies another emaciated boy with a gunshot wound to his left hip; it's clotted with flies. My stomach turns. Soldiers shot him in June or July. He can't remember. Shot here in Adre while working in a grain mill. Janjaweed attacked his village in Darfur in 2003, but he was shot here. He smiles. I clamp my hand over my nose and mouth against the smell, try to convey with my eyes that I appreciate his sense of irony.

Another boy. Shot in the buttocks in January by the Janjaweed. He lies on his stomach, urine bag spilled on the floor. A nurse steps on it, shakes it off her foot.

A fat bandage covers the boy's wound. It hasn't healed. The doctors don't know why. Perhaps the heat. Perhaps the lack of medicine. Perhaps it is just bad luck. They shrug, helpless.

"What are you doing here?"

I turn and face a doctor with Médecins Sans Frontières. We don't have his permission to be here. This part of the hospital belongs to MSF, he says. Do we not understand the danger we are in? Have we not seen all the soldiers? Everyone is watching everyone. Even now, as we speak. My God! No one is safe. MSF cannot be seen associating with us. What if we offend the Chad government? What would happen to his work then? If we want to talk to "the blacks," we must go over there.

He points to a collection of dejected buildings, a courtyard where fowl nod in the afternoon heat beside men and women sprawled beneath gnarled leafless trees.

"I don't know what they do there," the MSF doctor says. "The blacks operate that. It is not MSF. You can go there if you must."

"Even if we offend the Chad government?"

"This is very dangerous. A war. You put yourself and us at risk by being here. You must leave our side. I will talk to Doctor Adam."

He spins around and stalks down the corridor, trailed by a nurse. Black orderlies in white coats follow at a respectful distance.

We leave the hospital and follow a rutted street draining sewage. Our windows are open, dust blows in. Wide-eyed children stare from open doors that lead into darkened halls wet from mop water. Squatting men eat with their fingers from tin bowls. The air stands heavy with the funk of cows and goats and sheep that have passed this way to market. Many of the mortared huts provide empty reminders of the dozens of families who once lived here.

Abdullah parks outside the compound of Secedev, a Chad NGO that provides agricultural assistance. We get out of the Land Rover, dust covered and sore. Inside the gates a man scoops pasta onto a large plate. He inserts spoons all around the plate, and the staff and we sit in a circle on the ground and dig in. Flies ignore the food, descending instead on us.

"Janjaweed come together in great numbers and attack and take the animals of farmers," Ndoyengar Narisse says after I tell him about the MSF doctor. "It is very insecure. The SLA is in Adre. Sudan troops are in the hills across the wadi. This morning we go to Goungour, less than a mile from the border. The security there is OK, but villages near it have been attacked, and all the people flee to Goungour."

We drive forty minutes through the bush, following Ndoyengar, the soft sandy ground sucking at our wheels. Some spots are lushly green from rain. Goats rise up on their hind legs to graze on leafy trees, and farmers till the ground in fields of sorghum.

In Goungour village fencing made from twisted branches encloses empty corrals; dust churns up from the bare feet of children fleeing our advance. A generator hums through the warm wet air. An old man lays straw mats on the ground. We sit and he pours mud-filmed water from a plastic National Diesel Oil jug into a bowl.

"This is our water," Ndoyengar says before he drinks. "Taken from the wadi."

The village elders join us to share the water, their cheeks drawing in like the gills of a fish with each sip.

"This is the biggest village in this area. We had a police station, but the police left for Adre."

"There's no security now."

"Yesterday the Janjaweed took twenty-six cows."

"In July they took 150 cows and eighteen camels."

"They always come back."

"On horses and camels. White turbans. Sunglasses. Khaki pants. Rifles."

"They look for villages with animals."

"We miss our cows."

"We miss our land."

"We miss the people who are dead."

The afternoon creeps up on us without warning. We leave Goungour, return to Adre, then Farchana before nightfall. Ndoyengar takes us by another route he says is faster. My stomach turns, perhaps from the water. The sun swims in the sky, rainbow rings throbbing from it with each hole the Land Rover strikes. I drink from my water bottle, which I left too long in the heat. I'm woozy from the Benadryl, mouth pasty. My back itches. I bounce from my seat, flopping like a marionette as we hit another hole.

What is that? A ravine? We dip into it, drive ahead. Or is this the border wadi? Are those hills Sudan? Where the fuck is Ndoyengar taking us? The heat. I'm burning. I drink more water. I don't know Ndoyengar. Is he taking us to Sudan? More rainbow rings. Oh, shit, what's going on? How much can he get for us? Yellow sky, Arizona desert, except those are not Apache warriors on the sunned buttes. No, they're Janjaweed. Oh, Jesus, TV fucking Westerns, what am I thinking? The skull of a cow. Its sightless eyes hold the sky and me in it. Jesus, is he taking us into Sudan? Why can't anyone hear me? Where are we? *Where are we?*

"Stop, stop! Stop the fucking car!"

Abdullah stops, looks uncertainly at Mustafa, who reaches for my hand.

"What is wrong?"

Ndoyengar drives on. Then he stops. He gets out and walks back to us.

"Where are we?" I ask, my voice coming out in gasps. "Why are we crossing the wadi into Sudan?"

Ndoyengar scowls.

"Sudan is a mile away. What is the problem? I have work to do."

He walks back to the Land Rover. Abdullah starts the engine. I sip more water. Hot wind dries my face. I'm sweat soaked. My back itches. I pop a few Benadryl and close my eyes. Day-tripping. Let the land take me where it will.

We spend the night in the Farchana compound and then return to Abeche in the morning. After we stow our gear Darren and I join Claude in the cafeteria. A bottle of beer is on his table.

"The gendarmes say they need an increase in their incentive pay," Claude tells us. "The U.N. has approved a 6 percent increase. We're worried it will become a subsidy. It's already more than their salary. We're not sure how much of the salary they use. They might just sock it away."

Darren and I buy beers.

"The U.N. voted to deploy troops to Sudan. But Sudan won't accept them. So—"

Claude throws up his arms.

"There're rumors of a new offensive in Darfur," he continues. "Who knows what will happen now on the border. Will the rebels flee into Chad? Will Deby let them? Does he have a choice? The border guards and rebels are all from some tribe. If Deby lets them stay, will Sudan support another coup attempt?"

He pauses to sip his beer.

"It's about oil. There's oil in northern Sudan, oil in southern Sudan. Chances are, there's oil in the middle. Move out black Africans and put Darfur under Arab chiefs, and the oil is theirs.

"It's about Arabs versus black Africans, herders against farmers, Darfur population versus Khartoum leadership. But don't forget the oil."

In the morning we fly to Bahai, where the Oure Cassoni refugee camp was established in 2003, literally feet away from the Sudan border in the Sahara Desert.

Beneath the wings of our plane, the land transforms from a thin layer of green to rolling sand dunes. We land on a rock-strewn runway and stop beside a shack with a torn tin roof that is rattled by bursts of hot wind. A U.N. Land Rover awaits our arrival.

An African gazelle, a gift from the village elders, sits in the sandy lot of the Bahai compound and watches with wide dark eyes as we swing by it and park in front of the administration building.

The compound's administrator, Comlan Spero Guy, offers us chairs. He asks his assistant to provide us with a security briefing.

The people of Bahai are Zaghawa. The camp is twelve miles from here and less than a mile from the border. We travel in convoys only, at least three Land Rovers. A 6 p.m. curfew is in effect. "Be careful of looking at Zaghawa women. The men will harm you if you approach their women. If you kill a woman, you will pay at least a hundred camels. A man, you will pay countless camels. Understand?"

"Where would we get the camels?"

"Please, just try not to kill anyone."

"Right."

"It is very hot. The winds are dangerous here. Sandstorms cover the sun. What else do you wish to know?"

"You tell us."

"It is not easy to distinguish rebels from soldiers. They have the same guns, wear the same uniform. But no one will admit this to you. Chad and Sudan have an agreement. Chad is not to support the rebels, Sudan is not to undermine Chad's government. We will see, eh? Just on Sunday we saw Sudan forces deployed on the border, watching the camp. There may be some Janjaweed there as well. Questions?"

After lunch we drive to Oure Cassoni through a treeless desert landscape like the bottom of an ocean. Diesel-spewing jeeps loaded with armed men pass us. Some men wear desert military garb, others T-shirts and khaki pants. Rebels? Soldiers? Both? Who can say?

The camp sprawls for miles, the tents so covered with sand that at first I mistake them for dunes. I smell nothing. Instead the still air feels as vacant as the stares from families who sit immobile outside their tents in the harsh light.

We stop at the market, where the Shell insignia glints off the aluminum siding used on some of the stalls. An elderly man offers us tea. Beside him, other men take off their argyle socks and pour water over their feet in preparation for the time for prayer.

"My tea shop is called Gahwatu Alatilleen," the old man tells us. "It means if you have no work, come here."

He laughs. A young man approaches, asks where we're from.

"America."

The old man is his uncle. The young man, twenty-five-year-old Izeldeen Khacter, shows us a business card from Brigham and Women's Hospital in Boston.

"I have worked with doctors from this place."

"I want to talk to the rebels," I tell him. "I want to know what is happening in Darfur."

"Yes, you can do this. Come."

We follow him out of the market toward his tent in Zone C, Block L. The camp is divided by villages and tribes: Zaghawa, Fur, Masalit, Grron, Dagno.

In Zone C live families from Furawiya, Sudan; Zone A, Korunie City, Sudan; Zone B, Awmrow, Sudan.

Izzy left Furawiya with his parents days before the Janjaweed attacked it. From the road to Oure Cassoni camp, he could see Furawiya burning.

"I have no work papers. I only have refugee card for food. People say, 'Since you are Zaghawa, won't Deby help you?' In New Orleans people were American like your President Bush. Did he take them in?"

We stop at a tent that serves as a small library. Izzy manages it every morning. He attended university in Tripoli, where he learned English. Inside he retrieves a Thuraya satellite phone.

"Tonight I will call people in Sudan to speak with you tomorrow."

"How do you know the rebels?"

Izzy shrugs.

"Are you a rebel?"

"If I support George Bush and another man supports John Kerry, is that man a rebel? That is me. In America I would support John Kerry. I don't support Sudan government, but I'm not a rebel."

Evening at the Bahai U.N. compound. Vast blue-gray sky tinged with the rust color of an approaching sandstorm. I play with the gazelle, its black tail wagging like a dog's as I tug on its horns.

"We have three kinds of this deer," Mustafa says.

"This one is biggest?"

"Small."

The wind increases, stirring the sand at my feet. Sheets of burlap toss in the air and twist away toward an obscured moon.

"Do you know we have Janjaweed in Chad?" Mustafa says. "I see them, know them. They leave their problems in Sudan. Their generals rob them. They get tired of fighting or join the Chad army for better pay."

"Why would Chad let the Janjaweed come in?"

"The defense minister and minister of foreign affairs are both Arab. Deby says nothing, so they don't try a coup."

"Why doesn't he buy them off with oil money?"

"All the oil money goes to war: war with Sudan, for rebels, to generals protecting Deby. What do you think?"

"It makes sense."

"Yes. Because none of it makes sense."

Mustafa laughs. We shield our eyes against the wind, so much sand in the air now that I cannot even see the compound walls. Then Mustafa disappears. The wind howls.

In the morning we wait for Izzy outside the library tent. We pass the time by visiting with a man chained to a tree. He is crazy from war, we are told. There are about fifty people in the camp like him. He lives on a moonscape of rocks and boulders, the skulls of animals. Children observe him at a distance. Dressed in red rags, his sister swings a metal pole and talks to herself. Warns us away.

Izzy finds us, excited that he just sold a goat. He tells us he called rebel commanders the night before. There is heavy fighting in Darfur, they told him. They were too far away to meet us. But he will call them again so I can speak to them on his Thuraya.

I want to see the border. Our U.N. driver takes us toward a water tower next to Wadi Hawar, which separates the camp from Sudan. He radios the dispatcher at the compound and gives our position. His voice shakes. I hear frantic talk from the dispatcher.

"What is he saying?"

"Don't get killed," Izzy says.

We park by rubber tubes connected to the water tank. Sparse shrubs thrive in the wet ground around the tubes, but beyond the tubes little else grows, except in the wadi, where tall grassy weeds wave above the water.

Across the wadi we see Sudanese jeeps, machine-gun mounts, and soldiers. A Sudanese soldier follows us with a telescope. Izzy points to a hill where he says rebels once camped. A soft wind ripples the water. Long-legged birds strut through the weeds.

"I lived in that direction," Izzy says and points over the wadi, a short distance that is as far from here as the moon.

He calls Abdallaha Xaya Ahmad, a spokesman for the NRF, and interprets.

"The Sudan government is killing everyone. They are attacking us even now. Three days ago they bombed Umseeder village. Right now Umseeder is still smoking. Many killed. I don't know how many. Yesterday, Janjaweed attacked people between the villages of Kutom and Disa and killed seventeen persons.

"At this moment all civilians can't move between Kutom and Disa. Fasher University was attacked. Many students killed because they support rebels."

Izzy hands me the phone.

"He wants to talk to you."

I press the phone against my ear. I hear gunfire.

"What is your name?"

"Malcolm."

"Malcolm," he says, struggling with his English, "we stay and defend our rights and people, even if we are killed. What kind of name is Malcolm?"

"I don't know," I shout above the noise on the other end. "Scottish. My mother gave it to me."

"Very nice to meet you, Mr. Malcolm. God's blessing to your mother. Call anytime."

Then nothing but the silence on the other end of the phone and the quiet breezes blowing over the wadi.

When I lived in San Francisco and counseled Salvadoran and Cambodian refugees, I thought I learned from them the meaning of war and loss. But what I've seen here confounds my sense of earned expertise. Chad swirls around me, a seething waste of lost souls where years of war have shaken its steady heart, its proverbial moral compass—its way out.

Refugees live hopelessly in the camps. Government officials, aid workers, gendarmes, all are out for themselves, because nothing and no one represents anything larger—especially American diplomatic globe trotters who dance the dance of nonintrusive intervention, urging other countries to stand up against the war, knowing none of them will without U.S. leadership.

I came here suspecting that oil companies were war profiteers, cynical oppressors of an already impoverished people—the obvious scapegoats, the villains. I don't hold them blameless, but they may be the most honest among the dishonest. They arrived to find a moral vacuum, a willing bureaucracy that places more emphasis on titles and courtesy calls and the stamping of travel permits than governance and prefers personal gain to the protection of its own people.

While we were in the bush, President Deby accused Chevron, and Petronas, which is owned by Malaysia, of failing to pay taxes totaling $486.2 million. When Chevron produced official agreements showing that the amount it owed had been paid, Deby suspended the underlings who signed the documents and publicly denounced the taxes as mere crumbs. Chevron and Petronas, along with ExxonMobil, have already promised to invest $4.2 billion in an underground pipeline from landlocked Chad to the Atlantic port of Kribi in Cameroon, but that's no longer enough. Now Deby wants another half-billion dollars in taxes. Now he is demanding 60 percent of their profits. And what can even the petroleum giants do? If they refuse, Deby will boot them out, and another company will fill the void.

Long ago, oil executives must have learned, as I have, that one's position here determines rank and place in the pecking order of trickle-down payoffs. There's no obvious way to fix it, only a way to work it. Because it's not what you do but where you stand in line—and if you want to improve your standing, you have to do it by force. So strongmen set up shop and make their own rules and take what they can before the next coup. The American companies didn't make these rules; they're just willing to play by them in order to get the oil you buy to fuel your car.

So acknowledge your own place in this order. Step in line. Be ready to change allegiances with chameleon speed. Play along and pray you don't get trapped in the middle.

The music drumming into my brain from Le Carnivore has improved little since Darren and I were here three weeks ago. The sound system has been repaired. A few U.S. oil workers sit in folding chairs. One apologizes to a server for his behavior the previous night.

"You're back," Princess says.

We offer her a seat, but she demurs. She wears a pink blouse, tight jeans, and impossibly high platform shoes. She sits alone until a man kneels behind her and puts his hands over her face. She grins and turns around.

With luck he will carry her away to England, where she can become the soccer player of her dreams. With luck he will offer her more than $10 afterward. As someone who sits here pleasantly plastered after too much time in the bush, knowing that I will fly out to Paris in a day, I can indulge in optimism.

Just an hour earlier we had taken a cab to the airport to check our luggage. A sticker on the windshield read, "bin laden. Mai gaskiya yana tare da allah" (Osama bin Laden. Praise be to God). Darren tipped the driver a dollar, and the man smiled and pumped Darren's hands with both of his.

"That's how we defeat terrorism," Darren said. "One goddamn U.S. dollar at a time."

I gave the driver a dollar, too. Just for backup.

Princess and her escort get up together. She pauses at our table, holding his hand.

"How was your trip?" she asks.

"The fighting continues."

"Yes."

Princess and her man walk away to pursue their tryst in the alley, a pickup, or some rotten hotel room. She doesn't give us so much as a backward glance. Soon Darren and I will do the same, put the whole lot of it behind us. The music, the oil workers, the hovels of refugee camps, the killing. All of it. Let it be gone with the daybreak, gone with the rains. What else can we do but wish it away?

There is no promise, Mustafa. You got that right.

4

Who Is in the Power?

Kabul: August 2009

August 8 | Round one.

The birds entwine their heads like lovers, then separate and rear back, stabbing with their beaks. Blood spurts from one bird's eye. Men encircling the pit shout, throwing money into the filmy air, watching it fall and kick up dust from the dry ground. The wounded bird wanders blindly as the other bird jumps on its back. Two men in the pit thrust egg-shaped bamboo cages over the birds, separating them.

Break.

Within the circle of onlookers a translator, Aziz Ahmad, stands not far from his employer, an "Americaniste" journalist here in Kabul for the presidential election. They have worked together every year since 2001, when the journalist first came to Afghanistan after the September 11 terrorist attacks. Posters of the major candidates, including current president Hamid Karzai, cover the trunks of trees, but few onlookers notice them, even though the election is less than two weeks off.

"Don't ask me about the election," Aziz overhears one man tell the journalist. "Ask me about these birds."

"We want good men to take responsibility," another man says. "But we have more than twenty-five fucking candidates. How do we know who is good?"

Aziz and the journalist turn back to the fight. It was the journalist's idea to meet here, across from his hotel. Aziz had no interest in a bird fight, but the journalist insisted, saying it would make for good photos. Now Aziz must concede, if only to himself, that he is happy to be here. The fight engages him. A devout Muslim and a student of the Koran, he seeks its meaning. Otherwise, why would he be so fascinated?

He watches as one man in the pit fans the birds with a prayer shawl while another man splashes water over the injured bird. He coils a wet rag, lifts the cage, grips the bird by the head, and pushes the rag down its throat to clear away blood and feathers. He withdraws the rag and lowers the cage as the other man continues fanning the birds. After another moment he puts the prayer shawl away, and both men lift the cages.

Round two.

The injured bird clamps onto the other bird's neck and drags it down until blood patterns the dirt. The men separate the birds again with the cages.

Break.

The birds cluck loudly, backs to one another, beaks open, sucking air through the bamboo bars until the men raise the cages again.

Round three.

The birds circle one another, exhausted. Neither will die. The point is to fight. Fight and fight and come back for more until they can no longer continue. Then the fight will conclude, bets paid off to the owner of the bird that better held its own. A week later the birds will battle again.

Break.

The message of the fight, Aziz concludes, is that Afghanistan is its own pit, Afghans the birds fighting within it. The blinded bird, he tells the journalist, represents Karzai. Still in power, strong but weakened. The other bird represents the Taliban. Strong but not strong enough. The onlookers are like all the countries of the world, watching Afghanistan and betting on the outcome.

The journalist glances at Aziz and nods as if he is reading Aziz's thoughts, but Aziz suspects he does not understand. If he expects death and a final victor, they will be here all day.

Round four.

Aziz tells me the fight will last hours. I don't want to stay that long. I just needed a few pics for a feature. I tell him we need to visit a military checkpoint at the edge of the city for a story about the worsening security situation. About a forty-minute drive beyond the checkpoint lies Wardak Province. During the 2004 Afghan presidential election Aziz and I drove there. These days, with the Taliban controlling the province, we don't dare.

Five years ago it would have been unthinkable that the Taliban could dominate territory so close to the capital. At the time Hamid Karzai was heralded as a new type of Afghan leader, committed to modernizing the country and freeing it from the dominance of warlords and their militias. The future looked promising.

But cracks were showing. Even then southern Afghanistan was unraveling with a resurgent Taliban. The unfulfilled promises of international aid angered a once-expectant public that saw little in the way of job creation and infrastructure. Cities congested with returning Afghans strained aid agencies dealing with thousands of unemployed families.

Yet for a moment these problems were overshadowed by the triumphant public relations campaign heralding Afghanistan's first presidential election, with Karzai the victor. An energized populace rose above cynicism and voted in droves. The spin of pundits and policy makers alike suggested that the transformation of the country from a terrorist state to a democracy would be complete once the votes were counted, leaving open the door for American troops to be transferred to the all-consuming Iraq war.

Karzai had actually been an interim leader since December 2001, when he was appointed chair of the Afghan Transitional Administration. He was elected with 4,443,029 votes, or 55.4 percent, in 2004. But his victory never matched the hype. Over the years unemployment worsened. Farmers resorted to growing poppies and turned Afghanistan into the largest opium producer in the world. The insurgency spread from Kandahar, the birthplace of the Taliban, into the once-secure North. Aid organizations began to leave as the violence worsened.

Fast-forward five years, to this day in August 2009 when Afghans everywhere are preparing for a second presidential election. Expectations are low. Many citizens assume things will go wrong somehow, an assumption that will later seem spot-on, painfully and inevitably so. In this election forty-one candidates are vying for the top spot, a field so crowded that Afghans openly mock the process. Public confidence in Karzai has all but collapsed. Security hardly exists outside Kabul, and the central government has little power even within the capital. Later pundits will say Karzai was always expected to win because, as Aziz says, he's "in the power."

Afghanistan has always been a tribal culture. When the international community abandoned its pledges of billions of dollars of aid, Karzai resorted to the age-old creation of alliances among tribal and ethnic factions. His allies receive what aid trickles in and disburse it according to their own loyalties or simply keep it for themselves. Corruption is epidemic. People at the highest levels of the Karzai administration, including Karzai's own brother, Ahmed Wali Karzai, have been accused of cooperating in the country's opium trade.

On our way to the Wardak checkpoint, Aziz tells me a joke he overheard at the bird fight: Village elders meet with Karzai, pleading with him to stop the corruption in their province.

"Of course I will do this for you," Karzai tells them. "But first, how much will you pay me?"

Aziz and the journalist get stuck behind trucks carrying cattle to market, and it takes them almost an hour to reach the Wardak checkpoint. Aziz parks behind a hut where soldiers of the Afghan National Army stand smoking cigarettes. The journalist gets out and asks a soldier about security.

"As long as you are with us," Aziz says, translating what the soldier says, "you're OK. But by yourself, it would be too dangerous for you. Beyond the checkpoint is all Taliban."

The journalist asks the soldier if he may take photos of the cars and trucks being searched at the checkpoint. The soldier tells him, "No problem."

Aziz watches the journalist snap pictures of families gathered in small groups as the soldiers peer into their cars and beneath them. He hears someone shout behind him. Turning toward the voice, Aziz is pushed aside by the checkpoint commander, who strides past him toward the journalist and shoves the American to the ground. The commander picks up the camera that has fallen from the journalist's hand and shouts at him in Dari. Of course the journalist does not understand. He scrambles backward on the ground away from the commander, like a crab.

"What is happening?" he yells to Aziz.

"He wants to know why you did not ask him if you could take your pictures," Aziz says.

"I asked the soldiers!"

Aziz says nothing. He knows it's all bullshit. The soldiers gave their permission. That should have been enough, but the commander pretends to be insulted. He wants to show his power.

The commander rants at Aziz about what would happen if the journalist were kidnapped and his camera fell into the opposition's hands. They would see how vehicles are searched. They would devise ways to fool the soldiers at the checkpoint. Then what? Wardak is under government control, but the villages around it belong to the opposition. A Swiss journalist was kidnapped not far from here, he says. The commander has yet to find her. She is likely in one of the villages. Who knows what she has told them?

He tells his men to take the journalist to a vendor's hut. They push him onto a bench beneath a sagging shelf stacked with cans of Pepsi. Two soldiers stand outside. Another stays inside, his gun loosely pointed at the journalist. The commander demands the journalist's passport and then calls his superior on a cell phone. He reads the journalist's passport number, struggles to pronounce his name. After a moment the commander closes his phone. His superior will call him back, he tells Aziz.

"Get my camera back!" the journalist yells at Aziz.

Aziz does nothing. In the mujahideen time, when civil war reduced Kabul to rubble, he would run to the bazaar just for some rice, head down, as rival tribal factions shot at one another with Kalashnikov rifles. When the Taliban arrested his oldest son for listening to music, Aziz had to pay five hundred dollars to get him out of jail. After the Taliban left, his youngest son lost three fingers when a mine exploded. Aziz carried the screaming boy in his arms, looking for help. Kabul was deserted. Finally a man stopped and led him to a British doctor. In his fifty-three years Aziz has never been able to stop the violence around him and his family. Like now, he has always been trapped between the opposing sides.

"Advocate for me, Aziz!" the journalist yells. Aziz keeps quiet. A soldier tells the journalist to shut up. The commander's phone rings. His superior. The commander says a few words and snaps it shut. He tells Aziz to follow him into the hut. He motions for him to sit beside the journalist. The commander pushes aside sacks of sugar to make room for himself. He waves off flies and gives the journalist his camera.

"Erase your pictures," he tells him. The journalist deletes the photographs of the checkpoint. Speaking while Aziz translates, the commander tells the journalist, "You won't be able to come back here because you have been seen. The opposition has spotters. You want to avoid a pattern. The Taliban has no information on you yet, but now that you've been at the checkpoints, you should not come back for a while. A system has been activated. Information is passed on, money exchanges hands. The number of hands is too much now. The money too easy."

"I don't understand," the journalist says.

"Do you see all the bumps in the road?" the commander asks him. "They are the same potholes that were here last year, and the year before that and the year before that. No one has a job. Today people work from money pressure. I give someone five thousand dollars to kill a journalist. That is money pressure," the commander says. "You are like chocolate."

"What does he mean?" the journalist asks Aziz.

"A sweet for the terrorists," Aziz says.

Aziz and I drink tea with the commander and share a plate of crackers. I apologize once more for the misunderstanding, and the commander waves his hands in the air. Forget it. All is forgiven. We shake hands and the commander walks with us to the car. I say little to Aziz on the drive downtown. I'm pissed he didn't stand up for me. That's what I pay him for.

But Wardak is done. I have other things to do. I want to take a bus to the northern city of Kunduz. The region has turned into a battleground. The Taliban have returned and are gaining more and more support among the local population. A further example, I think, of how even the North, despite the domination of international troops, has deteriorated.

"You were very excited about your camera," Aziz says after a long silence. "You were lucky I was there or you might be spending the night in jail." I give him a look and he says nothing further.

We reach downtown and stop at a bus depot and inquire about a ticket to Kunduz. The bus driver asks for a copy of my passport. Why? I want to know. So he can alert the U.S. Embassy after the opposition stops the bus and kills me, he explains. I decide against buying a ticket.

On the way back to my hotel, Aziz warns me not to take cabs or wander around alone at night. "Kabul is very different than when you were last here," he says. "Now everyone is looking for money. They all look at the Western person and think, 'I should kidnap him.' I do not see Westerners on the street anymore. They all go around in trucks. This is not a game, my friend."

Aziz pulls up to the hotel, parks, and reaches for my hand. I give him a rueful smile. The day's over. No reason to stay angry. I got my camera back. We left the checkpoint in one piece. That's what matters. We agree to meet in the morning, and then I jog up two flights of stairs to my room and flop on the bed.

From my hotel window I watch cranes lower concrete blast walls dividing the ten-block street in half. Election preparations—in case terrorists attack the Ministry of Interior and the Indian Embassy down the street. The Indian Embassy was hit early this year, killing scores of people and demonstrating the ability of the Taliban to penetrate Kabul. Afghan soldiers stand in armored vehicles parked beneath trees and watch traffic. Children scramble over the tops of the blast walls, a new game that infuriates the soldiers and the police.

I take my map of Afghanistan from my backpack and look at cities outside Kabul. Throughout the country major urban areas have assumed the status of city-states, ringed by checkpoints that leave outlying rural villages to fend for themselves against the Taliban insurgency, which many Afghans now call "the opposition," a word that implies a certain legitimacy, like a rival political force rather than a terrorist organization.

I can't drive to Gardez, just four hours away, because all the areas between here and there are under Taliban control. The three-hour drive to Jalalabad might be OK, but I'd have to drive through Sorobee, a Taliban stronghold. I could drive to Ghazni if I leave at the crack of dawn, dress as an Afghan to fool passersby, and don't stop for any reason. Too chancy, I decide.

I look out the window again. Nothing to do but stay inside.

Aziz stares at the ceiling from his bed, unable to sleep. He survived the Russian time, the mujahideen time, the Taliban time, and now this time. Well, this time is not over. He takes Xanax to sleep. One night he did not have a pill and sent his youngest son to a pharmacy to buy him more.

All the pharmacies were closed. His son found a man who sold him a pill for four dollars. Everyone has become a thief, Aziz thinks.

On this night the pill does not help him sleep. After he dropped the journalist at his hotel, he applied to the Ministry of Reconstruction to build an addition to his house. His application was approved. But in the evening his district representative told him he had to pay one thousand dollars for a building permit. But I have been approved by the Ministry of Reconstruction, Aziz objected. I don't give a fuck, the representative told him. I control the district, not the ministry.

Aziz does not have one thousand dollars. The addition will not be built.

Today he asked the journalist for gas money and a phone card. The journalist gave him a little bit of money but not much. He told Aziz he was not responsible for the gas Aziz used and the calls he made after work. The journalist does not appreciate how much driving they do together, the number of calls they make, how prices have risen. Aziz rolls to one side of the bed, hands under his head. Even the journalist cheats him a little.

Aziz and the journalist met a man today outside the Secondary Courthouse who said the government took his property and told him to move into the mountains. The man, Abdullah, appealed. He gave some money to one court bureaucrat, who gave him a letter and told him to see another man. That man took more money, gave him another letter, and referred him to another man. It has been going on like this for two months. Finally he showed all his letters to the Ministry of Interior, but he was told that the name used in the letters was not his name. He returned to the court and gave the bureaucrats more money for new letters with his correct name. He thinks he has spent two thousand dollars on letters.

The land belongs to him, Abdullah said. Everywhere he goes, secret men follow him. He doesn't know who they are. He thinks they want his letters.

Aziz stares into the dark and decides to take another Xanax. He knows this election will come and go and not change anything. If Karzai loses, there will be new people in the power to pay off.

He tips his head back and swallows the pill. The new addition would have overlooked the garden and the red roses his wife plants. He will let the car run out of gas tomorrow so the journalist understands how much gas they really use. He wonders how Abdullah will sleep tonight.

August 11 | This morning Aziz and I stop at a Kabul bus depot that receives passengers from Kandahar. Families disembark in droves, overwhelmed by the fat bundles of clothes they drag across the rocky ground. Dogs flee before them to parked buses and the hot shade offered beneath.

A man waves us into his tea shop. Men seated on red carpets watch us approach and sit beside them. After our tea is served, I ask them about conditions in Kandahar.

"In center of the city it's OK," says Allah Dad, a bus driver on break. "But if you drive or walk to a village, it is difficult. The opposition comes into the villages. The Americans find out and send Afghan people in to negotiate. If they cannot negotiate, they start shelling and kill everyone."

I sip my tea. I know the seriousness of civilian casualties, how they have eroded Afghan support for the United States and increased cynicism and suspicion toward Western forces. Civilian deaths in Afghanistan from U.S. and NATO airstrikes nearly tripled from 2006 to 2007, exacerbating the problem and fueling a public backlash.

In the first seven months of 2008, at least 540 Afghan civilians were killed in fighting related to the armed conflict. Of those, at least 367 died during attacks by the various insurgent forces and 173 died during U.S. or NATO attacks. At least 119 were killed by U.S. or NATO airstrikes.

The men listen without expression as I ask my questions. Aziz tells them I am from India, but he fools no one. They know I belong to the people who shell them, just as I know some of them likely belong to the opposition.

"The Americans took all of Afghanistan in a few days, but not Helmand Province or Kandahar," a man sitting across from me says. "What stopped them? Nothing. They want to continue the fighting. At night Americans and Taliban eat and drink together, laughing. They have some plan. What is it?"

"I wouldn't know."

"With the Afghan army and police, it is a little bit possible that the Taliban would have tea with them," Aziz says. "But American forces, no."

He pulls on my elbow and together we stand. I reach to shake hands, but only a few of the men return the gesture, allowing me to grip only the tips of their fingers. Then they look away and sip their tea. An uneasy silence follows us out the door.

We drive to a truck stop that receives buses from Logar Province. Aziz parks beside several drivers seated on a blanket lumpy from the uneven ground. They share bread and tell us they have been stuck in Kabul for two days because of fighting in Logar.

"All the countries of the world come to Afghanistan, but they do not help us," a driver complains. "You see, we are trapped here. The government can't stop it."

"The Americans stop us in long lines," another driver says. "Three, four hours. I am going back to my home in Khost. I called a friend, and he said Khost is so bad it's suicidal. But we see killing every day. Why worry?"

"What do you think about the election?" I ask.

"It does not matter," one man says. "I would be as good as any of them."

The drivers laugh. I smile, glance around for a possible photo, my back to them. I see nothing but flat ground and parked red and yellow trucks ablaze in the fierce afternoon sun. I sip water from a bottle. Aziz takes it from me while I'm still drinking, spilling it across my shirt. He reminds me of an appointment. I don't have an appointment, I tell him, but he assures me I'm mistaken.

"What are you talking about?"

"Not here," he says.

We drive onto the road. Aziz keeps glancing in the rearview mirror until he appears satisfied that no one has followed us. Then he pulls to the side of the road and shuts off the engine.

While my back was turned, Aziz overheard one truck driver tell the other men not to talk to me any further. "He's a reporter," the driver said. "Don't tell him anything. He'll tell the army and they will bomb us."

"We should take him," another man then suggested. "What do you think?" They all agreed that it was an idea worth considering. They were not sure what to do about Aziz. He did not wait for them to decide.

He starts the car and looks at me. I don't know what to say, and he doesn't seem to expect a comment. I'm not scared, just discomfited, like hearing someone call my name when no one is around. Creepy. A vague notion of a threat I don't feel because I didn't know of it when it happened.

After a moment I give Aziz twenty dollars.

"For gas," I say.

He puts it in his pocket without a word. Money carries more weight than thank you.

After dinner Aziz, his wife, their four sons, and two daughters join his brother's family to discuss whether to vote in the presidential election. They talk until close to midnight, with little debate. Seated in a circle on the floor, supported by thick pillows against the wall, Aziz voices his opinion that voting doesn't work. "The people don't have power. Ask one man, he will vote for Karzai. Another will vote for someone else. Everyone says different things, but the election is still the same. Karzai will win.

"Look around us," he continues. "Our houses are in bad condition. The roads have holes. Prices are up. A president should solve these problems. But in the last four years he has not."

Aziz's wife agrees. "If something goes wrong," she says now, "God will say, 'Why did you vote for him?' It will be a negative point for us, our neighbors, and friends. People will say, 'You voted for Karzai and he is not working.'"

"He is very clever, though," Aziz says. "Karzai tells his supporters, 'Don't vote for me, vote for people who work hard like me.' Karzai is in a very good position. All the ministers are with him. Police, army, secret police. The other candidates are in a poor position. They go to a campaign rally and the people say, 'Fuck off. You're not in the power. Karzai is in the power.'"

Aziz pauses, pours water into a glass. This evening, after he left the journalist, security was very tight. He was stopped several times and told to take a different route. A bomb had exploded on a nearby road. The police did not know the number of people injured.

"All of Afghanistan is not happy," Aziz says. "Ask one hundred, two hundred people, and the answer will be the same: 'We are not happy with the government, NATO forces, aid organizations, all of it is going down.' Just people with money and power on top. They go to their offices, have one glass of tea, do nothing, and go back to their homes."

Aziz considers again what some of the men coming in from Kandahar had said. America is just going with its own plan. They have occupied all of Afghanistan but can't control two provinces, Helmand and Kandahar. Why can't they do it? It makes for hundreds of questions. Why does the fighting continue? Because of the opposition? Because of an American plan? Because of what?

The men in the bus station would not shake the journalist's hand. They were ordinary men, not officials. They showed what they thought: We hate all of you Americans.

Aziz reaches for a slice of watermelon.

"No," he says. "I will not vote."

AUGUST 14 | Aziz and I sit in the office of Karnail Najeebullah Samsoor, the District 3 police commander. He and Aziz were neighbors when the Taliban ruled, and Samsoor was a police officer in District 10. Aziz bought fuel for Samsoor's car one afternoon when he ran out of gas. "Anything you want, I can help you get," he told Aziz in appreciation. One day the Taliban stopped Aziz's son Nabil and accused him of possessing photos of naked women. Samsoor got Nabil out of jail. Aziz didn't even have to pay a bribe. Since then the men have traded favors.

Today I am the favor. At the right moment Aziz will tell Samsoor that I will give him a bottle of Black Label whiskey in return for information about insurgent activity in Kabul on Election Day. The government has forbidden ministries and local news organizations to report violence, fearing it will reduce voter turnout, so Samsoor's intelligence could prove invaluable. Protocol requires me to step out of the room before Aziz makes the offer, so I pretend to need the bathroom. Samsoor cannot accept a bribe directly from me, a guest in his country, but from another Afghan it's no problem. Aziz will deliver the whiskey after he drops me at the hotel.

I return minutes later to the crackling of a police radio on Samsoor's desk. He ignores me and frowns, holds the radio close to his ear. The chatter is loud enough for Aziz to hear.

"A suicide attack in Wazir Akbar Khan," he translates in a low whisper. "Near the U.S. Embassy. One of the cars was full of dynamite. Made a big hole. Car destroyed. Parked cars behind it destroyed also. The U.S. Army has encircled the area. No one allowed in. Police ordered to check all cars."

"We are in the deep shit," Aziz says.

Samsoor paces, eyes darting about his office, a worried look etched into his face. An officer barges in, snaps to attention, and introduces him to an agent of the National Directorate of Security, Afghanistan's CIA. The NDS agent says he was in District 3 at the time of the explosion and took it upon himself to inspect police checkpoints, all of which he found fully staffed and functioning.

Samsoor slams the radio down and shouts that no one, including the NDS, can inspect District 3 without his permission, no matter how many bombs explode. The NDS man scowls and is about to respond when Samsoor's commander calls him on his cell phone with orders to secure his station. Samsoor snaps out a command to an adjutant. In seconds I hear police officers run outside. They take positions by the front gate and unroll spools of barbed wire across the entrance. Samsoor rifles through papers on his desk and hands the NDS agent a white sheet. He shares it with Aziz.

"This letter says nobody can be elected," Aziz tells me. "It is not the time for these forty-one candidates. Islam won't allow it. God will not be happy. It is signed by Hizb ut-Tahrir, an Islamic opposition political party."

"Maybe they set the bomb?" the NDS agent says.

Samsoor shrugs and sets the radio on his desk. "We found it last night [while] inspecting polling stations. The opposition wants to make trouble for politicians, and politicians want to make trouble for the opposition."

Aziz's phone rings. A friend who works in a bank and receives security updates from the U.N. tells him that a notice has been issued warning of eleven attacks today. Businesses and aid agencies are closing for the afternoon.

"We should be a little bit careful today," Aziz tells me.

"You can't leave," the NDS tells Aziz. "All the roads are blocked."

We sit back on a sofa, confined to Samsoor's office.

"The Pakistan situation became worse when the Taliban was kicked out of Afghanistan," Aziz says. "Now Pakistan is exploding, and the Taliban are coming back to Afghanistan."

The NDS agent agrees. Samsoor slouches in his chair and thinks out loud. He has reinforced security. Today's security breach did not happen in his district. He is not responsible. He sighs, releasing tension. He tells his secretary to bring four soft drinks.

"It's war in Afghanistan," he says, cleaning the Pepsi can tops with a Kleenex. He inspects the dark smudges and makes a face before opening a can and offering it to me. "These things happen every day."

The next morning Aziz is on his way to pick up the journalist when a police officer waves him to the side of the road. He stops as cars ahead of him continue into the exhaust haze of morning traffic. The officer asks Aziz for his license. He glances at it briefly and then tells Aziz to get out of the car and sit in the officer's. Another police officer asks Aziz for his car keys and slides behind the wheel.

"What is happening, where are we going?" Aziz asks.

"The station in Khayr Khana."

"Why?"

"I have a report that your car was stolen and you are a Taliban spy."

"I have been in my house all morning. Check with my family. Check with my boss. Where did you get this information?" Aziz shows him his press badge.

"That doesn't work here," the officer tells him.

Aziz says nothing more. The police have the power. They drive in silence to the station, past walls plastered with campaign posters, past trucks with loudspeakers blaring the names of minor candidates with no chance of winning the election, past long lines of vendors oblivious to Aziz and the election and the police, just sweltering in the heat, which is made more annoying by the persistent pleas of beggars.

"Where do you live?"

"District 3," Aziz says. "Call the police commander. He's my friend."

"No. You work with U.S. people and then call the Taliban."

"I hate the Taliban."

"No. We have a report on you."

At the police station Aziz is led into a damp mildewed room and told to sit in a wooden chair that wobbles when he shifts his weight. A Commander Hoja sits behind a desk strewn with papers. Hoja asks Aziz for his phone.

"Call my friend in District 3."

"Don't talk."

Aziz feels his heart beat too fast. His chest aches and his mouth is dry. He asks for water and tries to prevent his hand from shaking when a glass is offered to him. Warm. Two men in black suits and ties enter the room. They speak English to one another. Excellent English but with an Afghan accent. They greet Hoja in Dari. The three of them talk in low voices so Aziz can't hear. They glance at him and return to their conversation.

"What have I done?" Aziz asks

"We have a report," Hoja says.

"A report is not enough," Aziz says, anger overtaking his fear. "You should check with my family. With my friend the District 3 commander."

Hoja ignores him, writes the numbers recorded in Aziz's phone, and then returns it to him. The two other men take the list of numbers and leave the room.

Hoja turns to the arresting officer.

"Did he have a gun?" he asks.

"No."

"Drugs?"

"No."

"Put his name in the computer and search his car."

The arresting officer leaves the room.

"What candidate are you voting for?"

"I am not voting," Aziz says.

Hoja shrugs.

"For which company do you work?"

"An American journalist," Aziz answers, regretting almost immediately that he answered the question. Will he get the journalist in trouble? Will the police arrest him too? Will he go to the jail?

"Where does the journalist live?"

"I don't know," Aziz lies. "I pick him up on the street and drop him off on the street."

The arresting officer returns to the room. He has found nothing in the car. Hoja leaves the room. He comes back minutes later. Nothing has come up on the computer.

"Yesterday was a very bad day with the bomb," Hoja says.

"I don't know anything about it," Aziz says. He notices how wrinkled his shirt has become from sliding and sitting up again and again in the stiff chair.

"OK, we'll let you go," Hoja says. "Give us money for lunch. Two hundred dollars."

Aziz takes out his wallet. The journalist had just paid him $350—seven days' wages. At least they didn't ask for $400. He would not have had it and would likely have spent days in jail until his family or the journalist came up with the additional money.

"You should vote," Hoja says, taking the cash from Aziz. "It is your obligation."

August 18 | Eight people, including a NATO soldier and two Afghans working for the United Nations Mission, are killed midmorning in a suicide car-bombing on Jalalabad Road in eastern Kabul. More than fifty people wounded.

Aziz and I rush to Wazir Akbar Khan Hospital, where the wounded have been taken. Women wail on the cracked steps leading into the hospital lobby, piercing cries that rival the screams of children.

Aziz takes my hand. We enter the hospital and proceed down a dank green hall, the tile floor sticking to the bottom of our shoes. We walk up three flights of stairs and push through two swinging doors. Bleeding patients lie on gurneys, arms hanging off the sides. Aziz covers his nose to avoid the foul odor.

Heads, so swallowed in gauze that only the eyes blink through, turn toward me. Young men sit against a wall, their heavily bandaged hands resembling boxing gloves. Yellow intravenous tubes snake into their arms. Numb looks that no longer question what happened, just as they no longer interpret the activity around them. Rushing doctors, gowns bloody. Shouting. Cell phones ringing. My camera click, click, clicking. They see and hear me but without comprehension. Stunned senseless, the life around them a film in another language without subtitles.

AUGUST 20 | Election Day. Aziz and I drive down empty streets. Perhaps the bombings scared off voters. Perhaps apathy, lives lived without expectations. All I see are a few dogs luxuriating in the emptiness of the warm pavement and weary police officers standing in desultory abstraction within the rising heat. Then, for no reason, something within them comes to life, and they wave us to the curb so a German shepherd can inspect our car.

"You are both old men," the police officer says. "If you were young, I'd give a hard time."

We stop at Habibia High School, a polling station, at 8:15 A.M. Voting should have started at 7:30 across the country, but this polling station remains closed, as will others Aziz and I visit this morning. No lines of waiting voters extend along the school's fences. Torn posters encouraging people to vote hang without purpose beside one lone security guard.

An explosion breaks the silence and seals my ears shut, as if they've been crammed with cotton. I press my hands against my head and stumble backward. I shout to Aziz to call the District 3 commander. I ask him several times before he hears me.

"Nothing," Aziz says when he gets off the phone. "An old ammunition dump, the commander said. That's all."

I don't believe him. I look around. The security guard has fled, the school abandoned temporarily to the uncertainty of this day, except for one man who dashes, hunched, across the road as if he expects gunfire to open up around him any minute. "I want to vote for our next leader," the man says. "But not like this."

We leave him to the empty school and try another location, Rabia Balkhi High School. It's a little after nine. A security guard tells me voting here has just started. A short line of men stands outside. The guard waves a metal-detecting wand over their bodies before allowing them through. In a classroom desks have been piled in one corner in such a haphazard and precarious manner that everyone avoids the cardboard voting booths near them.

Three poll workers sit behind a table and inspect a voter's registration card. They apply a hole puncher to the card so it cannot be reused, but the puncher cannot penetrate the plastic seal. The workers discard the puncher and tell the voter to dip a finger in indelible ink, a measure to prevent him from voting twice. Ballot in hand, the voter steps into a booth.

"In my opinion I voted for the future good," he says, after casting his ballot. "I live in a very poor tent. I came to vote for the future. I don't want to be the top man, the rich man. I just don't want to be the poor man."

I see three women in blue burqas voting in another classroom.

"Women are still in the deep shit," Aziz says, commenting on how they cannot vote in the same room as men. But his sympathy does not run deep. Stepping outside, we see more women approaching the school. None of these women, however, wears a burqa, and a few have on eyeliner and lipstick.

"See the stupid women in makeup?" Aziz says in disgust. "Everywhere there are women like this. There is too much of this kind of woman."

His phone rings. He speaks briefly into it and then turns to me. "The commander says not to go far from the city. He has reports that people have come to kidnap Westerners."

Aziz and I leave the school. We hear another blast, farther away this time but still loud and unsettling. But the commander gives Aziz the same explanation: another ammo dump detonation.

"Bullshit," I say.

On the car radio a BBC correspondent reports that at least five bombs have exploded in Kabul in the last few hours. The police have been exchanging gunfire for more than an hour with a group of insurgents in District 5. So much for ammo dumps.

"I wasted a good bottle of whiskey," I tell Aziz. "Your friend's a liar."

"He was very pleased with it."

"I bet."

"How much did you pay?"

"Forty dollars."

Aziz shrugs off my anger as we drive to another nearly empty polling station.

"In Afghanistan, if you are not lying, you're in the deep shit," he says.

Round one.

The men in the pit release two birds from cages and chase them toward one another. One bird charges, throws its head back, puffs its chest. The other bird thrusts its head forward, its beak a spear, and blood flies.

I look away, the cheers of men around me loud in my ears.

Barely twenty-four hours old, the election already seems like ancient history. Insurgents have already killed twenty-six Afghans in scattered attacks around the country. Preliminary vote counts will soon trickle in showing that 40 to 50 percent of the country's 15 million registered voters cast ballots—far lower than the 70 percent who cast ballots for president in 2004. We won't know the results for months.

In the end Karzai will win. Accusations of fraud will be extensive enough that thousands of ballots will be disqualified by a panel of experts appointed by the U.N., denying Karzai the 50 percent margin he needs to declare outright victory. The United States will convince him to participate in a runoff election with his closest challenger, the former foreign minister, Abdullah Abdullah.

But Abdullah will drop out of the runoff election before it can be held, arguing that the second round of voting will be no less corrupt than the first round was. In November, with no one left to challenge Karzai, Afghanistan's election commission will declare him the victor. He will vow to clean up his government. He will offer few specifics. Meanwhile the war continues.

"Nothing will change except who is in the power," Aziz says.

Turning back to the pit, I see the bleeding birds separated and pushed beneath their cages. Their heads jerk this way and that, pecking through the bars. They are enraged, driven by adrenaline and the madness of the moment.

Break.

Ramadan begins today, and for the next thirty days Aziz and other practicing Muslims around the world will fast from dawn to dusk. During this time, Aziz tells me, nobody is angry with anyone else. Nobody will fight with anyone else.

"Except during a war," I say, watching a man fan the birds with his shawl.

"According to the Koran, God will note this," Aziz says. "This month, if a suicide bomber attacks, he will go straight to hell, and the innocent will go to paradise."

"And after Ramadan?"

Aziz sighs and points at the birds as they are released from their cages. They are running toward each other, mouths open in yet another charge, one among the countless charges they will engage in this morning and tomorrow and each day of their existence.

Break.

Round . . .

5

The Dead Lieutenant

Khost Province, Afghanistan: July–August 2011

"You heard about the lieutenant, sir?"

"Which one?" I say.

"The dead one, sir."

We're sitting outside the mess hall of Combat Outpost Tereyzai. The soldiers smoke, flick ashes into a trash barrel. They have been here since January. Heads shaved. Each wearing the same beige desert uniform, the same beige lace-up boots, the same beige caps. The one who asked me about the dead lieutenant stares at me for a long time without saying anything further. "What's the matter?" "Nothing, sir." "What then?" "It's just that it's been a long time since I've seen a civilian, sir."

I ask some questions: How old was the dead lieutenant (twenty-six), what happened (he stepped on an IED), when did he die (two months ago)? The soldiers never call the dead lieutenant by his name. As if he never had a name, as if when he was taken from life, death consumed him totally and assumed his identity. The soldiers won't tell me their names, either. Worried, maybe, that they'd be jinxed if they said I'm Harry or Jim or Alan in the same breath as they spoke of the dead lieutenant. That their essence too would vanish beyond the disparate memories of soldiers they barely knew.

"I'm sorry about the lieutenant," I say.

The soldiers turn away from me.

"It doesn't matter," one says.

They all look the same. The dead lieutenant could have been any one of them.

I arrived at Combat Outpost Tereyzai in a convoy that had left Forward Operating Base Fort Salerno in Khost Province, southeastern Afghanistan, earlier in the day. We had not driven far from the FOB when the convoy was forced to drive around an IED found earlier in the day. The armored vic I sat in smelled like puke. "Antifreeze leak, sir," a soldier explained. "Smells horrible." "Yeah, take about a hundred bottles of water to wash this out, sir."

We put up with the funk until we jounced through the gates of COP Tereyzai less than a mile and a half west of the Pakistan border. I got out of the vic and stood on gravel burned white from the sun. The gravel shifted underfoot like sand, because the ground beneath it was wet from the previous night's rain. Members of the Afghan Uniformed Police shared the base with the Americans. They stood in groups, keeping their distance, and watched us heft our gear from the vics. Hesko barriers (protective walls) and barbed wire encircled the base, cutting us off from the desert we had just driven through. The tops of distant hills disappeared into low-hanging clouds and formed a fogged-in ridgeline rising and falling toward Pakistan, where I'm told the bad guys retreat after lobbing mortars. In the morning I leave with a patrol for Cherkowtah, an Afghan district even closer to Pakistan, to search for weapons caches.

About a dozen soldiers from First Platoon, 126th Infantry Regiment, gather around the LZ the next morning and wait for the 6:30 briefing before the four-hour drive to Cherkowtah. They put their packs and guns and grenade belts on the ground, hang out in groups of twos and threes, smoking, chewing tobacco, pounding energy drinks. The day is already pushing 100 degrees.

"Afghanistan is fucking biblical, man. Like those movies of Jesus and shit I've seen."

"I'm from San Bernardino. We go back home in November, December. No one knows. I had two weeks' leave in April. Now I got all this time in front of me.

"The dead lieutenant died on the way to Cherkowtah," the San Bernardino soldier tells me. "In a sun-bleached wadi. A smile on his face. Like he was asleep. That was hard. We were crushed."

Gravel crunches underfoot. The soldiers look up, watch the acting sergeant approach.

"Listen up. Who's here?" The acting sergeant reads off three names, stops. No one answers.

"I guess we're not ready to go yet," the acting sergeant says. "I guess 6:30 meant seven fucking o'clock. Here's the fucking word. I'm not the platoon sergeant, but I see things the same. I been doing shit to get ready, and all I see are two fucking team leaders doing their job. You feeling me? Your job is to make sure these motherfuckers are here and ready!"

He glares at us until we all look at the ground. He starts up again.

"I see bags full of trash. This is shit. Guys, when we leave the area of operation, we leave it spotless. And God damn it, don't advertise the energy drinks. We have a crazy first sergeant. He'll scream about dehydration and crack on that shit. No iced coffee, no energy drinks. Guys will fall out behind that shit. Now I want a couple of guys to bag up the garbage and find the rest of you."

A soldier nicknamed Pops jogs off.

"I want it to be someone other than Pops!"

Pops stops. A short, wiry, gung-ho trooper. Called Pops because at thirty-two, he's ancient compared to the other grunts. Lives near the Grand Canyon. Built houses, the economy tanked, he joined the army. Married at eighteen, two kids. Teenagers. Marriage got rocky behind money problems. Hasn't killed any bad guys yet. Carried a dead baby once.

Pops returns to the group, and two other soldiers break off and jog to the mess hall, shouting names. By 7:30 A.M. soldiers crowd the LZ. The sergeant begins roll call again. Everyone answers. He turns the briefing over to the first lieutenant in charge of the mission.

"Hopefully on the way to Cherkowtah, IEDs won't be an issue," the lieutenant says. "Gunner, same shit as always. Be aware. If there's a threat, know where the fuck it is. Use secondary weapons. M-4s. Don't need to level a whole fucking village. Scan ridgelines. Look for shit minesweepers might have missed. Don't relax on the IED threat. Keep heads below fucking shields. That's what they're for. Don't get sloppy. Tuck shirts in. Whole fucking uniform. It's the standard. Do the little things right. Let's mount up."

Four of us sit cramped in the back of the rear-armored vic. The ramp closes, sealing off the outside. Bars limit the view from two windows not much bigger than portholes. Netting stitched with small metal balls hangs over the vic to stop rocket-propelled grenades. We follow three minesweepers. The minesweepers move inches at a time, dragging out the drive to four hours.

A medic sitting across from me says, "This is where the dead lieutenant died." I look out the window at the dry, rock-filled wadi the vic lurches through. We've been driving for about an hour and a half. The bright sky spreads low over the wadi, and a solitary bird soars, dipping and rising on the whims of air.

The medic says he was talking to a buddy when the dead lieutenant stepped on the IED. "How far to Cherkowtah?" "About a click away," his buddy said. Then a boom. "Lead vic's been hit," the soldier driving said. "Anyone down?" "Dunno." Finally the medic heard the order to dismount and the ramp lowered. He remembers jumping out of the vic and running toward the dead lieutenant. He knelt beside the body. He didn't recognize the lieutenant. The medic thought the dead lieutenant was an Afghan soldier because of all the dust on him. Right forearm severed. A sergeant was screaming. There was nothing the medic could do. Every time he comes to Cherkowtah, he sees the dead lieutenant. No matter how many movies he watches. He hasn't told his family, he says, lowering his voice. His commanding officer suggested counseling, but the medic doesn't want that on his record.

Maybe because the vic is driving over the dead lieutenant's deathbed, I am struck by the difference between Afghanistan 2011 and Afghanistan 2001. In 2001, 2002, and most of 2003, you drove from Kabul to the southern city of Kandahar. It took fifteen hours bouncing along war-shattered roads, and when you finally made it into the city, you could buy cans of vodka for about $15. You stopped at villages and drank tea, and the villagers thanked you for visiting them. Girls attended schools. Songs by Madonna played in the streets. Movie theaters reopened, and mine removal projects allowed farmers to return to their land. You could drive east to Jalalabad and go through the border at Torkam and drive into Pakistan. You'd see the Hindu Kush and old trains abandoned on railroad tracks that date to the days of the British Empire. Really. You could go anywhere then and not worry about a thing.

The combat outpost in Cherkowtah stands on a barren scrap of rocky land. One building serves as the HQ and hooch. It reminds me of a shed on an abandoned farm somewhere off Interstate 80 in the middle of Iowa. Inside, bare bulbs hang from wires and bob from the ceiling in a narrow hall. A refrigerator on the porch holds bottled water. A generator pumps water for showers. We shit in plastic bags, tie them off, and throw them in the trash dump. Bags of Meals Ready to Eat lie strewn on one side of the porch. The food tastes of the plastic encasing it. The soldiers like the meals that include Cheez Whiz. You put the Whiz on and it kills the plastic taste.

Night descends, revealing a sky so empty that the moonlight casts a blue hue across the ground. No cities, no towns for miles around. Not even the lantern light from a farm. Dark. This must have been what it was like back in the day, the soldiers tell me. The days of cavemen and shit. This is as close as we will come to Earth's creation. Embarrassed by their own profundity, they move on to things they understand.

"Six-thirty's usually hit time."

"Oh, the hajis haven't hit here in two weeks, since that time we fired back at them."

"Remember that time they fired a mortar and blew themselves up?"

"Then there was an IED that blew up two of them. The minesweeper driver carried a head under his arm."

"A bird was eating a foot."

"Fucking poetic justice."

The voices of the soldiers penetrate the thin plywood walls of the HQ and drift in muffled tones in the empty hall outside a closed door, where the medic sits on his bunk watching *Transformers 3* on DVD. The film was just released. The DVD is a bootleg of the movie someone shot in a theater. The medic laughs when, in the middle of a scene where everything is blowing up, a guy in the audience stands and leaves his seat. The quality is fuzzy, but what the hell, he doesn't have to wait until he goes home to see it, does he? Despite the noise and mayhem on screen, his attention wanders. He has dreams. Vivid. Blood on rocks. Blood everywhere. The dead lieutenant was his first field trauma. The medic fights back tears. His face wrinkles into a dozen cracks. "Other medics have seen a lot worse," he says. "But the first trauma in the field stays with you."

The next morning the sun stains the sky a gauzy pink. Guys stumble from their cots into the dank hall of the hooch, hair askew, faces puffy with sleep. "Morning." "Morning, sir." Slumped and yawning, they wander to the porch and grab bottles of water, rinse their mouths, spit. A few consider eating an MRE. "I'll regret it later if I don't." They sit, squint at the reddening sky and all the empty space beyond the Hesko walls, and bum cigarettes. "You getting a tattoo?" "When I get back." "What of?" "Marine helmet." "I had a friend get a tat. Said, 'God's forgotten children.' He got kicked out later." Look at how the retreating shadows reveal little other than sand and sagebrush and a burgeoning heat that seems to rise out of the ground. Shit.

"Here's the deal," the acting sergeant says at the morning brief. "Weapons cache clearance today. Fucking soon as we get there, understand, we will be only 1,600 feet from Pakistan. Here's what's going to happen. The road bends east, then west. Leave the vics behind a hill so they can't be seen from Pakistan. Rear truck has rear security. Gunners need to be fucking scanning. Be aware of the country—east is Pakistan. Anything on the Afghan side happens, light the fuck up and kill it. But if we take fire from Pakistan, we break contact and get the fuck out of there. We're not firing rounds at their combat outposts on the border. If the only way out is to shoot, we drop some bad news on them and get the fuck out as fast as we can. But if it's coming from one of their outposts, do not shoot at that fucking thing. If it's random assholes in the hills, fire back. OK? Mount up."

(*muttering*)

"Can't shoot at Pakistan, fuck that."

(*shouting*)

"Oooeee, I'm up for some fucking killing today!"

(*backslapping*)

"Hey, pimp daddy, let's fucking roll!"

An hour later I follow Pops up hills along donkey trails into mountains, thorny branches cutting into our pant legs. An empty road below us twists toward Pakistan. Truck from Pakistan. "How many?" "Four in the back. They see us. They're turning around, back to Pakistan." "Don't follow." We look under trees, under rocks, continue following the donkey trails higher. "I found this. Looks like one of our mortar canisters." "You think? Where'd you find it?" "On the fucking ground, sir." The trails wend higher and higher, and some of the soldiers stop, squat, and rest, suck water from their camel packs. Their expressions hidden behind goggles. A sense of discouragement in their stoic solitude. "We won't find anything," Pops tells me. "I hate coming up empty-handed, sir." The loose ground crumbles underfoot, and cries of *shit* and *fuck* follow a rush of gravel and cascading rocks as soldiers slip and slide feet at a time down the mountain before they jam the butts of their AKs in the ground and stop. "Look at this rock, those lines," the lieutenant says. "Yeah, these lines could be from shrapnel." They lean a mortar tube against the rock, fire it, and it scratches the rock. "Yeah, OK, we got something. Take a picture." No one moves. They stare at the rock. A rock. Breathing hard, sweating. Tip their helmets back, rub their foreheads. Turn away. Fuck. The sky seared white, the burning sun.

"I came here to kill, sir," Pops says.

We drive back to the COP. Some of the guys go inside to watch DVDs. Others lounge on the porch, hang their shirts to dry off the sweat. "How was it?" "Nothing. We found nothing." A U.S. civilian law enforcement contractor training Afghan Border Patrol teams sits in a chair and rolls his eyes. A soldier leaning on the railing nods. Another soldier sits on the steps and nods, too. Two soldiers stand by the fridge and offer no reaction.

The contractor: My job is to train Afghans with the Border Security Patrol in law enforcement techniques. When I arrived in Afghanistan, I was told about corruption in the BSP. A General Gul Dad Kahn, who commanded all the BSPs, extorted trunks coming from Pakistan, but no one could prove it. Finally he was removed and replaced by a Lieutenant Colonel Atiq Ullah. Dirty as shit. Ullah liked gifts, put on big meals. He wanted to be adored. He had seven bodyguards. He took caffeine pills to stay up at night. Paranoid as shit. He fled after the Americans came down on him. Now I deal with Taj Mohammad, the second in command under Atiq. Dirty as shit, but he's in charge now of all the BSPs. His second in command was caught running an illegal checkpoint and extorting money. When I talk to Taj, I watch his body language. He twitches, sweats. His foot shakes. He asks if anyone has been arrested for corruption and would he be arrested if he was corrupt. Why would he ask if he wasn't dirty as shit? I hate it here. Think of the lieutenant. What happened to him. He died for guys who shake down jingle trucks. Even the fucking camels growl. I hate it here.

The soldier leaning on the porch railing: We had a kid burned real bad brought here one time. Chemical burns all over his body, hair gone. We wanted to medivac him out, but the brass shot that down. Not enough birds to spare. Just three for this area. Fucking kid died. That sucked. We sent him home. Nothing we could do. He had stopped crying by then. His dad looked like a Taliban. Black beard, turban, and shit. Maybe he burned the kid just so he could look around the COP? I don't know.

The soldiers by the fridge: My mom sent me some cigs.
Yeah? That's a good mom.
It's nothing. I smoke weed with my stepdad.
I smoke dope with my dad. He's sixty-eight.
That's a good dad.

The soldier sitting on the steps: I'm from LA. I joined the army to give back to my country. I'll do my three years so I can say I did something. I worked at a Budweiser plant. Stocking. Things weren't going so good because of the economy. Budweiser just got bought by some European company. I joined in '09. From our drill sergeant, we were told we would take a lot of contact. We haven't seen a firefight yet. We found five IEDs, counting the one that killed the lieutenant. He stepped on it. He was a good guy. One of those guys you felt like you knew your whole life. He died by going up front. He was supposed to stay in his vehicle and send a small team to clear the wadi. It was just him and my squad leader. I was in the front vic. Me and another guy got to him. I could tell he was dead. Like a genie in a bottle. Poof and he's gone. First few weeks, I had images of his body in my head. I thought of

> other things to remind me of him when he was alive. He was always in the gym. When he got here on his first day, he greeted everybody, even the guys in the guard towers. A whole lot of guys don't trust the Afghans, because they figure it was an Afghan that laid that IED, and that doesn't say much for them, if you know what I mean.

I do know, because that trust died before it could be built. When I first arrived in Kabul, barbershops had reopened, and everyone was getting his beard shorn off as a way to show he was free of the Taliban. You would go to press conferences and listen to a U.N. spokesman rattle off how much money such-and-such a country was committing to aid. It was billions and billions. You'd leave and tell your translator, and he would tell his family, and everyone expected jobs. You'd go out and celebrate by buying CDs and DVDs, which had been banned under the Taliban. Everyone would crowd around you in the bazaar because they had never seen Westerners before. You were a curiosity, someone they had only heard about. You were a herald of great things to come. Later, at other press conferences, you began to notice fewer and fewer announcements of aid. Instead the talk was of how little money was coming through. And then the Iraq war started. But there were still insurgents fighting outside Kandahar, although your editors no longer cared. But by then there were no more press conferences. By then you felt you were the only reporter in Afghanistan, and you watched the Iraq war on TV, and you noticed that, unlike Kabul, Baghdad had real roads, all paved and shit, and that made you envious as hell. In those days how old would the dead lieutenant have been? About sixteen or seventeen, right?

In the morning a private and I catch a supply chopper to COP Tereyzai. The private has a two-week leave coming up. I skip the morning brief. The private can't wait for his leave to begin. Wants to know how long pot stays in your system. He'll be piss-tested when he comes back.

"Three days," I tell him.

"Three days, really?"

"Three days."

"No problem."

The briefing is done, and Pops is shouting: "Let's get some killing done today, boys!"

I tell the private that tomorrow I'll leave Tereyzai for Border Security Patrol 6 on the Pakistan border, not far from Cherkowtah.

"A real shit hole," the private says.

"Really?"

"Yeah."

"Oh, well."

"Three days?"

"Yeah."

"You sure?"

"Yeah."

An hour later we land on the Tereyzai LZ. The sergeant splits to his hooch, making up a little ditty with "three days" as the chorus line. I wander to the interpreters' hooch. They live below the watchtower across from a makeshift gym. The terps boil water, offer me tea. They left Afghanistan after the Russians invaded and moved to the United States by way of Pakistan, Asia, and Australia. One lives in New Mexico. Another in New York. Still another in D.C. They tell me they work for the army to be a part of history. To tell their kids they were a part of freeing Afghanistan from the Taliban. The New York terp says he worked with the dead lieutenant and was sad for two days after the lieutenant died. "The dead lieutenant hadn't been here but four, five months maybe," the New York terp says. "Yeah, his death was bad, but it's war. After he died, things went back to normal, a new normal, but it became an old normal after a while."

Border Security Patrol 6 stands at the top of a desolate muddy hill. The gray sky presses down, and we follow a slick mud road, slip and slide, careening toward the edge, until we round a curve and drive onto a flattened plain ringed by Hesko bags. We wait at a checkpoint while an Afghan guard calls someone on a walkie-talkie. Taj Mohammad appears minutes later, gives a hard stare, and then waves us through. The lieutenant in charge of this mission didn't expect Taj Mohammad to be here. "Be careful. The Afghans don't want us on their base." Weeks earlier American troops had busted Afghans at Border Security Patrol 7 for shaking down truck drivers entering Afghanistan from Pakistan for about 3,000 rupees. The lieutenant heard that the Afghans at BSP 6 were also extorting jingle trucks. "We want to check them out and show them some love," the lieutenant says.

The soldiers call the terp on this mission James Dean. No one knows how the name originated. James Dean has thick black hair that hangs loosely around his shoulders, and he wears dark sunglasses that conceal his eyes, and when he stands and faces the wind, his hair trails behind him and his sunglasses reflect the sky and the soldiers unpacking the vics. "Afghan soldiers will do what their commanders tell them," James Dean tells me. "If they are told to take money, they will take it. They want to make money. They'll stay up here and make money when we leave."

Taj Mohammad tells the lieutenant he is here to inspect the base. He swears he is cracking down on corruption. He wants to go on patrol in Tereyzai to get a Taliban guy he says drives into the district every night. Is he saying this to kiss the lieutenant's ass? Does he really want to get bad guys? It doesn't matter. Tereyzai is under the jurisdiction of the Afghan Uniformed Police, not the Border Security Patrol. Taj Mohammad would need at least one AUP officer to accompany him and avoid a turf battle, but only thirty-five AUP patrol all of Tereyzai District. There are none to spare for Taj Mohammad. Besides, the AUP never leaves its barracks without U.S. forces. And the U.S. forces don't patrol with them because the IED threat in Tereyzai is too high. So whatever his motives, Mohammad will not get his man.

Taj Mohammad asks if the Americans will continue bringing BSP 6 supplies: water, food, ammunition, and money to pay his soldiers. The lieutenant suggests that supplies should be brought in by the Afghan government on jingle trucks. "But they would be stopped by the Taliban," Taj Mohammad says. "Well, we have to try something," the lieutenant says. "We won't be here forever."

After lunch the lieutenant tells the soldiers to set up a perimeter. Taj Mohammad told us that the bad guys typically mortar BSP 6 in the afternoon. The Afghans never engage them. Instead they stay inside a bunker. "It's unlikely they will attack with us here, but you never know," the lieutenant says. "Can always hope. Don't fire into Pakistan."

I sit with the lieutenant beneath a tarp overlooking a valley. Wind blows, pushing empty plastic water bottles across the rocky ground. No sound other than the static on the lieutenant's radio. "Did I just hear a boom?" the lieutenant asks. "Negative," a voice says through the static. "OK. I guess I'm just going crazy," the lieutenant says.

The lieutenant tells me he was a friend of the dead lieutenant's. They attended officer training school together at Fort Benning. The dead lieutenant died near a village. People were questioned. Said they didn't know anything. "But you know what?" the lieutenant says. "For people who didn't know anything, you didn't hear about any of them dying from an IED just 2,000 feet outside their village, did you?"

The bad guys don't shoot at BSP 6. After two hours the lieutenant radios the soldiers to stand down. One of the soldiers wishes he had fought in Vietnam. "We don't get direct fire," he says. "Just IEDs. How do you fight people like that?" "Can't spend time wishing for the war you want," the lieutenant tells him.

The lieutenant allows the soldiers to fire into a hill near the Pakistan border. The soldiers fire their AKs, .50 cals, mortar guns, and M240s at once, and the air fills with jolting bursts of *boom, boom, boom.* Piercing whistling noises spiral out of the booms and curve around the hill like boomerangs and race back toward us to abruptly dissipate into silence, a trailing wind rushing against our faces. Even without holding a weapon and despite cringing at the noise, I feel a rush in the convulsing power reverberating through my body, a rush that leaves me drained during moments of silence and yearning for more.

Later I sit with James Dean on a rock overlooking the valley below us. A few figures shrunken in shadow walk toward a mud hut. Taj Mohammad's men. Behind us soldiers sprawl on the hoods of their vics and try to sleep. Fog hovers all around and assumes the color of ink as evening merges into night. "We're all going to die," James Dean tells me. He doesn't care about death anymore. He did before, but now he doesn't. As a boy, it was easy for him to take his father's gun and go into the mountains and kill as many as twenty birds. Today the Taliban kill people like birds. James Dean tells me about a time when the bad guys dialed a cell phone and blew up an IED in Tereyzai District. Two Afghans were killed and two were blinded. "You know about the dead lieutenant?" I nod. "Better to die than be blind,' James Dean says.

We leave BSP 6 in the morning. The lieutenant won't wait for the minesweepers. "*Audacity* is a word I'm bringing back into vogue," the lieutenant says. He charts an off-road route he thinks the bad guys would not mine because they would never suspect we'd use it. We drive down the hill and at the lieutenant's command turn off a bridge into a wadi. Rocks and mounds of dirt tear up the vics. One vic stalls. At the lieutenant's instructions we leave the wadi for a road. He knows roads are mined. Shit. He radios in for minesweepers.

Halfway to Tereyzai the minesweepers discover a hundred-pound IED. While we wait for it to be detonated, we turn off the road to inspect a vacant village of stone huts shaped like igloos. The walls of some of the huts have crumbled to the ground in an avalanche of disuse. The lieutenant squints at the cloudless sky as if he is trying to read it. Two graves covered with rocks lie behind the lieutenant. "We need to verify these are graves and that someone's not hiding weapons," he says. "Can I piss on them, sir?" a soldier asks. "Don't desecrate them," the lieutenant says. The soldier begins tossing rocks off the larger of the two graves, revealing nothing but dirt and bits of cloth. "It's an adult's grave and a child's grave," James Dean says. "I think it's a mother and a baby. The mother probably died giving birth and the baby died, too." James Dean begins piling the rocks back onto the grave. "You know that hundred-pound IED we found?" the soldier says, watching James Dean. "If we had hit it, all of us would have been fucking dead."

Standing beside the soldier, I think that if the dead lieutenant was with us, I would tell him that his fellow soldiers worry they might die as innocuously as he did. That they won't go out in a blaze of glory in some defining battle but in some anonymous burst of bad luck that leaves no impression other than one man's obituary. That everything they know about weapons and fighting and manhood would lose the chance to be tested. That they would die incomplete.

I would tell the dead lieutenant that I thought the war was over in 2002 when you were still a teenager and had not yet enlisted, but I was wrong. I'm not sure when I realized I was wrong. Maybe in 2003, when the people in the bazaars greeted me with silent sullen stares instead of joyful curiosity. Or maybe it was later, when I was told I could not drive the newly paved road from Kabul to Kandahar because insurgents controlled it. Or it might have been even later, when the town of Wardak, forty minutes outside Kabul, was overtaken by the Taliban. Or maybe it was on this trip, just before I left for Fort Salerno, when insurgents killed nine people in the Kabul hotel where the 2001 press conferences promising massive aid had been held. I thought I knew what U.S. soldiers died for in the years before your enlistment. I don't know now.

Back at COP Tereyzai I sit beside a soldier at a picnic table outside the mess hall. The soldier rolls up his sleeves and shows me a tattoo of blue veins and red muscles extending down both arms. Frowning theatrical masks are falling through the veins. He asks what I'm doing here.

"I'm a reporter."

"Yeah? You hear about the lieutenant, sir?"

"Which one?"

"The dead one, sir."

"Yes," I say. "Yes, I have."

6

Revolution Download

Aleppo, Syria: January–February 2013

An explosion. Followed by another.

"Downloading," Nizar says in the dark.

He applies the language of the Internet to the live video game outside. Incoming fire from the Syrian government he calls downloading. Return fire by the rebels is uploading.

"It's going to shit something," his cousin Radwan says. "What do you think, Uncle?"

He calls me Uncle because I am more than thirty years older than he. When we drove into Aleppo five days ago, my shoulders jerked in fright at every burst of gunfire, at every explosion. Now I've stopped reacting unless it stays quiet. Then I feel uneasy.

"It sounded close," I say.

We sit on the floor wrapped in blankets, shift closer to a wood-burning stove in the center of the room and the dying embers inside it. Amer and Bassel, friends of Radwan and Nizar, sit beside me. I wear three pairs of long underwear, tops and bottoms, two pairs of socks, jeans, a wool shirt, sweatshirt, coat. No power, no heat in the apartment, in the building, in the block, in all of Aleppo. The brittle January air tastes metallic. Ice films the ceiling. Sometimes we refill the stove with wood, sometimes not. It depends how desperate we feel, how much more cold we can stand. Burning wood warms us but creates another kind of misery.

Much of the wood comes from the debris of buildings shit-kicked by mortar rounds. Busted-up doors, chairs, sofas. The glue used to seal joints emits a foul odor when it's burned. We cough, our heads pound. Better to freeze. See your breath kind of freezing. Too cold to bathe. We douse our funk with the overripe sweetness of perfume snatched from the dressing room of an abandoned apartment. We crept into the apartment, down a hall and through a dining room, as if we didn't want to disturb the absent family. Bread on the table, a plate of chicken. They were about to eat (lunch? dinner?) but instead fled. In another room Mickey Mouse sits in an airplane suspended from the ceiling. The plane spins above an empty bed (a boy's?), the sheets folded back.

Radwan gives in to the cold. He stands, opens a balcony door to retrieve a sack of wood for the stove. Frosty air rushes in. Beyond the balcony young men, many of them former university students, roam the streets. They belong to their own militias within the loose conglomeration of rebels known as the Free Syrian Army that is fighting the government of President Bashar al-Assad. They carry pistols, Kalashnikovs, rocket-propelled grenades, and move openly, almost casually, in the street like pied pipers followed by chanting boys.

"God bless the FSA! God bless the FSA!"

The rebels' passion for the revolution is real. But they have no plan for the future other than the immediate one of ousting Assad. They live day by day, with only the authority that comes with carrying a gun as their guide.

The lines separating FSA forces and government troops zigzag between them, splitting neighborhoods into a puzzle of forever shifting, disputed territory. Many streets remain deserted, their apartments and businesses empty, controlled by government snipers.

In the night, if the snipers see no one to shoot, they will kill stray cats and dogs, Radwan says. Even birds.

Every morning we see dead animals.

We avoid open areas. Instead we move through a maze of houses like interconnected caves. We enter one house, walk over a couch and through a wall blasted open by a rocket-propelled grenade, and enter another house. We continue in this way, house to house, until we reach our destination. One time I got confused and emerged from a house and onto a street covered by a sniper. Radwan yanked me back inside. "You want to die, man?" he said.

Although they are not part of the FSA, Nizar and Radwan carry guns. Nizar owns a Schweizer, a German-made pistol. Radwan carries a Kalashnikov. Nizar makes a big show of clearing the Schweizer's chamber every morning. He likes shoving the clip in and taking aim at imaginary targets.

Tonight he points it at me. "I will kill you, Malcolm."

He jokes, I know, but I also know he wants to shoot. To feel the heft of his pistol and the kick it gives when it's fired.

There are many ways to die in Syria now, Nizar says.

The Syrian uprising was almost two years old when I decided to visit Aleppo. It is the largest Syrian city and considered strategically important. Fighting between the rebels and government forces began there in July 2012. Rebels quickly seized several neighborhoods, but six months later and about the time I planned my trip, the battle developed into a bloody stalemate with heavy street fighting that left neighborhoods in ruins and forced thousands to flee.

I had no idea how to enter Syria until a friend introduced me to a Syrian doctor in Utah. She put me in touch with her cousin, a Syrian activist in Turkey. He introduced me to a group of FSA supporters through a Skype chat group. The lead member of the group used the moniker "Aleppo Rad." He would not reveal his real name because, he said, it would put his family and friends in Syria at risk. He already had a younger brother in jail, and his father had recently fled to Turkey to avoid arrest. Aleppo Rad offered to get me into Aleppo, where his family had an apartment. We agreed to meet in Hatay, a Turkish town about an hour's drive from the Syrian border.

Four weeks later I stood at the entrance gate to Mustafa Kameel University in Hatay. I called a number on my cell phone. A voice on the other end, Aleppo Rad's, told me to raise my right hand. I did. Looking around, I noticed three men standing by a white van. One of them waved. They had on heavy winter coats and wool caps. One wore glasses and had a patchy beard covering his face. I walked toward them. They hurried me into the van. I slid across the backseat. A sticker of a black flag associated with jihadists filled a corner of the windshield.

I glanced back toward the university, the throng of students, the sounds of their voices. Then the bearded man slammed the door shut.

His name was Nizar, aka Aleppo Rad. He drove. He was twenty-six and had been an architecture student at the University of Aleppo when the uprising started. He attended his classes and marched in demonstrations. Later, when the FSA entered Aleppo, he threw Molotov cocktails and worked as an FSA medic. Now he was "in media." He shoots YouTube videos for the FSA as part of a public relations effort.

Twenty-two-year-old Radwan rode shotgun. He was stocky, with a thin beard and nearly shaved head. He too had been an architecture student. He moved to Aleppo after the uprising had spread to his village, Taybet al-Emam, just outside Hama. In 1982 Assad's father, Hafez al-Assad, crushed a rebellion there.

One day a friend told Radwan the Syrian army was coming to their village with tanks. Radwan drove his motorcycle to the main road but saw nothing. Then he heard a tank. A soldier walked behind it. When he saw Radwan, he started shooting. Bullets thudded into the ground behind and around him. Radwan bolted across a field. That was his first encounter with a Syrian soldier. Since then he has faced hundreds more.

"You sure you want to do this?" he asked me.

At the border we stopped at a Turkish police station. An officer copied my passport and thrust a sheet of paper at me. It explained that Syria was in the midst of a civil war. Consequently the Turkish government bore no responsibility for my welfare. I signed it. He stamped my visa. I walked outside, passed through two security checkpoints. Nizar and Radwan waited for me on the other side of a gate. I followed a line of people through it.

The rebels controlled the border and no Syrian entry authority approached me. Burned tanks listed by the side of the road.

"Welcome to Syria," Nizar said.

We met up with Bassel, another member of Nizar's media team. Bassel shot video in Idlib, Syria, where his family lived. He was twenty-six, thin, and stoop shouldered, but he had an easy grin and patted me on the back, as if to assure me I would be fine. Last year the police in Idlib had detained him, but he escaped. He had not seen his family in seven months.

"Show me your balls, man," he said to me and laughed.

Bassel, Nizar explained, spoke little English. However, he loved quoting the lines of bad guys in low-budget American movies.

"Show me your tits, bitch," Bassel said.

We drove about a mile and then turned off the road at an FSA aid station. A blue tarp covered sacks of rice for Syrians who had lost their homes in the war. Nizar, Radwan, and Bassel entered a warehouse. They came out moments later carrying guns.

"For protection," Radwan said to me.

We drove south, passing through small villages congested with street vendors, cars, and mule-drawn carts. But as we continued, we saw fewer and fewer people, and the air turned noticeably colder. Shuttered shops threw long shadows, casting shrouds over those things that signaled the absence of activity: a stray soccer ball, a door open to a ransacked shop, a bucket swaying above a well.

We stopped at the house of Abu Saif, another member of Nizar's media team. He lives in the Aleppo countryside. He showed us video he had shot of FSA soldiers. In one video a soldier crept forward across a meadow. "Move slowly," a soldier behind him said, "or the birds here will reveal our position." In the same video moments later the soldiers raised their guns, then lowered them. "Don't shoot, civilians," the first soldier said.

"Syrians are fighting against each other," Saif said when the video ended. "It upsets me, but the truth is, we are right. We protested and the regime shot us, so we had to use guns to defend ourselves. It's a revolution. There is an end to everything. Dying is just a habit now."

An hour later we entered Aleppo. Shuttered stores stood submerged in darkness, black hulks, bleak outlines against the fathomless depths of the night. Flames rose from trash fires, and sparks drifted into the sky, and I saw lines of people huddled outside a bakery waiting for bread, a bright light inside glossing the pale brown loaves like oil, and the flames outside rose higher with the wind, and the faces of men and women shuddered and danced, their distorted shadows climbing up the sides of the closed shops. Mortar holes yawned open until the wind settled and the night closed over the subdued flames.

An empty freeway arched above an intersection. Beneath it, an FSA checkpoint. Nizar shut off his headlights. A government sniper held a position on the far side of the freeway, he explained. If he saw our lights he might shoot. Yet without our lights we risked marooning the car on the huge chunks of blasted concrete that covered the road. Nizar flashed his lights on and off, swerved around the looming obstacles. A sharp snap of gunfire. I sank low in my seat. An FSA soldier peered inside our car with a flashlight and waved us through.

Nizar stopped at an apartment building a few blocks away. We got out, and he opened a metal door, and we filed into a dark hall and felt our way up the steps to an apartment on the fourth floor.

Inside we took off our boots and walked into a large room with two sofas and a wood-burning stove. I met twenty-two-year-old Amer, yet another member of Nazir's media group. He stays in the apartment when Nazir is away. I sat beside him, blew on my hands.

"Where are you from?"

"Chicago."

"Chicago. Al Capone," Amer said. "I like how Capone controlled everything."

An explosion. And then another.

"There's no control here," Amer said.

Now, days later, I slip out from my sleeping bag, arms squeezed at my sides against the cold, and hurry toward the stove. Radwan and Nazir lie on the couches covered with blankets. Bassel snores on the floor. Socks and underwear hang from hooks above the stove. Ashtrays overflow with crushed cigarette butts. Amer peers at me, squinting, his hair matted down with sleep.

"We used all the wood last night," he says. "This apartment is like fucking Siberia."

He sits up, offers me a cigarette, and shakes Nizar. "We need wood, Nizar," he says.

Nizar burrows deeper into his sleeping bag. Amer shrugs. He and Nizar met at an antigovernment demonstration. At first Amer opposed the uprising. The regime, he thought, could not be challenged. But many more people believed that the regime would fall, as Mubarak had in Egypt. However, instead of collapsing, the government ordered its security forces to shoot demonstrators. Amer got involved then. Out of respect for the martyrs. He distributed leaflets denouncing the government. "Don't worry, Syria," the pamphlets read. "Freedom, it is coming."

A taxi driver asked him, "What is freedom to you?"

"To do what you want without hurting people," Amer said.

"Do you think we have freedom here?"

Amer didn't answer. Why, he wondered, was a taxi driver asking him these questions?

Later that day six security officers arrested him in an Internet cafe.

"See this?" one said, waving a leaflet the taxi driver had given him. "You want freedom?"

They dragged Amer outside, hitting him in the back with batons. He was shoved into a van and taken to a police station. The beatings continued. "Say good-bye to your mother; you will never see her again," they told him. They tied his wrists and suspended him from the ceiling. Only the tips of his toes touched the floor. After six days a friend bribed members of the security forces, and Amer was released.

"What happened to me was nothing," Amer says. "It happened to everybody."

After Nizar and Radwan reluctantly relinquish the warmth of their blankets, we walk to the Old City of Aleppo.

Built in the twelfth and sixteenth centuries, the Old City is a city within walls and remains contested territory between the rebels and government forces. Its ancient stones loom above destroyed pickup trucks and ambulances. We hunch over and sprint across a road covered by a government sniper, then enter the Old City through one of its twelve entrances.

A hive of cobbled streets and alleys twists below towering stone mansions and smaller apartment buildings with cell-like rooms, all abandoned. FSA soldiers mill on street corners. Some sit on sofas hauled out of a vacant home.

One soldier, fifty-year-old Yasser, was in a firefight with the army early that morning. About 3 A.M. he heard whispering coming from a government-held position. Get ready, he told his men. Don't shoot.

Let them get closer. He saw a line of government soldiers reflected in a bedroom mirror he had positioned at an angle on a shattered wall. He fired the first shot. A man behind him threw a grenade. Yasser fired into the dust rising from the explosion and kept shooting. Ten government soldiers died in thirty minutes. Yasser allowed the survivors to remove the bodies.

"We are fighting for God!" he shouted at them.

Yasser leads us deeper into the Old City. The sun catches the pink bandanna wrapped around his forehead. He follows some FSA soldiers into what had been a hotel. They stop on the second floor, consider the numbers on the guest room doors. Two, three, four, five. By our feet, Crest toothpaste, a comb, a brush. Deodorant. Dead plants. Bird shit. A teddy bear. Clothes in a closet. Sweaters, dresses. We wander back outside. An FSA soldier squats amid twisted metal and broken stones of a collapsed building. Baskets, shutters, milk crates, cans of tomatoes, a toilet, a chandelier. Cats prowl.

The scene stirs echoes in my mind of the voices of people I've encountered and the stories they told:

> *A barber:* Three rockets struck three buildings in my block. A large piece of metal tore through the door. I counted one hundred explosions in an hour. Jets came with bombs. Shrapnel struck the building like rain.

A government sniper fires a shot from a white building blocks away. We look through a hole in the cream-colored walls. Near the building we see a mosque and brown smudges of smog and a billboard advertising canned beef.

We wander back outside. An FSA soldier squats amid twisted metal and broken stones of a collapsed building. Baskets, shutters, milk crates, cans of tomatoes, a toilet, a chandelier.

More voices:

> *A fruit vendor:* People lay on the pavement bleeding. Some of them called for help, but no one stopped. A neighbor lost a son, his only boy. A jet[plane] fired, exploding

> burned cars with burned people inside. The government was sending a message: Without Assad, you will have no milk, food, schools, hospitals. Come back to us. Think again or die.

The FSA soldier plays a trombone pilfered from a music store across from the rubble. Another soldier beats a drum. A third blows on a harmonica. Some soldiers nearby begin dancing to the distorted sounds.

"You want to see me shoot somebody?" Yasser asks.

> *A teacher:* At the slightest noise I remember that night. I see bodies again, hear people screaming.

He jogs to a wall and aims his Kalashnikov at the building used by the government sniper. He squeezes the trigger, but the gun jams. He clears the chamber and reloads. Fires. One, two, three, four. Each shot like a slap. He lowers his gun, has no idea if he has killed the sniper. If not today, another time. He saunters back to where the soldiers dance.

"The cheapest thing in Syria," Yasser says, "is life."

Abu al-Majd, an FSA soldier, stands at an intersection not far from where the soldiers dance. He was in the Syrian army before he defected to the FSA. He saw soldiers kill demonstrators in the countryside of Damascus. People who escaped, escaped. Others died or lost an arm, a leg. Al-Majd would only fire his gun in the air.

He defected and moved to Turkey. When the war came to Aleppo, he joined the FSA there. He was twenty. Because of his military background, he became a sniper. One time he saw a government soldier praying. He wept and put his gun down. He could not shoot a devout Muslim. He cries telling this story. He taps his feet in a puddle, splashing water on his white sneakers, and his fingers drum against his knees. Every day he worries he might shoot a friend with whom he served in the army. He asks God, "Please don't let me kill someone I know."

Some days he asks more from God: "God, please don't let me see any government soldiers today, good or bad. I don't want to shoot anyone today."

When he visits his wife, he tries to forget the war and all the souls of the people he has killed. In his dreams God asks him, "Why are you killing?"

"I have to kill," al-Majd says, "or I will die. It's hard. I am sorry."

From Old City we drive to Said al-Dawlah, a neighborhood in west Aleppo. We race through intersections covered by snipers. Shower curtains and blankets strung across streets provide some cover. Blown balconies hang like broken jaws. Doors list on their hinges. The ripped side of one apartment exposes a kitchen cabinet, a table set with silverware, a bowl-shaped light above it. A clock on a wall frozen at half past two. All of it somehow undisturbed.

We park by four FSA soldiers. A small stick fire burns at their feet. One of the men, Az-Addin Salem, offers to show us his clinic. We walk behind him, through the gate of an apartment building and down a flight of broken steps to a patio. On the wall, a painting of a beach. Palm trees and bright yellow sand. Someone wrote, "Allahu Akbar" (God is great), beneath it.

Stepping through a blasted wall, we drop down onto a sofa and emerge into a dim living room. A table filled with tweezers, forceps, and cotton stands alongside an entertainment unit: TV, VCR. A box of antibiotics, expiration date 2010.

Salem was an engineer before the revolution. He knew the war would eventually come to Aleppo. He did not want to carry a gun. He looked at himself in a mirror, at his gray hair and gray beard. The lines in his face, his sagging chest. At fifty-eight he knew he was too old to shoot. To prepare for the coming fight, he stopped by a hospital and asked to be taught first aid. He learned how to take blood pressure, how to drain a chest of fluid, how to stitch deep cuts. Then he joined the FSA as a medic.

He sees two or three soldiers a day, often for sniper wounds. He always asks about the people he has cared for, but no one seems to know anything about them. Whether they returned to the front or not. When he is alone, he thinks about them.

Salem introduces us to his commander, Abu Ali. Ali is forty-four, a thin wiry man in white sweatpants, a yellow hoodie, and sneakers. His graying hair is perfectly combed, a line of stubble neatly trimmed.

"Come, come. Come, come," he says, barely taking the time to shake our hands. He jogs into an apartment building and through a sacked bedroom. Climbing through a hole in the wall, he emerges into a courtyard. We hurry after him, cross into another apartment building, and make our way down a hall. A faded map of the neighborhood, tacked to a wall above a plastic duck, rustles from our movement. Ali holds the duck against his cheek and smiles, blinking his eyes like a flirt. Assad has a mistress who calls him Ducky, he says. Then he drops the duck and rushes on. "Please, please, come, come."

We climb a flight of stairs to a bedroom, the walls painted pink with white clouds. An FSA sniper lies on his stomach, peering through the scope of his rifle. He offers the rifle to me. I look through the scope. Across a courtyard I see two men in green uniforms on the deck of an apartment. The Syrian flag flies above them.

Ali tells the sniper not to shoot. He doesn't want to give away their position. Not yet.

We retrace our steps to where we started. Ali leads us to an expansive stone building with about a dozen rooms. Here he lives with his wife and four children. One room holds a large cache of weapons: seven Kalashnikovs, gas masks, mayonnaise jars filled with TNT, tank bombs, jet bombs, plastic explosives, and a bomb converted from a blown water heater. Molotov cocktails in Chivas Regal, Black Label, and Johnny Walker bottles stand on a table.

Ali looks at his watch. Four p.m. "Enough for today," he says.

He shoos us out so he can spend this time with his family. He devotes at least two hours a day to them. He has a boy and three girls. The girls are Sarah, a Jewish name, Ali points out; Helen, a Christian name; and Farrah, Arabic for happiness. His son is Mohammad, a Muslim name. Ali has no problem with Christians and Jews. Everyone can live together happily so long as they believe in some kind of God.

Yesterday he borrowed a generator and watched part of the *Lord of the Rings* trilogy on DVD with his wife and children. After the movie they listened to gunfire. When the fighting first started, the children would vomit from fear. Now, months later, they play war games during the day. One child pretends to be a Syrian army soldier, the three others FSA. The FSA always wins.

"We live together as a family," Ali says. "Live together or die together."

We leave Ali and return to Nizar's apartment. We put wood in the stove and prepare for another night of sitting in the dark when the lights snap on. We look at one another, blink in disbelief. My God, we have power! Bassel doesn't miss a beat. He turns on the TV and flips channels to a Dubai station that shows music videos. Four women dance across the screen, singing in Arabic. Their skimpy outfits leave little to the imagination.

Bassel pulls his shirt up and points to his chest.

"What is this in English?"

"Nipple," I tell him.

Radwan, Nizar, and Amer join him in front of the TV, their sexual desires colliding with their fundamentalist beliefs. Women, Radwan says, violate the Koran if they have sex before marriage, dance, don't wear head scarves, and expose their bodies. Amer agrees. He blames Assad for introducing nightclubs to Syria. Places where men go to drink alcohol, meet girls, fuck, and get AIDS, he says.

None of them, however, can keep their eyes off the TV.

"That girl in the video shakes her ass like Shakira," Nizar says.

"I love Shakira's ass, man," Radwan tells him.

"I love California blondes. I hear they rule the house," Amer says.

"You take the house, I'll take the blonde," Radwan says.

They laugh. Then Radwan turns serious again. "When Assad falls, the new leadership will have to teach people real Islam," he says. Step by step. Islam is very clear. Do this, do that. Women can't just walk around nude. People can disagree, but if they do, they must disagree in secret and keep their opinions to themselves.

"And this?" I say, pointing to the video.

"Right now, we are making a mistake," Radwan says. "But after we watch this, if we say, 'God forgive us,' we will be forgiven."

Midnight. We lose power. The TV snaps off. We sit in the dark.

Radwan: The paper, Uncle, the one you signed at the Turkish border said this was a civil war?

Malcolm: Yes.

Radwan: That was wrong. This is a revolution. The people against the government. Do you understand?

Malcolm: Yes.

Radwan: There are three levels of people fighting the government. First level: FSA soldiers. They hate Assad. They just want freedom. They shout God is great, but they don't fight for God. They like material things. They steal. They are not always friendly to civilians. Not all but many of them. OK, the second level: They are good Muslims, but they don't have a strict interpretation of Islam. They don't think women need to be covered all the time. The last one, the third level: They are true Muslims, true jihadists. They will do anything for Islam. They like death more than life. They will die to open the door to paradise. They are like the Special Forces. They have no fear. They are our best fighters. They will fight anybody to have their interpretation of Islam in place.

Malcolm: Which one are you?

Radwan: When we have no power, I am third level. When we have power and the TV is on, I'm second level [*laughs*]. But I will be third level when the war is over because the jihadists will kick the FSA's ass.

Malcolm: So it is a civil war.

Radwan: No, not now. Now it is a revolution.

Midmorning, next day. We are meeting with Ali when we hear gunfire erupting near the Old City. Lots of it. *Poppoppopoppoppop!* Ali shouts at his men, and they shout at one another and scream into walkie-talkies: "What's happening? What's happening?" Ali runs one way and then another, screaming, "Get in the van, Get in the van," calling names, "Khalid, Nabil, all of you, get in! get in! get in!" and Ali jumps into the van behind them, "Go!" and the van races downhill, beeping, leaping over the debris of toppled buildings, bouncing against the curb as a fighter hangs on to the van's open door, his legs flying out from under him, *beepbeepbeepbeep,* kids cheering, shouting, "Allahu Akbar," Ali screaming, "Movemovemovemove!" and he raises his Kalashnikov and fires rounds into the sky, *popoppopopop,* Movemovemovemove!" and the van plows through a bazaar, overturning vegetable carts, bicycle riders, "Gogogogogo!"

Then, just like that, Ali tells the driver to stop. He listens to a voice on his walkie-talkie. His men watch him.

"The shooting has stopped," Ali says. One civilian dead. Another martyr. "Allahu Akbar."

We follow Ali back to his command and into the ammunition room of his house. He begins filling the rocket made from a water cooler with plastic explosives. The shooting outside the Old City will not go unchallenged. He tightens the cap and wraps it in plastic to keep it dry. A chemical engineer and a car mechanic taught him how to make bombs. He twists a drill bit in the nose of the rocket to trigger the explosion. Satisfied, he wraps a black scarf around his neck, tossing one loose end over his shoulder.

"Terroriste," he says.

Carrying the rocket, a copper wire switch, and a plastic pipe, Ali walks outside. We follow him across a ruined park to a house. We make our way to a kitchen. Outside the kitchen, a deck. On the other side of the deck railing, a stepladder. We hear a government sniper shooting close by.

Ali waves us forward. We clamber over the top of the railing, lower ourselves to the stepladder, jump to the patio wall of another house, and lower ourselves by grasping a tree branch. We jog through this house and run across an alley divided by a laundry line of blankets to yet another house. Up a flight of stairs to the second floor. There. Through a window we see government soldiers in the same building we had watched days earlier when we met Ali's sniper.

Ali presses a finger to his lips. Sound carries. *Shhh.* He hums Beethoven's Fifth Symphony, *da, da, da, dommmm,* and twists a fuse into the end of the rocket. He positions the rocket out the window. He lights the fuse.

Da, da, da, dommmm—

The explosion throws me on my ass. The building across from us lurches like a man punched in the stomach. Smoke and ash rise, and it begins to crumble. "Allahu Akbar! Allahu Akbar!" Ali's men shout, and then we run back down the hall, outside and across the alley, gunfire and shelling rocketing the house, running, the laundry line of blankets dancing from the explosions, small bursts of dust where bullets strike the pavement, running, the noise of our feet against pavement, the feel of our arms pumping, reaching, lunging up the stepladder, rolling over the railing and dashing into the kitchen, running, gasping, running down a hall and outside, running into Ali's house.

Ali paces in the hall, breathes deeply, hands on his hips.

"Bullets so close to me," he says. "I was dancing like a marionette!"

"Calm down, calm down," his men urge him.

"Did you see the entrance to the building?" Ali says. "There's no entrance anymore!"

"Where are you going?" a soldier asks him.

Ali stops, listens to gunfire and mortar rounds smashing into the house from which he fired the rocket. He smiles. He walks toward his wife and children at the end of the hall. His gait is jaunty. He has no specific plan to follow up the assault.

"Perhaps tomorrow," he says, "when they won't expect us."

In the evening Yasser, the FSA soldier, meets in the Old City with new FSA recruits to discuss two kinds of combat: street fighting and siege. Street fighting moves slowly, building by building, block by block, city by city. Before you take a block, you remove civilians from the area. Then you put a sniper in a good location and deploy cars with big machine guns like a 12.7 or a 7.62 PKM. Russian made. It's really good. The sniper provides cover, and you start moving your men in. You have to get close to the Syrian army to have a good shot. You occupy buildings, blow holes in the walls, and shoot at the enemy. You try not to destroy government buildings. They have documents and computers that may bear useful information.

To take Syrian army bases and airports requires a siege. You have to be really careful. The bases have heavy guns, planes, and ammunition. You need lots of FSA fighters. You must organize as efficiently as possible. You surround the base and cut off electricity. You don't allow anything in, food, water. You do this for at least one month. Then you destroy a wall, storm a few buildings, kill, and take weapons. You move from building to building, forcing the army back. When they retreat to the last building, you shell it and kill them all.

In the evening Abu al-Majd, the FSA sniper, rests the tip of his long rifle inside a hole in the wall of an abandoned apartment in the Old City. The location of the hole is important. The hole needs to overlook a wide area so he can see lots of streets.

Al-Majd sits on a chair with two pillows beneath him. He asks God to spare him from shooting someone he knows. He adjusts his aim to accommodate the wind. He will remain at his post for four hours. He won't eat, piss, or shit. Just look through the scope of his rifle, through the hole in the wall. Some days he never fires a shot. Other days he shoots and they fall, and he runs to another room to avoid being shot himself by return fire. He makes a new hole in a different room and takes up his position. He asks God once more to spare him from shooting someone he knows.

In the evening we hear another explosion. I look at Nizar. Download or upload? He turns to me and shrugs. Radwan crosses his arms and shivers in the cold. Bassel and Amer stare out the window at the shaking night sky. I stuff clothes in my duffle. I return to Turkey in the morning.

"Some people have seen their brother die, their sister raped," Amer says, turning away from the window. "What will they do after the war?"

I continue packing. I don't know how to answer his question. I leave Syria believing this revolution is mostly ad hoc with very real people devoted to it but conflicted about what's being asked of them, while still others have found their life's meaning in war. Who would they be without it? Unemployed university students, many of them. The longer the fighting lasts, the longer they have a purpose. What follows should Assad fall is almost beside the point.

"I will kill you, Malcolm," Nizar says and points his gun at me.

". . . When it's all over, I just hope we can forgive," Amer says. "It's just a hope I have, that's all."

Ali finishes watching *Lord of the Rings* with his family.

PART 2

Lost and Gone

7

You Cannot Tell from the Expressions on Our Faces What We Are Feeling

Islamabad, Pakistan: January–February 2009

The Western diplomat cuts two lines of cocaine on his iPhone and snorts them with a 100-rupee bill.

"Pure Colombian," he says. "Don't be shy."

I shake my head.

"A bit of jet lag, I expect?" he says, glancing about my room and inquiring about my fourteen-hour flight from the States.

"Some, yes," I say.

We first met in Afghanistan in 2003. He was a source. We got to know each other and became friends in the way I become friends with people I use for information. Constant contact breeds familiarity. We remained in touch after he was assigned to Islamabad. I e-mailed him as I prepared for this trip, and he agreed to meet me at my guest house after I arrived.

"Tell me, how many bomb attacks in the last year?" he says, tapping the butt of a cigarette against the arm of his chair. "Basically every day, somewhere here, somewhere there, two a day at least. They are well trained, they know where to hit. It's different than Iraq but just as tragic."

He licks the coke off his iPhone and drops it in his coat pocket.

"Bush was prepared to fight forever and send military into perpetuity. Symbolically, Obama wants this to end by 2012. The civilized world looks at its watches. These guys don't have watches, but they have a hell of a lot of time. Fighting is in their blood. They use a sweet name, Islam, to give their fighting a purpose and to portray the feelings of a society."

Since I was last here, he continues, the people have become very cautious. Not so long ago they would walk to a park and enjoy a day with their children outside. In the evening houses filled with visiting family. Now empty streets reveal a city on edge. A man drives a motorcycle and starts shooting. Like a drive-by in America, yes? People don't run but lie down and wait for bullets, real or imaginary, to pass overhead.

Fear prevails. Afghan refugees have become targets of harassment for bringing their war to Pakistan. Overcrowded cells make prisons ideal recruiting grounds as fundamentalist inmates mingle with common criminals.

They discuss radical Islam, a former inmate of Chudaray Shabir Prison in Rawalpindi told me earlier in the day. They approach only young educated men who have good minds and can understand the reasoning behind their beliefs. They have representatives in each section. If you join, you get clean clothes and better food. They pay off the guards, who are in it for the money. They don't say the names of their organizations except to those who join. They approached my informant only once, he said, and offered to get money to his family. We'll help you if you do things for us, they said. But some other inmates advised him against joining them. Don't do it, they warned. They will use you and kill you.

Pakistan has settled into an anxious dichotomy, with a civilian government attracted to the money and power the West can offer, while its people increasingly feel like pawns in a corrupting chess game they never chose to play in the first place.

"This government is very weak," the diplomat says. "Most democratic governments expect to complete their term. Here we don't know how long democracy will last. So they use their time in office to get money for themselves. Fraud is part of surviving."

Corruption has opened the door to further violence. The current extremist campaign in Pakistan started in summer 2007, after the military stormed the Red Mosque in Islamabad, a radical stronghold, and killed about a hundred people holed up inside, an event that al Qaeda seized upon to call for an Islamist rebellion in the country. That insurrection led to the formation of a Pakistani Taliban movement that fought not in Afghanistan but at home and that linked up with older militant groups in the country.

There were eighty-seven suicide bombings amid 2,586 terrorist strikes in 2009, a 45 percent increase over the previous year.

In spring 2008 the Pakistani military began conducting operations to uproot the Taliban in Swat Valley after the militants had gained control of nearly the entire valley, destroying about 200 schools for girls, decapitating politicians, and terrorizing the population. After three months Pakistan declared its offensive a success, claiming to have killed more than 1,800 militants. But even the U.S. special representative for Pakistan and Afghanistan, Richard Holbrooke, questioned whether the campaign really defeated the Taliban. His comments suggest a growing sense of worry that, rather than crushing the Taliban, the offensive may have simply pushed the fighters underground.

Security forces acknowledge the danger of the Taliban's melting into the local population and staging guerrilla attacks. Military experts say it is difficult to identify who belongs to the ranks of the Taliban and what their strategic goals may be. The Pakistani army has been reluctant to take on all the Taliban's factions in all parts of the country, worried that the backlash from waging war on other Muslims may be beyond control.

"The Taliban does not necessarily want to seize territory but simply to keep the government, the military, and common people surrounded by fear," the diplomat tells me. "Their agenda is going to be to keep on reminding us they are a powerful force."

"Can I visit Swat?"

"Yes, but wear a *kameez* and *salwar* and *topi*. Keep your head down, don't talk, blend in. You won't pass as Pakistani. You're going to have to decide to say where you're from when you get there," the diplomat says. "Everyone wants Americans out. They hate you. They feel you've pushed the Afghan war into Pakistan. They feel they are fighting a mercenary war for America. What do they get in return? Bomb blasts. Here people think your government is making fools of its citizens."

He contemplates the floor as I straighten my room. I stuff dirty clothes in a chest of drawers, shove my boots beneath a chair, collect notepads on a desk. After the confusion of layovers and long flights and abrupt time changes, I seek order and try to assert myself on my surroundings and take command of the imbalance I feel.

The down side of this attempt at order is that I leave no presence of myself. The room feels empty. It is as if I am not here but remain suspended on a plane still in midflight. I carry this numbing disassociation with me during the day, as all traces of myself linger breathless and without form somewhere behind me.

Outside my window cats yowl, and I hear gates clang shut, sealing off sprawling residential properties from the street. I had wanted to lodge at the same guest house where I had stayed in 2006, but my fixer, Tahir, had warned against it. It was too close to a police station, a potential terrorist target.

"Whatever you do, don't say you're from America," the diplomat warns. "Don't say you're from Denmark because of the cartoon controversy. Don't say you're French because they want to outlaw the burqa. Don't say you're Swiss because Switzerland has banned the building of mosques. Say you're from Spain. Do you have a fixer?"

"Yes. A man I worked with last time."

"How do you know he hasn't turned?"

"We've worked together before."

I see the diplomat out. At his suggestion, I catch a taxi to the office of his friend, Afzal Ali Shigri, a retired inspector general of police.

Shigri became a police officer in 1969 and spent his first years in the semiautonomous tribal regions that border Swat Valley. In those days he confronted communists who opposed property owners. It was their land, they claimed. He sighs. Pakistan has always dealt with terrorists of one kind or another.

In 2004 the Pakistani army began scouring the region for al-Qaeda and Taliban fighters and bombed, burned, and bulldozed the homes and belongings of those deemed collaborators or merely uncooperative. Civilian deaths from increased American drone attacks have further fueled hostility toward both the U.S. and Pakistani governments.

It is unlikely, however, that the army will win through force. No matter how hard the army assaults the tribal areas, tradition forbids its people to turn over a guest to an enemy without a fight.

"Listen," Shigri says, "one time a man sought refuge, and a woman gave it to him. Another man came to her home and demanded to see the stranger in her house. 'Where is he?' She said, 'I don't know.' 'He killed your son,' the man said. 'It doesn't matter,' she said. 'He came to me for help. He is my guest.'"

"As you are mine," Shigri says, offering me tea. "Will you be in Islamabad long?"

"I leave for Swat Valley in the morning."

"Swat used to be a peaceful place. The middle class would take their honeymoons there until three years ago, when the Taliban moved in. Now the government has thrown them out and is urging people to come back, but I don't want to go there."

Years ago, Shigri says, he was assigned to the frontier city of Mardan. One day the son of an inspector killed himself. Shigri drove to his house to express his condolences. The father thanked him for coming. He said, "I'm lucky my son died in my house. If he had been outside in my field and died publicly, I would have to find those who drove him to suicide and take revenge." Shigri thought it was very strange for a father to lose a son and be thankful to God that he had died inside.

These, he says, are the types of people we are dealing with.

At dawn the next morning my fixer, Tahir, and I leave Islamabad for the Swat Valley. We proceed through dense fog, so fleeting images of bicycle riders and feral dogs appear and vanish in our passing. Men kneel on prayer shawls and pray at the side of the road, bowing their heads in the mist. I wrap a blanket around me against the cold. The vague outlines of shops become objects for the emerging sunlight to fasten on. Police stand on the roadside by small fires, and beggars stand a few feet behind, like shadows. We pass through checkpoints unhindered by security officers, weaving through a maze of yellow-and-black-striped concrete blocks stamped with police insignias, motor oil emblems. Laws call for a car to be impounded if it does not have the proper registration, but we are not stopped, though Tahir left his registration at home. The officers don't ask who I am, though as a foreigner I need an internal visa to travel to Swat. That too is a law intended to bolster security. But like other such laws, it goes unenforced.

Five hours later we descend a twisting mountain pass into the flat plain of Swat Valley. The morning sky spreads breathlessly clear and blue above us, revealing a barren dusty valley parched from lack of rain. Dust has replaced the early morning fog, and we wrap scarves across our faces to breathe.

We creep toward Mingora, the largest town in the valley, through rambunctious bazaars where cars compete with donkey- and horse-drawn carts laden with wood. Squeezed vendor stalls blend into one long ramshackle block, forcing a glut of shoppers into the narrow roads and rendering them barely passable. The ceaseless beeping of car horns releases vexation and creates more in the stalled traffic.

We stop in Kota Nova Kali, a village near Mingora. Gutted buildings pummeled by the army offensive stand as testimonies to a previous life. A blocks-long line of men stands outside a burlap tent that serves as a United Nations World Food Programme warehouse. Men wearing WFP vests distribute flour, tea, sugar, and beans daily to about 200,000 people, the manager tells me.

"These people were all affected," he says. "They lost businesses, shops, farms. Everything was destroyed."

I walk through the warehouse, spilled flour spouting clouds about my boots. Men fill wheelbarrows with sacks of food and wobble from the imbalanced weight toward the exit at the opposite end of the tent. I am impressed by the order, the calm with which people wait in line. It is similar, I am told, to the manner in which they left the valley when the military began its offensive against the Taliban.

Quietly and mostly on foot. Men, women, children, the elderly. They brought little with them and filled the roads with a quiet resignation that accepted the fighting in the same manner as a drought. Part of a natural cycle that disrupts life, then vanishes as the resolute flow of that same life resumes.

Mingora spreads before us in a cluttered mass of slouching buildings that appear to seek some sort of equilibrium on the uneven hillside. Streets navigate the hills with the randomness of streams filled with winter runoff, unfurling forward without a clear destination. Tahir and I drive on one street and back on another, turning in endless circles and backing out of unexpected dead ends until we eventually reach our destination: the Inter Service Public Relation, an arm of the military.

I want to ask its commander where he thinks the offensive against the Taliban in the valley now stands. We show a guard our Ministry of Information and External Affairs permit to visit Swat Valley. He calls a Major Mushtaq, who meets us at the door. In short order we realize the government's bureaucracy has failed us. Our names were not passed on to the major. As a consequence he considers our authorization invalid.

Major Mushtaq ushers us into a large room and motions us to a couch. He contacts his superior and tells him he has an American journalist who has illegally entered Swat Valley. He recommends arresting me but worries such action may cause an international incident. Not likely, but I keep this thought to myself. Fortunately for me his superior does not see a problem. "Let them stay," Tahir overhears him tell the major. "If they were not stopped at the checkpoints, what is the problem?"

Red faced, Major Mushtaq steps into the hall and begins ranting. "We have regulations!" Tahir translates. "They must be followed, or what is the point?"

Our presence insults his ego. His whole sense of himself lies in the power he feels while enforcing rules, issuing orders, wearing a uniform that represents his authority. Enlarged egos are viruses that affect bureaucrats around the world. An army that serves U.S. interests in a country dependent on the United States is going to have more Major Mushtaqs than most. If Tahir and I are allowed to stay without facing any consequence, our very presence renders his rules meaningless, his uniform meaningless, his life meaningless.

Seconds pass. Gradually Major Mushtaq lowers his voice. He speaks more evenly. I wonder what sort of resolution he and his superior are reaching and what it means for Tahir and me.

The major continues talking. Tahir can no longer make out what he says. Then we hear nothing. Footsteps approach the door. Major Mushtaq enters without looking at us, his face tinged pink from his still-fading anger. A man walks in behind him with a silver tray of tea and finger sandwiches.

"Please," the major says, pointing to a tray.

We don't move. He sits beside Tahir, smoothes the creases in his uniform. He hands me a cup of tea, a sandwich, and a napkin. He leans back and rests his head against the wall. After a moment he turns to me.

"You will be allowed twenty-four hours in Mingora," he says. "Not a second more. Understand?"

I nod. Tahir nods. The major asks for my business card. I pat my pockets. I left them in the car.

"Funny how the simplest of things becomes complicated," Major Mushtaq says.

Everyone I speak to in Mingora remembers the arrival of the Taliban.

Sheerzaman Khan, a barber, remembers first noticing them in 2007. They came on horseback and in jeeps. They had long beards, heavy jackets. They carried pistols and Kalashnikov rifles. Every area had a Taliban leader. They said they were Muslims and occupied the best houses. Khan liked them for their strict interpretation of Islam. But then they started killing other Muslims. Every day he saw many dead bodies. Sometimes they had no head or legs. The Taliban told Khan to stop shaving his customers. To protect himself he put up a sign: "Please don't ask us for the shave, dear customer."

Fazal Ghan, owner of a movie theater, had no objection to the Taliban at first, because he felt they represented good Islamic principles. But then they shut him down because they said movies were immoral. That was not part of the faith as he understood it. But people went along. They lived. Taliban leaders told the administrators at Saidu Shrief Maskan Girls' Orphan House to stop teaching. The girls needed to cover themselves as well. Some of the Taliban were not much older than the girls. Eighteen-, fifteen-, even thirteen-year-olds. The Taliban paid six dollars a day to its fighters. Not bad pay for a Mingora boy.

A teacher called the girls into a meeting. "Don't worry," she told them. "Be brave." But the girls were very scared. They believed deep in their hearts that they would die horrible deaths.

Near the orphanage lives the family of a police officer, Arshad Ali. They show me a photograph of Ali sitting at the edge of a garden. Red and yellow roses rise behind him. He wears tan slacks, a blue sweater with police epaulets on each shoulder. Sunglasses perch on his forehead, and his short dark hair shines. His clasped hands rest on his knees, and he squints against the light, a look of concentration creasing his angular face.

He was kidnapped while walking to the police training center in nearby Hungo. His family first heard about it when a neighbor saw him on television. The Taliban had sent a video of Ali to the station. He was sitting on the carpeted floor of a small room. "If they can kidnap me, they can kidnap you," he said into the camera. His face was expressionless, his voice flat, his uniform rumpled.

A few days later a second video was released. Ali appeared to be sitting in the same room. He said nothing. He looked like a sad old man staring into the camera. Six days later he was found dumped on the road, his throat slit.

But like the barber and cinema owner, Ali's family had no objection to the Taliban at first. They believed in an Islamic government and considered the Taliban a good step toward that end.

Once the army began its Swat Valley offensive, many Mingora families fled to Peshawar and the homes of relatives. Unfortunately for them Peshawar was anything but peaceful in 2009.

Some of the deadliest terrorist attacks began in the fall. In October at least ninety-five people were killed and more than 200 injured when a powerful car bomb ripped through a packed Peshawar market. A November bomb blast killed 190 Peshawar police officers. In a statement authorities said the officers had embraced martyrdom. Bombs continued to rip through the city in December, killing more than a dozen people and injuring at least fifty.

Abbas Ali is a twenty-eight-year-old doctor in Peshawar's Lady Reading Hospital. When Tahir and I arrive to meet him, we see patients outside in their beds, covered in blankets and rigged to IVs, while janitors scrub the wards.

We pass patients wearing the same blood-stained clothes they had on when they were injured weeks earlier. Water drips down the grimed white walls inside and collects in puddles on a concrete floor that several men work over with brooms. Strained sunlight illuminates exposed ceiling wires and flickering bulbs. More water collects in door frames and rains down on me as I enter Dr. Ali's office, which consists of nothing more than a couch, a desk, and a scale.

"January has been quiet, thanks be to God," Dr. Ali says in a soft flat voice. He explains the injuries he treats. Burns, fractures, shrapnel cuts, head injuries. Most people leave the hospital in four weeks. However, someone suffering from a gut wound spends more time. Sometimes up to six months.

I tell him he appears very calm. He shakes his head, crosses his legs, and folds his hands, as if to hold himself together. "We are in great grief," he says matter-of-factly in the same flat voice.

Dr. Ali has seen five to ten people from a single family die, some of them children. Many of the injured have been related to surgeons, nurses, secretaries. They become victims as well.

When he wakes up each morning, Dr. Ali does not know if he will live through the day. He has heard the noise of many bombings, some close to his home and the hospital. He has watched the black smoke darken the sky. At those times he and other doctors rush to the casualty department and get ready for the onslaught of patients. One hundred sixty patients can arrive within forty minutes.

The hospital does not have enough beds for all the injured, screaming, weeping patients. Men and women, wrapped in bandages, covered with blankets, take up the floor. Relatives of the injured and the police crowd the operating room. Dr. Ali often does not know who all these people are. Is one of them a suicide bomber? Will a car arrive, supposedly with a patient, and then detonate an explosive?

After surgery he sleeps. He feels so exhausted it does not matter to him where he collapses. The next day he feels sorrow. Then he can't sleep. He recalls a fourteen-year-old girl who was crying on the operating table. She could have been a twin for his own daughter. He still hears her cries.

"It is not fair that someone does these things," he says with a shake of his head, a hint of anger breaking the lifeless tone of his voice. "They are misguided to interpret Islam in this way." He blames the United States for destabilizing the region. "Everyone has a stake here," he complains, "except for Pakistan. It is too busy doing the bidding of Western nations to care."

A man approaches me in a Peshawar bazaar and begins talking in Pashto. He wears a gray turban and has a thick dark beard. I look for Tahir. He stands across the street, back to me, buying cigarettes. Why is this man talking to me? Do I pass as a Pakistani in the *salwar kameez*, a long tunic over pants, I borrowed from Tahir? If I speak, I'll give myself away. What would I do then? Would he assume I'm an American or a European? Would he ask why I'm dressed as a Pakistani? Why I'm trying to pass? Is he harmless or a threat?

I stare at Tahir, hoping to catch his attention. Two other men walk toward me. They know the first man. They begin talking to me as well. I point to my mouth and ears and make guttural noises as if I'm a deaf mute. Another deceit. Another reason to suspect me if I'm found out. Lie upon lie to keep me safe, yet now I feel at greater risk by fueling suspicion. I look again for Tahir. He is crossing the street, cigarettes in hand. He joins me and speaks to the men. It turns out that the first man is from Islamabad and was asking me for directions. He and his companions are trying to find the address of a friend to attend a wedding. Tahir tells them I'm a Spanish journalist, not Pakistani. They laugh and offer to buy me a cup of tea. I decline. They want to know how I can be a journalist if I have trouble speaking. Tahir doesn't know what to say. He asks me why the men think I can't speak. Now we must explain my subterfuge. More lies. More reason to suspect me, this Westerner among them.

In the morning Tahir and I return to Islamabad. On the long drive he fills my head with talk of "the coming time," similar to the end of times in Christianity. However, the coming time is not about the return of Jesus but an anticipated calamity when Pakistan falls into chaos because of advances made by Islamist extremists, increased government corruption, or both.

Tahir earned his paranoia in 2008, when he was nearly killed in a suicide bombing. He was in a section of Islamabad called Melodee Chowk, drinking tea at a small shop beneath a canvas tent. Round white plastic tables stood unevenly on the rocky ground. A man served his tea in a small cracked cup and was in such a rush it splashed onto the saucer. Tahir poured the tea back into his cup and let it cool. The warm day made him wish he had ordered a Pepsi.

At one table, among the men eating rice and chicken off tin plates and other men requesting more bread with their meals, sat a suicide bomber. Perhaps he too was eating. Perhaps he ordered only tea. Perhaps he sat alone, as if waiting for a friend.

Police officers stood at a roundabout in the stilled midafternoon heat, curtained by scrims of suspended dust and exhaust. A friend called

Tahir on his mobile phone and asked to meet him across the street. Tahir ducked under the tent, crossed the street, and walked about 300 feet when an explosion raised him in the air, and he ran forward to keep his balance and to escape the roar in his ears.

When he regained his footing, he turned around. He saw body parts seemingly suspended in air. He ran toward fleeing police officers. He saw their horses on the ground, their exposed teeth and shrill screams, and began weeping. "Why are you weeping for horses?" an enraged police officer in a torn uniform screamed at him. "Why are you not weeping for the police?" "I am crying for the police," Tahir said, "but the horses have done nothing."

"I never want to see that scene again," Tahir says, "but I always do."

Pakistan's thousands of fundamentalist madrassas are thought by some to provide training for little except jihad, so Tahir and I arrange to visit one the next day to hear what its teachers and students have to say. Then, weary from the drive, we call it a day.

Late afternoon turns to night. I am restless but stay put. Tahir warned me about kidnappers. The rise in kidnappings comes as a floundering economy leads more people to commit crime. It's also a result of the overall erosion of security as Pakistan faces spreading Islamist militancy. Criminals are suspected in most kidnappings, but the Taliban and other militant groups are thought to earn a slice of the money—perhaps millions of dollars.

I try to read a book but can't concentrate. I attempt to sleep but toss and turn. Finally I kick off the sheets and decide the hell with it. I have to get out. At least for a few minutes. Not far from the guest house, the noise of a bazaar carries into the evening. I walk toward it. Butchers, cobblers, tailors stand in the glow cast by bare bulbs and strings of lights. A university student stops me and asks where I am from. Spain, I tell him. He asks about Madrid. Never having visited there, I tell him what little I know. We stop by some vendors. Assuming I want to buy something, the university student offers to translate and perhaps, I suspect, receive a tip.

I feign interest in a pair of sandals and at the same time ask in the most casual voice I can summon how the vendors around me feel about the current situation in Pakistan. Their voices fuse together in their eagerness to vent. They catch me and the university student off guard. We step back and they step toward us. I am like a sponge, my head filling with the unintelligible noise of their frustration. The university student raises his voice above theirs and can barely keep up as he translates.

"It is not good, a very bad time we have here. The main reason behind this is terrorist attacks."

"We had two bombs here and are scared all the time. You cannot tell from the expressions on our faces what we are feeling."

"Slowly, slowly our lives have been poisoned, and things have come to this state."

Soon their complaints echo into a chorus of complaint against the United States.

"America makes nice military action and imposes it on us."

"They want us to get involved so they can get out."

"Our government gets the Americans' money and we get the bombs."

The barrage of voices overwhelms the university student, and he waves his hands and stops translating. I buy the sandals to divert attention before my Spanish bona fides become suspect amid all this hatred for America. I thank the university student for his help, give him 200 rupees, and hurry off before he asks me more questions about Madrid.

Tahir and I sit in a large spare room with three students at Jamia Muhammadia, an Islamabad madrassa. Red carpets cover the concrete floor but don't keep out the cold. Cracks converge across the walls near a glossy photograph of a mosque. I hear students in the next room reading from the Koran, and the sound mixes with the shouts of more students playing soccer in a dusty field.

"We are like missionaries," says their teacher, Abdul Koadoos Mohammadi. "We offer free education. We are not breeding grounds for militants." He complains that the United States fosters this misperception as an excuse to attack Muslims.

"We don't want to kill, but the other side keeps killing us. The U.S. would be more successful if it said, 'We want your oil and gas. If someone feels they can stop us, do it.' They'll never say that, but pragmatically speaking, it makes more sense if they would." Furthermore, he says, September 11 was "an inside job" planned by the American government so it could invade Afghanistan and then Iraq.

Nonsense, I tell him.

He responds with a flurry of questions: How do I define terrorism?

How would I feel if a Muslim country attacked America? Why did U.S. Secretary of Defense Robert Gates recently visit Pakistan's arch rival, India, before flying to Islamabad?

Every answer I offer results in another series of endless disassociated questions, the purpose of which fails me. The students laugh at my frustration. I end the discussion with a muttered thanks for his time. He offers us lunch. I decline.

Jawed, one of the students, follows us out and suggests in an aside to Tahir that we meet them at a nearby McDonald's. Had he suggested a local tea shop, I would have refused. I was in no mood for another assault of accusatory questions answered by more questions accompanied by endless cups of green tea.

But meet at a McDonald's?

Islamabad is just two years removed from a bomb attack directed at Westerners at the Marriott Hotel that killed fifty-four and left a crater sixty feet across and twenty feet deep outside. But while today the Marriott is surrounded by a noise-dampening blast wall with metal detectors for guests and visitors and barricades to keep cars far from the entrance, at the McDonald's we sit and watch crowds of university students file past a Ronald McDonald statue. There is a metal detector and a heavy police presence, but the tables are crowded with Pakistanis eating the most Western of foods, the Big Mac.

Our setting reminds me of a meeting I had recently in Lahore with Hafiz Khalid, the Pakistani deputy leader of the banned organization Lashkar-e-Taiba and the son of one of its founders, Hafiz Muhammad Saeed. The name Lashkar-e-Taiba literally translated means Army of the Righteous, or Army of the Pure. It is one of the largest and most active Islamist militant organizations in South Asia. It is based in Muridke, near Lahore, and operates several training camps in Pakistan-administered Kashmir. Lashkar-e-Taiba shares an ideology with the most extreme versions of Wahhabi Islam followers, including al-Qaeda—anti-Western, anti-Indian, anti-Jewish.

The only surviving attacker in the 2008 Mumbai terrorist attacks that killed at least 173 people and wounded more than 300 told police that the gunmen had trained for months in Lashkar-e-Taiba camps in Pakistan. Lashkar-e-Taiba denied any role in the attacks on Mumbai.

We had met in, of all places, a Holiday Inn. Khalid strode in with another man, an engineer. Both wore a kameez and a black waistcoat. They never travel alone, Tahir whispered to me. They like to show they have followers. Al-Qaeda is successful because it gets engineers and doctors. Educated people. They have the capability of buying whom they want.

We shook hands and embraced in traditional greeting. Khalid asked about my trip and if I had everything I needed. Yes, I told him. He nodded and looked pleased.

"They give a friendly posture but won't mind beheading you," Tahir said, smiling back at Khalid and pretending to translate for me. "They are great at it."

We sat near a gated restaurant where security guards stood holding military rifles beside a flat-screen television set airing a cricket match.

Khalid dismissed the government ban on Lashkar-e-Taiba as a gimmick to appease foreign governments, especially the United States and India. Indeed the group plays humanitarian and political roles within the country and would be difficult to shut down. That branch of the group, called Jamat-ud-Dawa, is involved with helping to run schools and hospitals.

It provided relief operations in 2005 when Pakistan was devastated by a major earthquake. It established an earthquake relief fund for Haiti just days before our meeting. Would this be an organization that killed? Khalid asked me. He did not sound angry but rather hurt at the suggestion.

I told him that dozens of terrorist attacks have been attributed to the group by people within and without Pakistan. Can they all be wrong?

"There are people in the government who want to crush us," he said. "They are under the influence of India and America."

I found it hard to confront a defense that offers no introspection but instead plays the victim. Anything negative attributed to the group was part of a coordinated India-U.S. strategy to discredit. It's a foolproof fallback position that can be applied to every question. And as I am an American, my questions can be dismissed as another part of the conspiracy against Lashkar-e-Taiba. The strategy is not for my consumption as much as for that of the people who Lashkar-e-Taiba wants to recruit.

More excuses: The Pakistan Taliban are not Taliban at all but proxies for the United States, to give it an excuse to attack Pakistan. The U.S. invasion of Afghanistan created a holy war against evil and therefore justifies the fighting there against Western armies. Nobody knows who committed the September 11 attacks, and therefore the invasion of Afghanistan was not justified.

"The international community applies pressure to Pakistan, and Pakistan applies pressure to us," Khalid said. "But we won't be pressured. The members of Lashkar-e-Taiba come from simple families. They live in the streets, shop at the bazaars. We have influence with these voters. The government knows this."

He looked at his watch and then excused himself to attend another meeting. He stood and paid for our tea despite my offer to do so. I was a guest, he said. We shook hands and embraced again.

"It was a pleasant surprise for us—not you, of course, but us—that Western governments are talking about talking to the Afghanistan Taliban," he said. "It's what we all want. Talk to the Taliban, give them their share in the government. This development is a sign of failure for America. It will have to take its troops out of the country. Success will come to the Taliban. Muslims believe you live your life for God. When you die, your life has been for God. That is why Muslims are a hopeful people."

He walked through the metal detector at the front door, paused, and looked back at me, a smile on his face.

Miles from Lahore, the three madrassa students and I share McDonald's milkshakes and discuss American heavy metal bands while talking jihad. Jawed insists I play an instrument but am too modest to admit it. My ponytail, he says, tells him I'm a musician.

At twenty-four Jawed is the most assertive of the three students and perhaps the most devout. "The purpose of life is to receive blessings from Allah," he says. That is possible only by studying Islam and acting on its principles. When he was not living a religious life, the world was too much for him. Something was missing. His heart was empty. He won't elaborate.

Asad, also twenty-four, studied at a university to earn a degree and find a job. But, he says, he was always tense and worried about making money. The day he enrolled in the madrassa, he felt calm. The school provided for him, and eventually Allah blessed him with the means to open his snack shop.

The third student, twenty-one-year-old Sham, first attended the madrassa as a boy. At eighteen he enrolled at a university, earned a science degree, and then returned to the madrassa to complete his religious education. When he finishes, he wants to enroll at a university again and study fine arts.

There are different interpretations of Islam, the students tell me. They concede that the people who set off bombs may be misguided. However, if a person willingly sacrifices his life, it means he is ready to die for his religion and therefore is not a terrorist.

Some groups misuse jihad, Jawed concedes. He won't name them. He does not want to give the impression to me, an outsider, that Muslims are divided.

"Muslims oppose these groups?" I ask.

"Yes," Jawed says, "but even they do not hate the people, only their government."

He waits for my response. Like his teacher, he wants to dismiss my questions and leave his convictions unchallenged. But unlike convictions, I am tangible. I am a physical representation of the amorphous American government that can reach halfway around the globe, deep into Pakistan's halls of power, and that these students loathe. They can see it, feel it, despise it by looking at me. It is why I lie and say I am from Spain. How else can I avoid being their victim?

"But you still don't understand," Jawed says. "We don't hate you. You are just a guest to us."

The diplomat knocks, enters my room, and withdraws two cans of beer from his coat pocket.

I tell him about my afternoon talk with the madrassa students and my failure to make even the smallest point.

"They were right, you know," he says. "You were a guest. At least in that setting. In another circumstance you'd be a target or collateral damage. And they'd be martyrs. Nobody gives a shit to die here."

On a positive note, he says, people are pleased with an agreement reached at the recent London conference on Afghanistan to reach out to some elements of the Taliban. It's what people want. Talk to the Taliban, get U.S. troops out. Stability returns. The end. The diplomat shakes his head dismissively, as if he has heard it all before.

I tell him Lashkar-e-Taiba has a different spin on the talks. They see them as part of an eventual Taliban victory. "What else would they say?" the diplomat says. "Listen. Look at the players involved. The real success of any diplomatic overture depends on Pakistan.

"Unfortunately," he says, "the Pakistan government has other objectives. It's blackmailing the world. 'If you don't help us, we could become the most dangerous country in the world if our nukes fall into the wrong hands. So you have to help us.' And they get the help. U.S. dollars. It serves American interests, the government's interests, and, in terms of recruits, the terrorists' interests."

He stands, finishes his beer, and tosses the empty can in the trash. He pinches his nose and sneezes. I offer him a Kleenex. He might take a holiday in Dubai, he says as he takes the tissue from me. This time of year, the weather would be perfect. Not too hot, right? He'd like to see that new building. The tallest one in the world, isn't it?

I think so, I say, and follow him to the door. He suggests dinner. Kabob? Sure. He waits while I get my jacket. He won't predict how all this war on terror business will end. The civilian government is weak and may not finish its term. The United States would rather do business with the military anyway. Less messy.

"Not soon," he says as I reach for my keys. "The real conflict is yet to come."

8

Missing

Islamabad, Pakistan: January 2009

Amina kept all the flowers her husband, Masood, gave her over the years. She kept the first bottle of perfume, the first scarf. She believes he will be back, as strongly as she believes in God. Tomorrow or the day after or next week or next month. She doesn't know when but someday. She must believe this to stay motivated. If she is a fool, OK, let her be a fool.

For years she was unaware of the miseries of the world. She never read newspapers. She decorated their Rawalpindi home, painted pictures, and wrote poetry. They met in 1977 when she stopped by a gallery he administered and inquired about hanging some of her paintings. He could organize things in an instant.

They married and had children. They loved to go hiking on weekends. They enjoyed impulsively packing up their son and daughter and driving into the countryside with no specific destination in mind. When it snowed in the mountains, they would go skiing on a whim, leaving behind the congestion of city life with all its problems and politics. Masood was openly critical of government corruption and of his government's ties to the war on terror, but otherwise he was not a political person.

Neither was she—until he disappeared.

I sit across from Shaukat Aziz Siddiqui, a lawyer who represents families of missing people, in his Rawalpindi office. Through him I will meet Amina.

The power has shut off, and he apologizes for being able to offer me only cold tea. Dusty cobweb strands hang from the ceiling. The mildewed books filling shelves on both sides of his office offer an odor suggesting wisdom lost to moisture and neglect and poverty.

Siddiqui tells me he does not know how many hundreds, perhaps thousands, of people suspected of ties to jihadi groups ("You know the ones, mullahs and their followers") are being held in jails throughout Pakistan in unknown detention centers as a result of the 2001 terrorists in New York and Washington and the subsequent alliance between the United States and the dictatorship of former president Pervez Musharraf. Suddenly, he says, everyone became a suspect, and despite promises of reform, the detentions have continued under the democratically elected government of President Asif Ali Zardari. Guilt or innocence is not the issue. To impose terror on suspected terrorists, to maintain a grip on power, ah, now that is a strategy, eh?

Siddiqui believes that some of the missing have been given over to U.S. authorities in exchange for cash and held in Guantánamo Bay, Cuba, or Bagram Airfield in Afghanistan. But who knows? Perhaps they are elsewhere.

"You will not be jailed in America if you say you hate the United States," says Siddiqui. "But I, as a Pakistani, cannot criticize the policies of America or my own government while in Pakistan for fear of becoming a missing person."

He pushes a stack of file folders toward me, and I catch them as they nearly slide off the table. Each folder has a name. Each one tells a story. I pick up one, Complaint of Amina Masood Janjua, and begin reading.

On July 30, 2005, Amina and Masood ate breakfast around nine. Fried eggs and toast. The day was sunny, nice. Their children were asleep. The morning heat increased as time passed. They knew that soon the streets would be dusty and clogged with traffic amid the pandemonium of the bazaars, and that the dust would cling to them.

Masood left the house to meet a friend, Faisal Faraz. Together they bought bus tickets to Peshawar, where they planned to spend the day with friends. They would return that night. Amina can still see him walking to the door, turning one last time to smile at her as he said,

"Good-bye, see you tonight." He and Faisal caught the bus, but something happened on the way. The bus arrived in Peshawar without them.

Amina, however, was not worried when he did not come home that evening. She assumed Masood had been delayed. Maybe at a rest stop along the way. Their only phone was a cell phone; he had taken it with him and therefore she could not call him.

The first night passed. Then the second. Then the third. By the fourth day of his absence, Amina felt her heart beating so hard it made her chest ache. She could not quiet her fear. After one week she could take it no longer.

Her father-in-law, a retired colonel in the Pakistani army, had been in the same commando training unit as Pervez Musharraf. Her father-in-law spoke to then-president Musharraf about Masood. Yes, we'll find him, relax, Musharraf told him.

Days passed and then weeks. No Masood.

Amina wrote letters to the Interior Ministry inquiring about Masood.

No response.

She checked with jails, hospitals.

No Masood.

Then mysterious men began standing outside the house. They had short haircuts. Black suits and ties. They would not speak to her.

Amina started receiving phone calls about the same time. We know where your husband is, the callers said. Don't make a fuss. He's OK. He will come home. They did not give their names. No call number appeared on her new cell phone.

One year passed. She started demonstrating with four members of her family outside the parliament. They had never demonstrated before and did not know what to say, worried how the police might react if they said anything. They held placards and stood silently.

"Mr. President," one placard read, "please find my loving father." Another: "Mr. President, please find my loving husband." Another: "Where are the human rights of my son?"

More days passed. The days turned into weeks, months, years. Still no Masood. Amina, now forty-two, alternates between fear, sadness, and puzzlement when she speaks of Masood's five-year absence. She can't imagine what she would have done had she known so much time would pass without him. Maybe, she thinks, she would have killed herself. But now, instead of despair, a weary hardened resolve to find him compels her. They had been married sixteen years when he went missing. Twenty-one years now, when she includes the five years he has been gone. She tries not to think what another five years will be like without him.

Mohammad Arshad lives in Kalawan village near Haripur, a town two hours north of Islamabad. Green farm fields unfold just beyond the open door, and donkeys walk gingerly on stone paths, their backs burdened with firewood. His plain square concrete home stands on a hill. A table, a handful of chairs, and a bed for guests to sit on emphasize a sparse atmosphere, in keeping with Arshad's grief for his eighteen-year-old son, Sheraz.

On December 3, 2009, the police knocked on Arshad's door minutes before midnight. They overturned furniture and searched the rooms.

"We arrested two guys, and they say your son has a rifle," the police told him. "Everyone has a gun," Arshad told the police. "To protect livestock." The police ignored him and woke up Sheraz, a slight university student with a patchy beard. They took him by his arms and pushed him toward their car, tugged a hood over his head, and shoved him inside. They left in a fury of stones spewed from beneath the tires, left Arshad alone in the doorway, shouting after them for his son.

The next morning Arshad walked to the Haripur police station. The police said they didn't have Sheraz but that the Ministry of Defense and the Inter Services Intelligence agency, an organization similar to a domestic CIA, were involved in his case. Arshad said he did not want trouble with the ISI. He simply wanted his son back. The police said nothing.

More than a month has passed. Arshad's wife often falls to the floor and weeps when she sees Sheraz's empty bed. Her weeping chokes her, and sometimes she vomits. Arshad helps her up and guides her into their room, where she collapses on their bed, inconsolable. Then he stands by himself in the front doorway and stares at the fields and cries quietly.

Why Sheraz? he thinks. Sheraz had a friendly attitude with everyone. He smiled easily but shyly. He helped older people in the village with farm chores by digging furrows in their fields and taking a hoe to the hard rocky ground. He always invited home for tea people he met at the bazaar. He wanted to join the army for the opportunities an army career would present to a young man born in a humble village. He also liked the idea of wearing a crisp ironed uniform, the way he would look in it.

"You know how boys are," Arshad says.

Gulam Farwo sits beside his nephew, Arshad. Gulam is much taller and stockier than Arshad, with a full black beard that reaches down to his chest. His own sorrow-filled eyes begin to tear.

Gulam's two younger brothers, Munir, twenty-six, and Mohammad, thirty, went missing the same day Sheraz was arrested. On that December morning Gulam saw them in the mosque praying. After their prayers the two brothers returned to their homes and tended their wheat fields. Gulam drove into Haripur. Two hours later he received a phone call from a neighbor. Two police officers and six men wearing black suits and ties took his brothers from their fields, and now they are gone.

Gulam called the police. They said the brothers would be released in a few days. After three days the police said, "We don't know where they are. Some agencies are involved. ISI. We don't know. You have to wait." Gulam asked what charges his brothers faced, what evidence resulted in their detention, but the police refused to answer. This was not police business, they told him.

Gulam is also searching for his twenty-eight-year-old nephew, Mullah Kari Sadiuk. He was in Arshad's house when Sheraz was arrested. "Who are you?" the police asked him. Sadiuk told them. "Oh, we're looking for you," they said. And they took him.

Only days before, two men with military-style haircuts had asked about enrolling their children in the village mosque, where Sadiuk teaches. Gulam told him to hide. Those men are trouble, he warned. But Sadiuk ignored him.

Amina spends her days in the office that Masood used as managing director of the College of Information Technology in Rawalpindi. Circles sag beneath her eyes. A purple-patterned scarf wrapped around her head frames her face. She adjusts a brown prayer shawl across a shoulder and uses it to wipe the screen of a computer monitor. Curled lists of missing people are tacked to the walls. Above her head hangs a photo of Masood. He would be forty-nine now. He smiles at the camera, head tilted to one side, as if he is trying to figure something out. His thick graying beard rings his face.

She uses his office to administer Defense of Human Rights, a group she founded in 2006 on behalf of missing people. She helps collect information on nearly a hundred cases that she then turns over to lawyers representing families of the missing. Each case needs as much detail as possible for a lawyer to take it. In some cases the families have no clue what happened to their husband, father, son. In other cases eyewitnesses have submitted letters saying they saw so-and-so taken by the police or by men in civilian dress with short-cropped military-style haircuts. She speaks so softly that many families she tries to help must lean forward to hear.

"If my son is alive, I want him here, and if he is dead, I want to know about his death," a woman dressed entirely in black tells Amina. Her son has been missing for a year. Amina holds her hand.

"We won't complain to anyone if he's dead," the woman says. "We just want someone to tell us."

"Do you have any clues? Did anyone see anything?" Amina asks her.

"No. He was just gone. Nothing was disturbed in his room."

"Tell me what you know."

"I want my son to be with me," the woman says.

Amina never asked Shakeel Ahmad Turabi to get involved in her struggle. He chose to, and now his son, Hassan, is missing.

Sitting by himself in his office, Shakeel, an editor at the South Asian News Agency, stares into space and recalls the night of March 13, 2007, when a car cut him off as he drove home. Two men dragged him out and pushed him into the backseat of their car and shoved him to the floor. His face pressed against their shoes. His kidnappers drove to a house and put him in a small dark dirty room. They removed everything from his pockets and turned off the light. About half an hour later a young man with major's bars on his jacket told Shakeel to introduce himself.

"Your duty is to introduce yourself to me before you question me," Shakeel said, trying to assert himself beyond his fears.

"You don't know who we are."

"No."

The major complained that the South Asian News Agency had republished a *New York Times* story about who would take over the government should Musharraf resign. The story claimed that the mood of the populace seemed solidly against both Musharraf and the army.

"Why publish a story critical of the army?"

"How was that critical?" Shakeel said.

"Do you know the number of missing people?"

"No."

"Do you want your name on that list?"

"No."

"Who would look after your three kids?"

"Allah. Don't worry about my children."

"Don't teach me philosophy. And don't publish bad news."

The major left and turned off the lights. One hour later they gave Shakeel his things. He had messages from his daughter, Fatima, on his cell.

"Who is Fatima?" the major asked.

"Don't be rude. My daughter."

"Tell her you will be home in one hour."

After seven hours he was released.

Six months later, on September 14, two men assaulted Hassan, then thirteen, after he was dropped off at school. The school called Shakeel and said Hassan was ill. He called his driver to go pick him up. But then the school administrator called him again. "You must come," he said. "Your son is in the hospital."

Hassan's legs were black and blue, and his face was bruised. His two assailants had told him, "We tried to teach a lesson to your dad, but he did not mend his ways. Hopefully after this he will mend his ways."

After the assault on Hassan, Shakeel was careful about what subjects he chose to write about. He was less critical of the government. For a time his family experienced no more problems. But then he met Amina at a demonstration on behalf of missing people. Her struggle was a good story for his news agency, but he also admired her tenacity. He told her his story, and she listened to him as if she had no problems of her own. Moved, Shakeel demonstrated with her when she camped outside the parliament. Days later he started receiving anonymous phone calls: "Why are you so active?"

He thinks about that question now, the implied threat in the voice on the other end. He thought at the time he must be very careful or he might be kidnapped again. He worried they might beat Hassan up again, but he never expected them to take his son.

On January 5, 2010, Shakeel's driver dropped off Hassan, now seventeen, at Islamabad College for Boys. He never came home. A teenager likes to stay out, Shakeel reasoned. But by evening he was concerned and started looking for Hassan. Desperate after five days of fruitless searching, Shakeel met with the inspector general of police.

"You can get your son on Monday the eleventh at 2," the inspector general said. Shakeel returned on Monday. The inspector general did not meet him until 3:30 that afternoon. "The army men who know about your son are not here," he told Shakeel. "Come Tuesday." On Tuesday the inspector general did not show up for the appointment. He never came to his office and did not answer his cell phone. On Wednesday he came to Shakeel's house.

"The army told me it's not your son," he said.

Other families of missing people have told Shakeel the authorities gave them equally mixed messages. With us, not with us. Nothing.

"But how can I stop looking?" Shakeel asks them. "You can't," they tell him. "You won't."

Shakeel takes pills at night but can't sleep. He tries to explain to friends how he feels, but he just breaks down, covering his face with his hands, feeling himself crumbling apart. His wife tosses and turns in bed, shouting out Hassan's name and asking, "Where are you?" Their twelve-year-old daughter said, "Father, give me a bomb. I want to blow myself up in front of the agency that took you and my brother."

It is natural to want to retaliate, he thinks, but no one can do anything in Pakistan. There is no rule of law. He avoids any criticism of the government when he writes a news story, even if that leaves the story unbalanced and incomplete. He lives every day hating the indignity of his compromises, but he has decided that he won't lose his son to his words.

In 2007, according to court documents, new evidence regarding missing people was provided to the deputy attorney general of Pakistan by a lawyer representing the physician Imran Munir, a former detainee who had been charged with espionage. In a handwritten ten-page statement to the court in English, Munir wrote that he was held in solitary confinement in Chaklala, a Rawalpindi prison. One excerpt reads:

> [The guards] didn't let me sleep every day except 3 hours a day and let me stand almost 15 hours a day in chains on my hands and both feet. They started giving me tremendous amounts of extra red chilies in my food every day and due to that I got external hemorrhoids and fresh blood started coming out through my stools and also got stomach ulcers. They didn't let me shower and didn't let me change my dress and therefore I got scabies.
>
> The guards who were guarding the 12 solitary confinement cells told me that . . . [the] only . . . way to get out from the hands of ISI is to cooperate with them and give them the statement the way they want, otherwise they will not release me and they might hand . . . me over to the U.S.A. custody in Guantanamo Bay or they might torture me further and they might kill me but will never release me. First I didn't believe them but when they let me spoke to the other three inmates . . . opposite to my cell and when I heard their stories . . . [of] how they were apprehended by ISI and they were never charged and never taken to any court, than I believed them and realized that . . . the only way to get out from the ISI custody [is] to cooperate with them. Out of those three inmates there was a business man Masood Janjua of Rawalpindi.

Two staff members at Defense of Human Rights give their resignation notices, effective immediately, to Amina. And the third woman on staff is ready to leave. Maybe Amina has given her staff too much work. She herself works day and night. She knows not everyone is so dedicated. The women work from 10 a.m. to 4 p.m. Amina does not consider that too much.

She sits, presses a hand against her stomach. She suffers from diarrhea, ulcers. She keeps to a bland diet, but still her stomach churns. She talks to keep her mind off her pain, recalling when Musharraf declared a state of emergency on November 3, 2007. He removed fifty-five of the Supreme Court's ninety-five judges, including Chief Justice Iftikhar Muhammad Chaudhry, citing interference with counterterrorism efforts. As a result, hearings for 485 missing people, scheduled before the end of the year, were delayed.

When the decree was lifted in March 2009, Amina spoke to the registrar of the Supreme Court. "When will there be hearings on the missing?" she demanded. "There are no hearings on the missing scheduled," the registrar said. She was heartbroken. "I am not going home," she declared. "I will stay here until you take our case." The registrar shrugged and said nothing. She had no idea how her children would manage without her. She went to the cafeteria and ate enough food for two people because she did not know how many days she would be gone from her home.

Amina arranged a blue tent on the damp ground outside the parliament building under overcast skies. Police watched her. She erected a placard outside her tent that said "Release the missing." A photograph of Masood was all she had inside the tent. Families of the missing began joining her. Within days forty people were camped outside the parliament.

The authorities tried to intimidate her. Men in dark suits told Amina that the people supporting her would be involved in car accidents. Their vehicles would be confiscated, and they would be sent to jail. They advised her to tell them to pack up and go home. Instead, Amina told supporters to take taxis. "Don't drive your car," she begged them.

She talked to her family by phone and cried afterward. Her children fought with each other, her in-laws, and the son of a brother-in-law—all of whom were staying in her house. Her daughter scolded her, "You don't come home. You don't care about your kids. What's the point? The government won't listen to you."

On November 13, 2009, twelve days after Amina pitched her tent, two men stood outside it and told her the registrar wanted to see her. She had been taking a nap and did not want to talk to them. Still half-asleep, she followed them into the Supreme Court beneath cavernous ceilings that made her feel small and vulnerable.

The court had agreed to hear the missing cases, the registrar told her as he shuffled papers on his desk. "Really?" she asked. "Are you sure?" "Yes," the registrar said, continuing to sort papers. "You are a big security risk. You have too many people with you. The chief justice told the attorney general to remove the problem."

The first hearing was held November 16, 2009. Since then five other hearings have been held. The court asks the government to respond to allegations that ISI and the Ministry of Defense have taken people. The government responds by asking for more time. Soon Amina will attend yet another hearing. And another and another. Into spring and then summer. Another hearing.

It's one in the morning on Saturday, January 26, 2010. Three men arrive at the Haripur Police Station minutes apart. The first man, Sheraz, the son of Mohammad Arshad of Kalawan, steps out of a van. He wears the same white *salwar kameez,* a long tunic over pants, he wore when he was arrested. A blindfold is removed from his face.

He starts walking.

He was held fifty-one days in a crowded cell. "What is the case they have on you?" he and his cellmates would ask one another. "Why are you here? Why are they keeping us?" None of them knew, and no explanations were offered.

A bare lightbulb in their cell was on all the time. Sheraz slept on the floor with a blanket and awoke every morning at four. Interrogators asked him what he did for a living, what his job was, and what his relationship was to Mullah Kari Sadiuk, the family member who was arrested with him.

"He's a relative," Sheraz said. "I'm a student. I have no job." He was asked the same questions day after day. His interrogators told him they were from the intelligence bureau. They talked to him for fifteen minutes at a time. He asked to contact family. "No," they told him. "Not now. You will be released soon."

Now he passes silent vendor stalls, hears the cries of dogs and the wind in trees, sees dark shapes in plowed fields beneath hundreds of stars overhead. He looks behind him, sees no one. Still he worries. They said they would check on him.

Mullah Kari Sadiuk walks not far behind Sheraz. The man who had been interrogating Sadiuk told him only hours ago that he knew he was innocent. A short time later Sadiuk was escorted to a van. No other detainees rode with him to the Haripur Police Station.

The police called him a terrorist and accused him of being involved in terrorist acts when they arrested him. They put a hood over his head and punched him in the face and kicked him, shouting, "Oh, you terrorist fuck." He had no idea why he was suspected of anything. He had a beard, wore a turban. He was a mullah, taught the Koran. He assumes he was faulted for that.

They drove for a long time before the van reached the detention center. He was held alone in a concrete cell. He heard other prisoners praying and reading from the Koran. All of them mullahs. "Without any evidence, why do they keep us?" they shouted to one another through the space between the bottom of their cell doors and the floor.

His interrogators would put a hood over his face and ask him, "Where is your home, where did you come from, where were you educated? Which schools did you attend? Do you know about so-and-so?"

He said he worked for a mosque.

"Who trained you? What organizations are they with?"

They asked him the same questions two days in a row. On the third day he was moved to another cell. He was never interrogated again.

In the silence of the night he wonders if they are still watching him.

Mohammad Hafiz, the missing younger brother of Gulam Farwo, stands in front of the Haripur Police Station, unsure whether he should go inside. His thin bearded face and sharp nose catch the moonlight and throw a slim shadow against the wall. He decides against going inside and starts walking toward his village. He does not know that Sheraz and Sadiuk have been released and that his brother, Munir, has not.

"How many brothers do you have?" an interrogator had demanded of Mohammad. "What is your name? What is your job? What does your brother do?"

On the thirty-sixth day one of his interrogators told him that he knew Mohammad was innocent by the expression on his face. Then, this morning, fifteen days later, he was released and driven to Haripur.

When he reaches his village, after he makes his way on the narrow stone paths leading to his home, after the hugs and tears and celebration, he will learn that his five-month-old daughter died during his detention. Standing over her grave, he will conclude that innocent people can do nothing to protect themselves. They only burn inside. He will decide that Pakistan is now his enemy.

Stacks of law books line the bland concrete walls of Courtroom A in Pakistan's Supreme Court building. Mildew spreads across the ceiling, and vast cobwebs consume cracked corners. The worn brown carpet bunches in waves across the floor, rolling toward a security guard asleep in his chair beneath a painting of a stern Jawaharlal Nehru.

Three Supreme Court justices ask Amina and a lawyer for the Ministry of Defense to approach. Amina carries a plastic bag stuffed with testimonials of families of missing people. She sets it down, letting the bag sag against her right leg, and then she straightens and stands immobile, a diminutive figure looking up at the justices. The Ministry of Defense lawyer walks from the other side of the courtroom and stands beside her.

"I have written letters to the Ministry of Defense and they have never responded," Amina tells the court. "I don't want to dishonor any institution. If they want any guarantee, I will not say a word if my husband is released. If that is the hurdle. I am ready for any compromise. I don't know whether what I am doing is right or wrong. I am only struggling for my husband."

"What material does the Ministry of Defense have about the missing?" a justice asks.

"There is no material, Your Honor. The Minister of Defense is like a post office. He passes information on to other agencies. He does not consider it."

"Are we playing a ping-pong game?" another justice asks. "I am looking at a one-page report from the minister about the missing and how he has passed information on, as you say. But it is obvious a low-level clerk drafted this report and that the Minister of Defense signed it without knowing what he was signing. Consider the spelling errors. You know it is not an effective report. We need a whole report. Not a page with errors."

"The ministry is cooperating," the lawyer says.

"The report is vague and one-sided. The evidence should have been examined. The report does not serve any purpose other than as a spelling lesson. The minister of defense, the minister of interior, ISI . . . all should be here with documents."

"We have many missing cases," the first justice says. "Who is responsible for this? Who investigates these cases?"

The third justice, who has yet to speak, crosses his arms and closes his eyes. Soon he falls asleep.

"We want answers straight away," the second justice says. He looks at Amina and then back at the lawyer. "Do you feel for her? Or have you become desensitized like a surgeon? Return with a credible report in two weeks. Not one written at a desk by some clerk. This is not just about Madam. We are talking about thousands of people."

Outside the Supreme Court seventy-year-old Abdul Ghaafar rides a rusting bicycle with a large poster of his missing son, Abdul, strapped behind him. The photograph shows a young man with a thick mustache staring intently into the camera without expression.

Ghaafar has also arranged a large piece of cardboard between the handlebars on which he has written: "My son is innocent. I am trying to find him. But I can't. I am a poor person. I need due justice from the government of Pakistan. My son did not take any steps against the government. Please release my son. This is my request to the government of Pakistan."

Ghaafar stops as many people as he can. He tells them, "I'm looking for my son. He drove a truck between Peshawar and Mardan. Have you seen him?"

The last day Ghaafar saw him was a warm hazy morning. Abdul drank tea and ate fried eggs and naan for breakfast with his wife and three children amid the noise of vendors setting up their booths on the teeming streets outside. He shaved, put on clean clothes. He told his wife, "Have a good day. I'm going to get my truck."

He never returned. He has been missing almost nine years. If he is alive, he is thirty-four.

In 2005 the police gave Ghaafar a photograph of a man killed in Kashmir. Blood ran down his forehead and across his nose. "This is your son," they said. "No, it is not," Ghaafar said. "Yes, it is," the police insisted. "Show me his DNA," Ghaafar said. The police refused.

The people crowding around Ghaafar near the Supreme Court feel his profound sorrow. They consider Abdul's picture and then stare at the old man before them with his heavy white beard and his sweat-stained black kameez and shake their heads. They do not recognize his son. Ghaafar gives them blue flyers to distribute. "Kidnapped driver not recovered yet. I am a poor man. I demand the release of my son. Police should do everything to get his release."

He rides away, the bike shifting to the left and right beneath him, his legs pushing down on the pedals. The people he has just spoken to wave their hands and wave the flyers in the dust-filled air and promise to pray for him.

Ghaafar diminishes in the distance as Amina walks out of the Supreme Court, a smile on her face. The court rejected the report signed by the minister of defense. The court means business. It was as though the justices asked about flowers and the minister's lawyer answered with talk about water. No related answers. The ministry provided no evidence to contradict the claim that it knows about Masood.

If the Ministry of Defense lawyer continues to stall, Amina will demand that the court call for the defense minister himself and members of the ISI to appear and to ask them for all the names of missing people.

She can always camp outside the Ministry of Defense. She can resort to that if she must. Sometimes she imagines Masood in a cell. How it looks. Dark, cold. How he feels. Lonely, grieving. Once she was stuck in a cramped bathroom. The door jammed and would not open. She laughs about it now, but at the time she panicked and felt claustrophobic and had trouble breathing. What must it be like for him?

Amina misses Masood most at night. Sometimes, alone in their bedroom, she weeps, with only the shadows cast by a flickering candle to comfort her. At these times she has no spirit left. She doesn't want to talk to her children, work in her office, attend Supreme Court hearings—nothing, until the moment passes and she gathers her resolve once more. In five years she has accomplished much in her search for Masood, but she regards it as nothing compared to what he gave her.

Gives her, she corrects herself. Gives her.

9

Here Everything Is Poison

Institute of Public Heath, Mitrovica, Kosovo: June 2009

Krasnici, Meba. Born 2006, Osterode. Blood lead level: 34.6

Seljimi, Arbenita. Born 2008, Osterode. Blood lead level: 22.1

The boy tilts his head back, Darren's camera close to his mouth. I make a face.

"Smile."

Looking at me, the boy starts to giggle. How old? Maybe five? He can't stop giggling. We are playing this game beneath gray skies in Osterode Resettlement Camp, in the ethnically divided city of North Mitrovica.

"Smile."

Darren's shutter clicks.

Cold winds carry lead-filled dust from a nearby slag heap, a hundred million tons of toxic tailings, and scatter it on clothes hanging from laundry lines, on open buckets of drinking water, on the dirt children play in, and on the feral dogs running down alleys in this former French army barracks housing about 250 displaced Roma men, women, and children.

Another resettlement camp, Chesmin Lug, Serbian for—appropriately—runoff, lies downhill from here, just past garbage-strewn railroad tracks upon which two dead dogs lie rotting amid melting spring snows. That camp shelters another forty-seven Roma families in ramshackle huts pieced together from scrap wood and warped two-by-fours.

In the distance stands the Trepča mining and smelting complex, once the largest mine in Europe—now slowly coming back online after a decade's dormancy following the Kosovo war. The ground around the complex, gouged open by water streaming down the slag heap, reveals black lines of lead and zinc deposits like rings on a tree. Both the ground and this boy's mouth are ravaged by toxins.

Click.

The boy bares all his teeth. I look closer, leaning over Darren's shoulder. The boy's left front tooth is almost entirely covered by lead that has emerged through the rotting tissue of his receding gums. Lead, more often than not, is an invisible killer. But in this boy's mouth it announces itself with a boldness that turns my stomach.

The boy sees my reaction and frowns. I shake my head, make another face.

"Smile."

He opens his mouth, grinning once more, tongue dancing. The lead glistens from saliva.

Click.

The United Nations built the Osterode and Chesmin Lug resettlement camps in 1999 to temporarily hold as many as 9,000 Roma—Gypsies, as they are more commonly known in America. The Roma neighborhood on the Ibar River straddled Serb-dominated northern Mitrovica and Albanian-controlled southern Mitrovica, and Albanians destroyed the neighborhood in the waning days of the Kosovo conflict when protective Serbian forces left the area. Without a country willing to claim them, the Roma have nowhere else to go.

The Albanians, furious at the atrocities to which they had been subjected by the Serbs, accused the Roma of collaborating with the Serbian army. The Roma, a traditionally down-trodden clan, say they were hardly in a position to do anything but strive for their own survival; they think the Albanians' grudge should be solely with the Serbs, not with them.

Whatever the truth behind the accusations and denials, almost everyone agrees that moving Roma families next to a toxic slag heap, onto land highly contaminated with lead, zinc, arsenic, and other metals, has caused dozens of families to suffer severe health problems and spawned a generation of brain-damaged children.

Lead blackens the children's teeth, blanks out their memory, and stunts their growth. Other symptoms of lead poisoning include aggressive behavior, nervousness, dizziness, vomiting, and high fever. The children swing between bursts of nervous hyperactivity and moody depression; they have fainting spells and epileptic fits.

According to internationally accepted benchmarks drawn up by the U.S. Centers for Disease Control and Prevention, 10 micrograms of lead per deciliter (mcg/dl) of blood cause the beginning of brain damage. When the World Health Organization tested the Roma's blood for lead in 2008, the readings for twenty-one of fifty-three children showed lead levels of 65 mcg/dl, which is the highest level the machine can measure.

Such children fall into the category of "acute medical emergency" and under normal circumstances require immediate hospitalization. Instead they have remained in the camps, ingesting lead through the air, through the dirt, through their food. Even before their birth, lead enters their bodies through the water their mothers drink.

Worse still, critics of the United Nations say the organization knowingly put the Roma on toxic land. Kosovo was administered by the U.N. from June 1999, after NATO bombed then-president Slobodan Milošević's troops in a bid to halt Belgrade's repression of the majority ethnic-Albanian population, which was seeking independence.

"In 1999, we had to respond to an emergency and founded the camps as a temporary facility," says Francesco Ardisson, senior protection officer of the office of Chief of Mission, U.N. High Commissioner for Refugees, in Pristina. "Unfortunately, we have been unable to find an alternative site, because neither the Albanians nor the Serbs want them."

However, U.N. staffers have raised questions about the organization's handling of the Roma. "The U.N. put the Roma in the camps even though the U.N. knew the place was poisoned," says Ilija Elezovic, the health department director for the U.N. Mission in Kosovo. "The place where the camps are, the U.N. had a plan to build a fence around it that said Danger. But they didn't do that. Instead, they put the Roma there."

Elezovic says his own blood lead level was 16 mcg/dl.

"Everyone is poisoned here," he says, "especially the Roma."

"They are conceived in lead," Paul Polansky, an American activist, tells me between questions to Tina Gidzic, his Roma assistant, who makes his appointments. The three of us are sitting in the lobby of my hotel drinking muddy-looking Turkish coffee.

Tina met Paul in a Bosnian refugee camp and started working with him in 2002, after she studied English through a program he had established for Roma people. She taught hygiene ten to twelve hours a day, five days a week, in the Osterode and Chesmin Lug camps. Within a year she began getting sick—vomiting every day and feeling dizzy. A test revealed her blood lead level to be 17 mcg/dl. She was treated with doses of magnesium and vitamin C. Now, at twenty-two, her joints still ache and she believes her memory is not what it was.

"These camps are horrors," Paul continues. "I know of eighty people who have died in the camps from lead. They have to be immediately evacuated from the camps and medically treated. The Albs and Serbs don't want them. The only hope is to get them abroad."

The Roma, however, are not considered refugees by the U.N. but "internally displaced people." That means they do not fit the U.N.'s criteria for financing their resettlement abroad—a penny-wise, pound-foolish accounting gimmick any bean counter would appreciate. Even if the Roma were classified as refugees, however, finding countries willing to accept them would be difficult.

"So far, no country has come forward to offer assistance," Paul says. "Gypsies are not the flavor of the month in any country. That's the problem. If they were another group, this wouldn't be happening."

A native of Mason City, Iowa, Paul left the Midwest in 1963 in protest of the Vietnam War. He settled in Spain, hunted big game in Africa, married, had four children, divorced, and moved to Czechoslovakia to research his family ancestry. There he discovered files documenting the deaths of thousands of Roma in Nazi concentration camps. Intrigued, he immersed himself in Roma history. He published volumes of Roma oral histories. He wrote poems about the Roma. The Roma became his passion.

In 1999, when the U.N. needed a Roma expert in Kosovo, Paul signed up—but quickly became disenchanted when camps were arranged on toxic land. He quit the U.N. and became a one-man Roma advocate. He is now head of a mission for the Society for Threatened Peoples International, a German-based organization dedicated to publicizing the plight of threatened peoples. After ten years his commitment and anger have only increased in the face of international disinterest.

His scathing indictments of the international community for, in his view, ignoring the plight of Kosovo's Roma caught my attention. Like most Americans, I had long since forgotten about the Kosovo war amid the years of our own conflicts and had never even been aware of Roma casualties.

I e-mailed Paul. It was clear from his response that I did not score points with my ignorance, but an ignorant journalist was better than nothing at all, and nothing was about all Paul was getting as he sought to bring attention to the camps. So, in March 2009, with little to lose, he encouraged Darren and me to fly to Kosovo to see for ourselves what war had wrought.

As Paul and I finish our coffee, Tina reads a text message on her cell phone. A concerned look crosses her face. "That was Demsit in Osterode Camp," she says. "His grandmother has died."

"Did she live in the camp?" I ask.

"One month."

"That's eighty-one dead," Paul says.

Of course he doesn't know if she died from lead poisoning. Like AIDS, lead attacks the immune system, resulting in secondary illnesses that are often the official cause of death—if a cause is determined at all. Most of those who have fallen ill in the camps have been treated in Serbian hospitals, and human rights groups have had difficulty getting medical records. Paul's anger, I think, causes him to jump to conclusions. It is the desperation that comes from being ignored.

Minutes later Demsit Jahiirovic, a lanky young man wearing jeans, a T-shirt, and black stocking cap, saunters into the hotel and up to our table with a gangbanger strut. But the gentle-yet-sad expression in his eyes suggests the futility of his posturing. He tells Tina that his aunt in Europe will send 250 euros for his grandmother's funeral. Paul offers to donate additional money.

"Two years ago Demsit tested 38 for his blood lead levels," Paul says. "He has not been tested since."

"They say the whole of Kosovo is polluted," Demsit tells me. "The administration of the camp doesn't talk about the future, because there is none. There is no hope for me and the whole camp. The camp is a catastrophe."

He had lived in Germany since he was an infant, after his parents fled his native Croatia in 1991. But they never applied for refugee status, and in 2005 the family was deported to Kosovo, where his father was born. Demsit has lived in Osterode ever since.

"How long are you here?"

"Two weeks," I tell him.

"There'll probably be another death by then," Demsit says.

In the morning Darren and I meet Paul for a quick breakfast and then, along with Tina, pile into his aging RV, a groaning, coughing rattletrap of a vehicle, a survivor of too many miles crisscrossing Europe. Paul affectionately calls it "the caravan." He lived in the RV for years before buying a house in Serbia after he left the U.N.

A surprising six inches of snow fell overnight. We jounce down an ice-covered, cobbled road toward Chesmin Lug. It can be hard to believe an armed conflict here resulted in a six-week NATO bombing campaign that by its own count caused at least 1,500 civilian deaths—let alone the consequences of that conflict, which led to the Roma's living on contaminated land. University students walk down streets singing to tunes on their iPods. Restaurants and Internet cafes bustle with business, and cars clog the narrow colorfully lit streets.

Despite the activity, anger from the war and the ethnic animosities that still haunt the Balkans reveals itself in not-so-subtle ways. Graffiti sprayed in thick red paint across the walls of old communist-era cinder-block apartment complexes castigate the U.N. presence. Vendors sell postcards with a black slash through *U.N.* and T-shirts—showing a sodomized Mickey Mouse—that dismiss the West with vulgarities. Other T-shirts promise that the Serbian army "will be back."

As we approach Chesmin Lug, I see the snow-covered slag heap that Paul calls "Moby Dick" lurking above the bare trees surrounding the camp. It appears to be rolling forward, as if diving back into the ground, a white hulk waiting to burst forth and spout its poison upon the Roma. We cross the train tracks, pass the rotting corpses of the dogs lit by thin slats of sunlight emerging between clouds. Small boys chase one another, throwing snowballs. The snow turns to brown puddled sludge beneath their feet, streaming into the tainted ground.

Glancing downhill, I see a jogging trail built by the U.N. for the Roma. It weaves beneath the trees toward the smelter. A sign, "Breathe in the Odor of Good Air," without a hint of irony in its absurd good cheer, was once posted by the trail—before the Roma tore it down, along with the metal exercise bars they dismantled and sold to recycling plants. Weeds push through cracks in the disused path. The broken ground winds past a soggy soccer field, the sagging goalposts a quiet salute to games no longer played.

I follow Paul down a lane, avoiding a small girl shoveling snow with a tray, pebbles scratching the metal raw. I squint against the glare ricocheting off tin-sheet roofs weighed down by truck tires to prevent the roofs from blowing away. Wood smoke rises from chimneys, the heat melting the snow in long teardrops. Windblown shirts bounce on laundry lines in a jittery dance of headless marionettes. A pair of black pants, suspended above the blue-painted door of the Smajiliji family, absorbs the dripping snow. Paul knocks. Rifadija Smajiliji answers, her husband, Muhammad, standing behind her. Tina translates. Despite his years advocating for the Roma, Paul has yet to master their language.

"Rifadija has test results," Tina tells Paul.

"Anyone explain the results to them?"

"No."

Paul is not surprised. Effective treatment for lead poisoning would require removing the Roma from the camps. The test results mean little as long as the people remain on toxic land, continually absorbing more lead and other poisons. It's as if the camps are laboratories where the Roma are observed and their deteriorating health documented for no reason other than to document it again and again—a Sisyphean experiment without meaning or application.

Rifadija sorts through a Winnie the Pooh bicycle pack in a small brightly carpeted room heated by a stove. She offers Paul papers from the Mitrovica Institute of Public Health. According to the papers, her four-year-old daughter registers 60 mcg/dl, six times the amount that causes brain damage. Their nine-month-old baby shows 37.8 mcg/dl. Still another child registers more than 65 mcg/dl. A greater-than symbol on the lab test indicates the results for this child were higher than the machine could register.

"The baby cries a lot. I don't know the problem," Muhammad says.

"Your children should be in hospital this minute," Paul says.

Muhammad begins to weep. Without being asked, his son brings him a glass of water. Muhammad squeezes two pills from an aluminum packet into his palm and tosses them in his mouth. Antidepressants, he explains, saying, "I can't take it anymore."

In the evening Paul and I sit alone. He sips a glass of red wine, removes his glasses, and strokes his beard. The Roma, he knows, can be their own worst enemy. He bought one woman three washing machines and three dryers to start a laundry business. He even built her a laundry room. The first month she was a tremendous success. Then one night she sold everything to buy her sixteen-year-old son a bride.

He shakes his head and taps the table with his glasses. It's maddening, this work. Most of the eighty dead were kids. He had known them since they were born. Watched them going downhill, month after month, year after year. Knew they would die from lead poisoning. An entire generation. No, two, when he counts the unborn offspring of the dead kids.

"People told me how dangerous it was to live here but what should I do?" Paul says.

How does he explain it? You can't see lead poisoning. It's not like a nosebleed. He observes kids over time. Gradually he notices they no longer walk the way they once did. They don't remember what they did seconds ago. They get sick too often. He sees the progressive deterioration. The mothers see it. They always see it first. Their expressions of grief swirl in his head.

"I feel very bad seeing my children dying. I saved them from war, but I cannot save them from lead."

The Council of Europe Commissioner for Human Rights, Thomas Hammarberg, visited the camps earlier in the day. Arms crossed, a frown on his face, he listened to camp leaders. He spent perhaps thirty minutes in each camp. I pulled him aside and asked for his thoughts.

"The lead thing is a grave tragedy. The Roma are victimized by that," Hammarberg told me. "It is sad the international community has not found a solution ten years later. The real solution must be to move them; I think that's right. There is very little treatment without moving them. It is the single most major environmental disaster in Europe."

Hammarberg's remarks pleased Paul, yet he does not hold much hope for action. He has seen many officials visit the camps. Hammarberg may be different. Or, like the others, he too may file a report, have it bound and put on a shelf, its spine even with the many other bound and dust-covered reports on the same shelf. But what will become of it? Nothing, more than likely.

"My grandchild is very sick. We have been in the camp three years."

Genocide. Say it. *Genocide.* No one wants to use the G-word, but Paul does not hesitate. Genocide. His parents taught him that if he sees an injustice, he should protest and call it what it is. Genocide. If the government would only move the Roma, Paul would be out of Kosovo tomorrow. At sixty-seven he has survived five heart attacks. He wants to live in a warm climate, read books, write poetry, continue his oral history projects. But he can't leave. Not yet. Tomorrow he may surprise himself and find someone who will listen to him. Really listen. He pins his hopes on another tomorrow. But doubt plagues him tonight. He does not know if anyone in the camps can be saved. He understands the bottom line.

They're Gypsies. Gypos. Who gives a fuck about Gypsies?

Djemailji, Baskim. Born 1999, Osterode. Blood lead level: 42.29
Hajdini, Senad. Born 1992, Chesmin Lug. Blood lead level: 38.16
Hajdari, Jakup. Born 1998, Chesmin Lug. Blood lead level 40.0

In Osterode Camp, Feruz Jahirovic (no relation to Demsit Jahiirovic) and his wife, Flanza, sit sorrowfully before me. They are the parents of Sara, a three-year-old with a blood lead level of 53.8 mcg/dl. The family has lived in the camp since 2004. Sara and her eight siblings are all sick. They need help now while they are alive, Feruz tells me. Joint pain, stomach pain, headaches. They don't walk properly, have trouble learning. They don't see or hear well.

Even when Feruz finds work and buys good food, his children don't eat. They have no appetite. Look at their nine-year-old son, Mussa. He has a blood lead level of 43.7. He does not look nine. He looks four. A very skinny four. His ten-year-old brother is skinnier and looks even younger. Feruz's parents were very good to him, and he wants to be the same for his children. He will even clean toilets to earn money to help them. But they are lost.

"I watch them dying and I can't help them."

Flanza rocks Sara to sleep. She faints often, Flanza tells me. When this happens, Flanza shakes her and pats her face with cold water, but often she does not awaken. They give her a bottle, but she does not take it. Desperate, they rush Sara to the hospital. The taxi goes too slowly. Flanza wants to get out and run with her to the doctor.

Her children are an example of why she should not have more, she says. She has induced miscarriages by deliberately falling on her stomach, lifting buckets too heavy to carry, drinking vile concoctions recommended by older women that make her violently ill. She bleeds a lot during these times and is sorry for the lost babies. But she does not want more children born with lead.

Food, air, water, she trusts none of it, she says, looking at Feruz. He nods, his sallow face drawing tight.

Here everything is poison, he says.

I walk the jogging trail with Tina. Slush oozes beneath my boots. The Ibar River, flooded with melting snow, rushes alongside, thick with roiling mud and the bobbing refuse of discarded bottles and all other manner of garbage. We pass the rutted ground of the soccer field; it is covered with dead weeds left over from the previous spring.

"Do you think it is good for eating?" Tina shouts to three fishermen, their poles poised over a small pond filled with the overflow of the Ibar. "This place is poisoned, no?"

"No, c'mon," one of the fishermen shouts back.

"What are we to do, not eat?" another counters.

The ruffled water sweeps past them, a brown ribbon spinning and turning, carried by wind and its own gravitational force, bubbling up around fallen trees and broken branches that collect discarded plastic bags, snap, snap, snapping in the wind like so many angry flags.

We continue on toward the smelter. A chained, rusted gate prevents further progress. A bird flies over a red-and-white chimney stack and calls out in the stoic silence enforced by the vacant buildings beneath it. Tina shifts uneasily beside me.

"Even the air tastes different here," she says.

Zoran Savić, a pediatrician, has seen many Roma children since he began working in the camps in 2005. He had been told the camps were temporary and the families would soon be moved to a place with less toxicity. He dispensed medicines. He treated more than 300 children and really thought he would be successful, but he was deceived. Year after year the families remained in the camps. When he stopped treatment, their blood lead levels continued to rise. So he avoided going to the camps. What was the point?

He knows of seventy-seven people who died in the camps between 1999 and 2008. Maybe more, as Paul says. Dr. Savić does not know how many were children. The grandchildren of one family have particularly high blood lead levels. More than 45 micrograms. One girl is physically retarded. Another has bad convulsions. All from lead. He has no doubt. His own blood lead level is 3 micrograms, well below ten, but he watches it.

Dr. Savić will see Roma children who come to his office. He tries to ease their pain but feels he is wasting his time. He can't imagine what the camps will be like in ten years. Lead poisoning takes a long time to treat but not as long as the politics of treatment, he says.

Some agencies have tried to move the Roma out of the camps, only to become ensnared in a funding limbo. Mercy Corps, an American aid organization, has budgeted $2.4 million to resettle fifty Roma families—about 250 people—this year in either north or south Mitrovica, away from the contaminated sites.

According to Catherine Rothenberger, a Mercy Corps administrator in Kosovo, most of the budget would be applied to new housing, although treatment for lead poisoning is also included. She says more families would be moved if additional donors agreed to support the program. "Resources are not an issue, but a clear plan is," Rothenberger says. "Donors are reluctant to invest unless it results in productive resettlement."

In other words, more families will remain in the camps than will be moved out.

Asanaj, Sevdije. Born 1998, Chesmin Lug. Blood lead level: 37.40
Ljatifi, Eruduan. Born 2001, Osterode. Blood lead level: 57.35
Audi, Valjentina. Born 2004, Chesmin Lug. Blood lead level: 54.14

On a Friday morning Paul announces that he must leave Mitrovica for his home in Niš, Serbia, a three-hour drive. He has to check on his two dogs, catch up on e-mail, plan speaking trips abroad about the camps. He has just finished lunch with a Roma leader from a third camp in Leposavić. That camp is not on toxic land, but Roma there often marry into families living in Osterode and Chesmin Lug, continuing the legacy of lead poisoning.

Paul is still trying to convince the Roma leader to organize a protest. To burn candles and hold signs that read "Save Us" on April 9, International Roma Day.

"C'mon, we have to do this."

The Roma leader offers a noncommittal nod. Just like the woman with the laundry business and the many others who also agreed but who eventually disappointed Paul.

"Get everyone behind this. It will draw the media," Paul insists. He turns to Darren and me. "Guys, you must stay until April 9."

"We can't," I say.

"You must."

"We can't."

Paul glances at his watch. He needs to pick up Tina's sister. His health prevents him from driving long distances alone.

"We have to stay on this," he says, the tired insistence in his voice revealing the resilience of his weary heart, beating still.

From my hotel window I see, beyond the brick tile roofs and somber squares of concrete apartment buildings, the dark shape of Moby Dick humped against the evening sky, darker than the night. I hear Demsit: "My family all feels bad, but we have not begun to look for food in garbage yet," and my thoughts race backward and forward as other voices converge in my mind—"My children have bad memories, when they start something they are confused and don't finish"—as if there is no past or present but only what is now, this moment.

I am Muhammad Smajiliji. I see my children jumping rope near fat puppies asleep against a shed stacked with firewood. The snow continues to melt in the still air. A nearby graffito reads, "Fuck nato." Always the laundry lines bend with wet clothes. A car moves up a muddy lane.

Sizzling green peppers cook on the stove. We huddle around the expanding warmth. Our shadows rise up the pink chipped walls, a bare bulb overhead. In the corner a broom to sweep the rug of black dust.

"Yes, the children vomit and have high temperatures," my wife tells Western visitors. "Our four-year-old has a blood lead level of 60 and is very nervous."

"They are all nervous," I say. "I am nervous. I start to shake, and it takes a long time to calm down. While we wait for someone to do something, I feel myself losing power. I am losing concentration. I feel like collapsing."

I am Feruz Jahirovic. My wife and I take the best care of Sara that we can. Doctors tell us she has three different illnesses in her heart. That's how I understand it. I don't have money for medication. She has been sick since 2007. She needs an operation. Many times we go for a walk, and she gets tired too soon and wants me to hold her.

My wish is to take my children out of the country, treat them, and save their lives. I wish I would die as soon as possible and leave this place, but as a parent I have to look after my children. But I would be very glad to die.

I am Paul Polansky. I am fighting off a cold. I can't stop coughing. Tina will worry about my heart. The hospital didn't have medication when I had my first heart attack, and I had to buy it myself. There was no bedpan. Tina bought a soda so I had a bottle to piss in. University of Pristina Hospital. Shit hole. I was later airlifted to Belgrade. The doctor there told me to try his homemade brandy. It will open your arteries, he said.

At one time my blood lead level was 20 mcg/dl, twice the level for brain damage. I felt a bit nervous, a bit aggressive. Treatment calmed me.

I survive but what of the rest of mankind? Americans are like the cheetah. It kills one animal at a time. When its prey is gone, the cheetah is gone. But the hyenas and other scavengers that eat garbage, they will survive. The West is so highly specialized. With all your money do you think you'll eat garbage? You can't adapt. But to survive a Gypsy will eat garbage.

Seljimi, Giltema. Born 2003, Chesmin Lug. Blood lead level: 60.42

Kuvelic, Dragica. Born 2004, Osterode. Blood lead level: 22.1

The day after Paul leaves, Tina and her friend Gushami Bekim take me across a bridge into north Mitrovica, where international aid organizations have, with the consent of the Albanians, built apartments for Roma families on the land of their old neighborhood. Gushami lives in one of the apartments.

We walk through an empty park that has no name and onto a construction site, where two- and three-story brick apartment buildings rise above torn ground. The interior of one building has been gutted of its electrical outlets and hall lights, probably sold by a Roma tenant for recycling. Looking out the window of a second-story landing, I see a jungle gym made of discarded tires in a garbage-filled sandpit alongside a seesaw and a swing set made from logs. Drying clothes and rugs hang off balconies, dripping water onto the sand. "They still think they live in the camps," Gushami says of the Roma. "That's why they mistreat this place."

His apartment stands in stark contrast to the ruin of the hall. Shined hardwood floors, kitchen, and a breakfast nook. Newly white-painted walls, bright red rugs, and a couch that absorbs me when I sit. Struggling to get up, I suggest we talk on his deck overlooking the playground.

"It doesn't matter that I have an apartment," Gushami tells me. "I need work, but I'm not safe to work here. I have seen many times Albanians beating up Roma here. We didn't steal. We didn't kill and burn down houses. It's not our people who want their own country. All we want is enough food for our children, and jobs."

He lived in Osterode before moving here last year. A 2005 test showed all his children had lead in their blood. He doesn't know if they still do. They seem more active here, he says. "In the camp, they were always sick. The conditions were bad, but at least then I had a job."

I ask him if he has considered moving to another country. Gushami smiles at the question, like an old man tolerating the question of a naive child. "I'd go abroad, but who would take us? We are not that lucky."

In the evening I stand with Alil Ahmit in Chesmin Lug. Darren and I will leave in the morning. Our time here over. But I have breathed in the toxins: immeasurably small amounts, to be sure, but now I carry this place in my blood, and its lead will follow me home.

Demsit was wrong about one thing. Other than his grandmother, no one has died during my visit. But lead kills, and whether any individual dies today, tomorrow, or next week, they are all dying slowly. Now, with the Trepča mines coming back to life—the deep shafts again producing ore, the smelter concentrating the ore into high-grade lead and zinc—the toxicity surrounding the mines will only increase. And given the world's love affair with high-tech gadgetry, the production of zinc for batteries and lead for solder is bound to go into overdrive.

I tell Alil about the new apartments in the old Roma neighborhood, but Alil says he is afraid to move there. Instead he will remain in the camp and raise pigeons. He keeps them in a green shed and, as the sun sets, opens the door and releases them. I watch dozens of gray and white pigeons soar into the air, circling high over our heads.

Families collect around us, cup their hands over their eyes, and watch the birds. Two of Alil's children have the highest blood lead levels in the camp, or so a doctor with the Institute of Public Health told Alil's wife. The doctor said they should take a lot of vitamins, but Alil does not think that will help.

We continue staring into the broad band of sky growing ever larger with the pink light that precedes nightfall. Alil supposes his birds too have lead but what of it? They can fly while he and his family remain here on poisoned ground, marooned by gravity, political indifference, and their need.

Sometimes he thinks he should free his birds. But then he would be denied the joy he feels with their daily release, the power that comes from knowing he alone can liberate them, the images that come to his mind when he sees himself flying among them, the camp a tiny speck beneath his wings. Man is selfish, he tells me. Besides, the birds need him. They no longer think on their own. They are like the feral dogs skulking around our feet, fighting over scraps, unaware they too are poisoned.

We watch the birds circling the camp, rising higher and higher in the wide sky. A boy stands on his toes and reaches up with his hands, as if entreating them to return—or, more likely, to take him with them. Winged shadows in the fading evening light, they ignore him and us. Unmoored. Floating onward in ceaseless orbit, above all harm.

10

Bed 18

Herat, Afghanistan: September 2010

In bed 19 a woman suffers from high blood pressure and burns to her feet from boiling water spilled from a pot. The woman in bed 21 burned herself lighting an oil lamp. The one in bed 20 fell against a water heater.

Then there is the young woman in bed 18. She looks no older than fifteen. Stray wisps of black hair lie limply against her cheeks. Rank-smelling blankets cover her bandage-wrapped body, flakes of charred skin peel off burns to her chin and neck, and she stares mutely at the ceiling. Beside her sits her pregnant sister-in-law, who looks about the same age. They live in Lashkar Gah, the capital of Helmand Province, a Taliban stronghold far south of Herat. They have never left their home before, have never been to their village bazaar and the cities beyond it. They won't look at us. This is the first time they have not covered their faces in the presence of men outside their families.

Dr. Naeema Nikzad, a psychologist who counsels burn victims at Herat Regional Hospital, considers both young women while adjusting a blue-patterned scarf around her head. When they came to the hospital, Dr. Nikzad told the sister-in-law to remove her burqa. The doctor gave the sister-in-law a smock, flip-flops, and a surgical cap and told her to put them on.

Dr. Nikzad then took the burned woman into surgery and told her, "Now I have to strip you. You cannot wear a burqa. No one will touch you. No one from your village will see you."

The woman felt Dr. Nikzad raise the burqa above her head.

"I am exposed," she said.

My Afghan colleague Aziz looks at the young burned woman with mournful eyes. He is dressed in gray slacks, blue shirt. Silver hair combed back, beard trimmed to perfection. But he has the drawn look of sleepless nights. I can only guess what he is thinking. The sister of his son's wife burned herself to death just two days earlier in Kabul.

The mother of a young man Aziz's relative liked had approached her parents for permission for the young people to marry. Her mother said that she would rather see her daughter burn than have him for a son-in-law. The daughter overheard and told her mother, "You will see me burn." She walked into the kitchen, poured kerosene over her head, and set herself ablaze. She burned 75 percent of her body and died in the hospital. She used to be white as a sheet, Aziz had told me, but in the hospital she was black.

"Our families are sad," Aziz told me. Perhaps more than thirty years of war and suffering have reduced grieving in Afghanistan to the bare minimum of expression. Something so common that loss no longer evokes shock. I don't know, but the gross understatement spoke as loudly to me as the monotone exhaustion I heard in his voice.

I had flown to Afghanistan to write about women who attempt suicide by setting themselves on fire. Despite the 2001 ouster of the Taliban regime, women still have few opportunities for education and a career. They rarely participate in choosing a husband and have little, if any, say in the mundane decision making of everyday life. The husband and his family dominate. Men rule, women obey. And for some women it becomes too much, and they set themselves on fire.

Herat, in western Afghanistan, is only a few miles from the Iranian border. Aziz and I would base ourselves in the burn unit of Herat Regional Hospital, one of the few facilities in Afghanistan that treats self-immolation victims. It's no accident the hospital was built in Herat. Iran has a culture of suicide by burning that goes back centuries, and the practice is now common in eastern Afghanistan.

But it was just a story, another assignment. It never occurred to me someone close to Aziz might do the very thing I had come to write about. To make matters worse, the dead woman's sister, Aziz's daughter-in-law, had recently given birth to a boy. Her family was afraid to tell her about her sister. They worried she might get so upset her milk would dry up and she would be unable to feed her son.

So they buried their dead daughter without telling her sister, and the next day Aziz and I flew to Herat.

She is very sad, Dr. Nikzad says of the young woman in bed 18. She looks to be in denial, shamed.

There's no problem, the sister-in-law says as Aziz translates. She caught fire cooking.

Dr. Nikzad does not believe her. In the first six months of this year, she has seen sixty-nine self-immolation patients. Two were men. One man wanted to marry a young woman, but her family refused him. The other man . . . Dr. Nikzad shrugs. She does not know why he burned himself. Sixty-five percent of his body. There were family problems. He was jobless. He felt the shame of his family. He probably wondered what his life meant. She supposes he decided it meant nothing. He will likely die.

Girls as young as nine burn themselves, but most are between twenty-two and thirty, Dr. Nikzad tells us. They are forced into marriage, tolerate it for two or three years, and then set themselves on fire. Or they are not married. They are just very young and frustrated with their lives. They don't understand how badly they will hurt themselves. They come into the hospital and their clothes stink of gasoline.

The fire came up with the wind, the sister-in-law says.

They have knowledge of self-immolation, Dr. Nikzad continues. They learn from other women it is a way to die. When they burn themselves, the family sees it. The young women want to make a demonstration of their unhappiness.

She looks at the burn patient and adjusts her blankets.

Maybe she has mental problems, Dr. Nikzad says. Maybe she is a very sensitive person. We have counseling centers for women, but they don't come. The families don't give permission.

"I put water on her," the sister-in-law says. "I called the family."

The patient in bed 18 falls asleep. Her sister-in-law appears worn out and can hardly keep her eyes open. Aziz and I decide to leave and return in the morning.

Outside, the cold clear air washes over our bodies. Aziz breathes it in and raises his arms. He seems rejuvenated to be away from Kabul and the tragedy that struck his family. He reminds me of someone who has come to town for his high school class reunion and for a moment occupies once more a distant time that was free of all restraints. While he is in this carefree mood, he reflects on the family he has temporarily left behind in Kabul and tells me how he met his wife.

"I have been married for thirty-three years," Aziz says. When he turned twenty-five, the age the Koran instructs men to marry, his mother began searching to find him a wife. Her friends suggested one family with an eligible eighteen-year-old daughter, the best time, the Koran says, for a woman to marry. She introduced herself to the girl's parents and after four visits asked if Aziz could marry her. She offered them $1,000 for the kindness of their hospitality, and they consented.

Aziz did not meet his bride-to-be until the engagement party, a week later. Which one is to be my wife? he wondered. He and his fiancée were seated together across from their parents. Looking directly at her before the engagement became official would have been rude, so his mother gave him a hand mirror. He stared at her reflection, at her long black hair, deep dark eyes, and wide full mouth, and approved. After the families formally announced the engagement to one hundred guests, Aziz told his fiancée's mother that he wanted to take her to the bazaar for twenty minutes to help him buy more food for the party.

Her mother thought twenty minutes was too much time for them to be alone together and told him he should be gone no more than ten minutes. But Aziz insisted on twenty minutes, arguing that walking to the bazaar would require ten minutes at least, and she relented.

Aziz did not tell his fiancée what he had told her mother. Instead he flagged a taxi and had the driver take them to a restaurant, where they discussed their future together. Did she really want to marry him? Aziz wanted to know. Was she willing to live with him in the house of his parents? Did she enjoy cooking? Did she want children? Then he stopped talking and just looked at her, and she smiled and he decided that she was very beautiful.

They did not share the same bed on their wedding night. Or the following night or the night after that. They had never slept with anyone before, and Aziz was so nervous he could not achieve an erection. He saw a doctor who diagnosed his condition as stress and advised plenty of rest. One night, thirty days after they had married, thirty days after they had begun sharing a house and meals and daily chores, thirty days after they would sometimes glance at each other and for no reason start laughing, Aziz looked at his wife and realized he was no longer nervous.

"Let's do it," he said.

"OK," she said.

Years later, after giving birth to three boys and two girls, his wife told Aziz, "Please, no more."

"OK," he said.

And they stopped doing it.

The following morning Aziz and I catch a taxi to the hospital. Our driver races down the wide streets, cutting in front of other cars and honking incessantly. We pass sidewalks crowded with crates of bananas and grapes, and slabs of raw meat hanging from hooks in a bazaar. Tuck-tucks—multicolored carts attached to motorcycles—whiz past us with families hunched together inside. Mud-brick buildings bristle with flecks of grass and twigs like a day's growth of beard, their towering, centuries-old wooden doors heavy with metal knockers. They stand as bulwarks against the commotion, biblical in their ancient solemnity.

Snow-capped mountains rise beneath a vacant sky far beyond the bazaar, and a frosty wind blows through our windows, carrying with it the shouts of vendors and the sharp smell of fresh dung and the clopping noise of donkeys and horses drawing carts sagging with firewood. The commotion stays with us, growing in volume until we turn off the road and enter the hospital grounds through an open pair of rusted red gates, past armed security and a glut of beggars assailing passersby.

The burn unit emerges from behind a cluster of clinics, dirt grimed and forbidding in its solitude. Nearby a weed-covered lot holds the broken remains of metal cots, swivel fans, and chairs. Aziz and I walk past the lot and up a ramp to the entrance of the burn unit. Wide cracks above the doors snake through the walls, pausing at vast holes where the plaster has broken off before the cracks continue in ruinous flows.

A nurse holds an infant whose head is wrapped in brown-stained bandages. The child peers at us through a lopsided window. A man tells us the boy is his nephew. He may take him to Iran. They can do nothing more for him here.

Inside a janitor leads us to a locker room and instructs us to put on blue smocks, torn rubber flip-flops, and surgical caps—the hospital's idea, I suppose, of sterile clothing. The smocks appear stained from bleach and smell of the previous user.

We follow a nurse down a dim green hall, past wards filled with the groans and cries of bandaged women and infants. Their charred skin rolls in waves across their chests and arms and legs like cooled lava. No, no, not all self-immolation, the nurse tells Aziz. Too often they light gas lamps that explode, showering themselves in fire.

The sister-in-law of the young woman in bed 18 tells Aziz her name: Balanaz. The patient's name is Shagufa. Neither knows her age. Balanaz spends her days and nights at the hospital. Shagufa's family will not visit. Her mother has other children to care for; her father must tend to his crops and farm animals. It remains for Balanaz to look after Shagufa.

"Did she take a capsule for pain today?" Dr. Nikzad asks.

"Yes," Balanaz says.

"Give her another one."

Balanaz fingers an ibuprofen tablet into Shagufa's mouth and offers her water, waves flies away from her face. Balanaz spoon-feeds Shagufa crushed pomegranate from a tin plate. Shagufa moans.

"Shh, be quiet," Balanaz says, stroking her forehead. "Your pain will go down."

Dr. Nikzad gives Balanaz small tasks. Throw this bottle away, empty that trash, go to the other room for more bandages. Balanaz dashes here and there with eagerness and an authority that comes from having stayed at the hospital for days and days, observing the doctors and nurses, and learning every nook and cranny of its wards and supply rooms.

I tell Aziz that Balanaz reminds me of when I was a small boy, happy to do chores adults gave me, because it made me feel grown, made me feel I was catching up to my older brothers, who were able to leave the house and go off with their friends. Aziz translates what I said to Balanaz. She listens, looks at me, and then turns back to Aziz.

"I don't know about his life," she says.

When I first came to Afghanistan in 2001, I hired Aziz's oldest son, Khalid, as my translator. At the time his wife had just given birth to a daughter. Now these many years later, Khalid has five daughters. He loves his girls, Aziz says, and as an Afghan man he is passing on a new kind of thinking: girls are not for sale, they should not be forced into marriage, they can hold jobs, they are as good as boys.

But Aziz's wife complains that Khalid's wife has yet to produce a son. "She is old school," Aziz says of his wife.

In 2009, when his son Nabil turned twenty-two, Aziz's wife selected a young woman for him to marry, but Nabil refused. "If I must marry, I will marry this woman I know from work," he told her. "Her name is Fadwa. She is a good woman, a nice woman, and I like her."

"Part of the new thinking," Aziz says.

They married a few months later. Aziz gave them money for a honeymoon in India. When they returned to Kabul, Nabil and his bride moved into the third floor of Aziz's house. They had no wish to start a family immediately, but Aziz's wife wanted more grandchildren, preferably boys, and threatened to beat Fadwa if she did not become pregnant. Fadwa quit her job as a computer programmer and a year later gave birth to a son, now four weeks old. Nabil sleeps by himself, leaves the baby with his wife, so the infant does not awaken him in the middle of the night to be fed.

"Old school," Aziz says.

Aziz and I take breaks from the hospital and loiter on its grounds by the lot with the discarded bed frames. We watch men with heavy black beards waiting outside clinics to see a doctor. They adjust their turbans, look at us, and I decide that the ones who return my greeting of a raised hand like Westerners. I think those who look at me without expression support the Taliban. A pointless engagement with paranoia that distracts me from dwelling on what I see and hear inside the hospital.

A doctor peeling skin off like cellophane as she screams

"He's one," I say. "He's a Talib."

Aziz says I am being ridiculous, but it becomes a game between us.

"What do you think?" Aziz says, nodding at one man smoking a cigarette and staring sullenly at us.

"Oh yeah," I say. "He's one."

Rotted flesh stuck to discarded bandages, the putrid odors

Our guess-the-Taliban game not only stops me from thinking about burned and disfigured patients but is grounded in a real concern for our safety that we first encountered in Kabul. After Aziz had picked me up at the airport, we stopped for lunch near my hotel. The restaurant fell silent when we entered. The stares were directed at me, Aziz explained, and reflected the anger Muslim people felt toward the Florida pastor who had threatened to burn volumes of the Koran on the ninth anniversary of September 11. The pastor backed down days before my trip, but the issue still inspired outrage.

We sat quietly absorbing the hostile looks. Aziz told me that in the days leading up to September 11, leaflets were distributed in his Kabul neighborhood exhorting people to kill at least one Westerner for every burned Koran. One leaflet even urged Afghans to storm the U.S. Air Force base in Bagram, about a forty-five-minute drive outside Kabul. "Many of us would die," the writer of the leaflet declared, "but we would at least get one of them."

I told Aziz about an Afghan man I sat next to on my flight from Dubai. His name was Said and he worked for the U.S. Army. He was born in Kabul but raised on Long Island, where he still lived. Married with two kids. Ran a convenience store. Then the recession hit. He lost his store and signed on with the army as a translator. Two hundred grand a year, three-week vacations every six months.

"The Americans," he said, "don't trust the Afghans soldiers they train with live ammunition." Army snipers peer down from parapets, ready to take out anyone who experiences a sudden urge for jihad. Said never tells the trainees when he leaves the base. They might call someone and have him shot for working with the Americans. "Now is a time of no trust," Said had told me.

One week later Aziz and I wonder who here in Herat might be hostile. "Look at that guy," I say nodding toward a man with a heavy black beard and black turban.

Aziz watches the man without comment. In some ways, Aziz says, life was better under the Taliban. He liked that they required women to cover their bodies and faces. A burqa, he tells me, prevents men from leering at other men's wives and daughters. It enforces respect. His wife wears a burqa when she leaves the house, as do his two daughters, both in their early twenties.

Under the Taliban, Aziz continues, there was no stealing. A man could leave $2,000 on a table and no one would take it, because if they were caught, their hands would be cut off. Sometimes a thief would bribe Taliban officials so they would not lose their hand. Then the police brought in somebody to replace the thief and that person lost a hand. The Taliban were not perfect, Aziz admits.

"There's one," he says. "What do you think?"

Terrified Shagufa is looking at me with suffering eyes as I take notes. I have no answers.

"What do you think?" Aziz says again.

"Yeah, definitely Talib," I say.

The hospital closes on Friday, a Muslim holy day similar to Sunday for Christians. Only one nurse and a doctor wander the empty halls. The sound of their flapping sandals rises and diminishes with each slow step that takes them past small wards designated with matter-of-fact simplicity: skin graft bedroom, emergency room women (where a baby suckles the burned breast of her sleeping mother), emergency room men, infected adult women, acute men.

Balanaz sleeps on the floor on a prayer mat at the foot of bed 18. Curled up, sandals beneath her head, bare dirt-grimed feet twitching against the floor. The red smock she wears is torn in back. A fan whirs the silence of her sleep into a soft wheezy breeze that rustles her hair. I smell sharp odors rising from pans stained with iodine. Somewhere I hear water splash.

Balanaz rolls over and looks sleepily at us. Pauses midstretch. Her eyes snap open and she leaps to her feet, flees to the far side of bed 18 and covers her face with a sheet.

"She thinks she is in Helmand," Aziz says.

"It's just us," I say, and Aziz repeats in Pashto, "Just us."

In the evening just before sunset dust collects above the city and slowly stitches together to form an airborne particle carpet. A few domed buildings poke through the haze before finally becoming submerged beneath a mantle of pink light, an Atlantis immersed until dawn, when it will rise once more into the light of a pale desert sky.

But for now, at the end of another day, Dr. Nikzad returns home and thinks about the patients she has left behind. She removes her white hospital gown and hijab, hangs them by a mirror, catches sight of her lined face, her bent shoulders, and decides to make tea.

She knows women feel they must burn themselves to escape their homes. They can't wait for change. She suspects all patients burned themselves deliberately. Including Shagufa. Dr. Nikzad has spoken to her several times since she was admitted. When Balanaz left her side this morning to fetch some bandages, Shagufa complained to Dr. Nikzad about her married brother who always criticizes her. She could do nothing right in his eyes. "Do this, do that," he tells her. "Why can't his wife do his bidding?" Shagufa wanted to know. Why must she?

As she prepares her tea, Dr. Nikzad wonders whether Shagufa set herself ablaze to strike back at her brother, articulating her outrage through the purification of fire, her shrieks flaming upward in some kind of horrific, present-day stone-age rite, exultant in its message of suffering.

Dr. Nikzad has seen many such patients. After three, four days they begin talking. They cry and admit it. Or, like Shagufa, they admit nothing other than their powerlessness and need to escape.

The situation in Afghanistan is not good for women. Why is this? Why are women and men always fighting? By thinking about these questions, Dr. Nikzad occupies her mind and copes with the pain she sees, the screams she hears, the curses of nurses who slap shrieking children because the supply of ibuprofen tablets has been depleted and they have nothing else to relieve the children's agony. It makes her sad. Pain is a way of life for Afghan people. She wants to know why this is. Her questions lift her mind into an abstract world of intellectual query far removed from the burn unit and the screams left lingering in her mind deep beneath her exhaustion. She wants to find a sensible answer to her questions, although she knows there is none.

One morning at the hotel restaurant, as Aziz and I eat hardboiled eggs and drink green tea for breakfast, Aziz overhears two women and two men talking at a table near us. The men offer to pay the women $16 for the use of their two rooms, plus another $22 apiece for sex. The women want $44 for the rooms and $160 apiece for sex.

"Not good women," Aziz says.

I remind him of Said, the Afghan man I sat next to on my flight to Kabul from Dubai. He had asked me where I had stayed in Dubai. When I told him the name of my hotel, Said shook his head and suggested I try the Broadway Hotel next time. Russian women will sit on your lap at the bar until you arrange something further, he said. Very young, very inexpensive.

Aziz makes a disapproving face, then recalls a time in the 1980s when he was a low-level bureaucrat in the Soviet-controlled Afghan government. In 1985 he was sent to Czechoslovakia for a year and trained to detect counterfeit money. He loved Prague, its wide streets, tall buildings, friendly people. Its entertainment. He visited nightclubs. A young woman asked him to dance one night. Later she asked him to come home with her. He was tempted, but his friends had warned him about AIDS. "No, I'm sorry," he told her, "I can't do this."

He still thinks of her sometimes. When they danced, he held her by the waist. "She was very soft," he says.

While Aziz is telling me about Prague, the five doctors and twelve nurses of the burn unit are holding their morning staff meeting.

"We have twenty-five patients total."

"We have two skin grafts for today."

"We have no supplies."

"Last night a patient died."

Balanaz hears the woman in bed 19 gasping. The harsh intake and exhalation of air. She watches the patient's mother try to feed her, listens to her put down the spoon and read from the Koran.

The dead patient is twenty-two. Burns on 90 percent of her body.

Balanaz sleeps, hears verses of the Koran, and knows she is dreaming. Then she hears her name, "Balanaz . . . Balanaz," . . . over and over, and realizes she is not dreaming.

"I put in a request to the government for supplies to cover poor patients. We have no medicines."

"Their clothes burn off, and we don't have clothes to send them back home in."

“The dead patient had severe burns to her lungs and larynx.”

“Balanaz . . . Balanaz.” Shagufa asks for water, and Balanaz wakes up and struggles to reach a plastic bottle by the bed. She notices a doctor standing by bed 19. The doctor asks the time of death. A nurse tells him. The mother weeps.

“Last week a man came in with five children. I bought milk for them out of pocket.”

“All the poor are dropped off here. Even the army and NATO drop them here.”

“The patient died about 1 a.m.”

Balanaz looks at the dead woman’s mother. She is crying. Balanaz feels sad for her.

Just after we finish our breakfast, Nabil calls Aziz and tells him that he will be leaving Kabul the next morning on a three-day business trip. Nabil works for the Kabul office of Roshan, an international telephone company, and his supervisor wants him to attend a training seminar in Dubai. Nabil has asked his mother-in-law to tell Fadwa about her sister while he is away. He does not want to be home when she finds out.

But no one speaks to her. When he returns to Kabul, Nabil knows he can no longer put off the inevitable. He talks to his in-laws and they agree to a plan. Nabil will drive Fadwa to her parents’ house, and her mother will take her aside and tell her. But on the drive there Fadwa senses something. By the time they reach the house, she is weeping and almost hysterical and does not want to leave the car. “Take me home,” she tells Nabil. He pulls her from the car, and when she sees her parents, their wan faces and red-rimmed eyes, she falls to the sidewalk screeching. “No, no, no!” Fadwa tears at her face, claws the air, and Nabil steps aside to let her mother hold her.

On our last day in Herat, Aziz and I stop at the hospital to thank the staff for their time. Dr. Nikzad tells us that Shagufa is well enough for skin grafts to her legs and abdomen.

Balanaz rests her hands on her stomach and watches us shake hands with Dr. Nikzad. She does not know when her baby is due. She does not know how old she was when she married. “I was young,” she says. Her father called her into a room and said, "I want you to marry this boy." Before she married, she had not been allowed outside the house. Now she can go to the barn and feed the farm animals.

While doing her chores, she has sometimes seen American soldiers standing far away. Should they one day pass her house, she would say, "Salaam." If they were to shoot their guns, she would run. She knows little about the war.

From her time at the hospital, however, Balanaz knows that women can become doctors. But she will not be one of them. "Educated women start school when they are seven," she says. She is older than seven. She has never been to school. She is about to have a baby. Her future was decided by her father.

"It is too late for me," Balanaz says.

I do not see Aziz for four days after we return from Herat. Alone, I walk to the restaurant beside my hotel, where he and I had ordered lunch the day I arrived in Kabul. The customers are different, but the hostile stares and overbearing silence remain the same.

Across the city, Aziz is spending time with his wife. They go to the bazaar and buy wood to heat the house in winter. She wears a burqa but removes the hood to cool her face. Aziz does not object.

Nabil's wife, Fadwa, leaves her parents' house after spending several nights with them, grieving for her sister. She lives again in Aziz's house with Nabil and their infant son. She is sad but no longer weeps at night. Nabil continues sleeping alone, although the baby does not cry as much now.

Aziz's younger daughter has a twenty-six-year-old suitor. The young man's mother saw Aziz's daughter answering phones in a medical clinic where she works as a receptionist and liked her simplicity: she wore no makeup, did not look directly at male patients, and wore a burqa when she walked outside. A clinic doctor told the woman that Aziz's daughter came from a good family and was just twenty-two years old. The young man's mother called on Aziz and his wife and asked them if her son could marry their daughter.

Aziz agreed to meet him. If he likes him, he will ask his daughter if she wants him for a husband. She will say, "It is up to you, Father." Aziz will then meet the young man's family. If he approves of them, he will make arrangements for the engagement party. His daughter will quit her job, marry, and have children.

"Old school," I say.

"A little old, a little new," Aziz says.

11

Pyramid Schemes

Cairo, Egypt: April 2011

Friday, April 8, 11 a.m. | She wants me to look at the sign she holds high above the heads of protesters and read the words she has written on either side of a photograph of her five-year-old grandson.

"From the revolution where are my rights"

"I'm an innocent child release my father"

And this below his picture:

"Bring my father out quickly

"Bring my father out injustice is not good.

"Bring my father out I want to see him

"I see everything dark without my father

"Bring my father out or you will go to hell"

Dozens of people push and shove, jostling around the grandmother, forty-eight-year-old Magada Ahmed Mohammad. They are spinning in circles, moving one way and then another, with no apparent purpose other than to escape the crush of bodies descending on Cairo's Tahrir Square for today's demonstration, a day of "cleansing and prosecution," as organizers have called it.

Two months earlier similar gatherings in the square forced Egyptian president Hosni Mubarak to leave office. Those demonstrations also had names: "The Day of Revolt," "The Friday of Anger," and, most memorably, "The Friday of Departure," when Mubarak quit the presidency on February 11.

Now the youth movement that defied him has grown impatient with the slow pace of change since he left office. The Supreme Council of the Armed Forces that now rules the country appears reluctant to prosecute Mubarak and his cabinet for corruption and human rights abuses. So the hundreds of protesters now clogging the square have decided to demonstrate once again and to stay until Mubarak and his cronies are arrested and charged with crimes.

Magada sits on a green railing, holding her sign aloft, her black hair hanging as loosely around her lined face as the baggy rumpled blouse that sags around her body. She is in the square for an altogether different reason than the protesters. She seeks justice for her thirty-year-old son, Abdel-Hamid Mohammad, the father of her grandson, whose wide-eyed photo stands out among all the hand-held Egyptian flags waving around it. Magada hopes someone in the square will see the photo and ask about it. Someone who has the clout to do something on behalf of the boy's father. She thought I might be that someone, until I explain through my Egyptian colleague Rashad that I am an American journalist covering the protest. She purses her lips and nods, giving me a look that lets me know I am of no use to her but rather another example of the bittersweet days following the fall of Mubarak, when hope spread throughout the country and region and even helped inspire a revolt in Libya, before those expectations began to be overshadowed by the lingering hangover of the despot's long reign: government corruption, including money laundering and profiteering; a nearly 10 percent unemployment rate; and the continued mass arrests of political opponents.

Magada tells Rashad that Abdel-Hamid was detained in November 2007 for marijuana possession and drug dealing and sentenced to ten years' imprisonment. Magada insists crooked police manufactured the allegations against him. She has left messages at the prime minister's office, at the district attorney's office, and with secretaries to the Supreme Council of the Armed Forces. No one responds.

As she tells her story, Magada's sense of isolation increases with the rising bustle around us. The commotion reminds me more of the Super Bowl than a protest. Vendors hawk black and red wristbands—the colors of the Egyptian flag—E-shaped key chains, and V-for-victory pins. Boys sell chocolate candy, peanuts, and popcorn. Bugs Bunny, Cinderella, and SpongeBob balloons bob beneath banners denouncing Mubarak.

The beaming white mustachioed face of Colonel Sanders, just feet away at a Kentucky Fried Chicken, offers American-style fast food and large glass windows for hastily scrawled protest signs taped crookedly across advertisements for family-friendly Variety Big Box Meals:

"The people want prosecutions!"

"Put Mubarak on trial!"

"We will not leave until a judgment is passed on Mubarak!"

Various demonstrations have used the square as a rallying point for years, including the 1977 Egyptian bread riots and the March 2003 rally against the U.S.-led war in Iraq. A large and busy traffic circle occupies its center. A statue of Omar Makram, who resisted Napoleon's invasion of Egypt, rises stalwart above the crowd northeast of the traffic circle near a mosque named after him and where Magada stays at night.

"The revolution will never die!" the demonstrators chant. An old man painting Egyptian flags on the cheeks of protesters holds out a cup of steaming tea to Magada. She reaches for it, her face an expression of weary thanks, but a shift in the crowd knocks the cup from the old man's hand.

I have to fight off a sense of drowning as I am driven deeper into the crowd, the pouting appeal of Magada's grandson eclipsed by upraised faces shouting into the sky, confident their every demand will be met if they simply occupy the square once more.

Rashad squeezes after me. He enthuses about the revolution in a voice that hints at a slight British accent but is combined with a street cockiness expressed through the liberal use of the word *motherfucker*. His father was a diplomat, and Rashad has lived throughout Europe, the Middle East, and parts of central Asia. But the Egyptian revolution has been the highlight of his life. He can't stop talking about it, recalling it, reliving it even now, amid the hubbub and distorted shrieks of static-cracked speakers carrying the increasingly hoarse voices of screaming protesters: "Who are they? Thieves and robbers. Who are we? The people!"

"On January 25, the first day of the revolution, 'The Day of Revolt,' I prepared some banners. I was in one group of twelve guys. If the motherfucking police watched us, my job was to draw attention to myself so the group could reach the square. That's how we began walking to the square, man. Groups of twelve from all over the city—small enough, we hoped, not to be noticed," Rashad recounts. "Hundreds and hundreds of groups of twelve. We were like the legs of a motherfucking spider stretching down all these streets marching. When we got to Tahrir, two things came to mind. Oh, my God, look at all these people. Then I thought, 'If this doesn't work, what will happen to us?'"

Magada watches Rashad and me disappear into the throng before she turns and faces a woman who has stopped to snap her photo.

"If I get my son released, then the revolution is fine," Magada tells the woman.

"Don't move," the woman says. She holds a cell phone in front of Magada's face and clicks a button. She looks at the photo and frowns.

"I had hoped my phone camera would work so I could take pictures and spread the word about you, but it looks like the battery is dead."

"Oh," Magada says.

She stares after the woman, who quickly disappears into the throng of protesters. Magada wants to unburden herself, release the anguish inside. But it must be to someone who can help her son. She sits silently, the weight of her loss left unspoken, bearing down upon her as much as the pressure of the sun's heat sears her neck, draining her of energy and hope.

On the day he was arrested, Abdel-Hamid had invited his parents to lunch. He and his wife lived in an apartment below them in Cairo's Imbaba neighborhood, a congested middle-class district of narrow broken roads and grimed apartment buildings interrupted by cramped clotheslines and dust-blown trees.

He stood in the street and shouted for his mother. She leaned out a window and told him they would be right down. Magada called to her husband, who was in the kitchen making tea. "Let's go," she told him. Then she heard yelling and looked out her window to see Abdel-Hamid arguing with a police officer standing outside a van. Another police officer sat in the van.

"What are you doing here?" the police officer demanded.

"What concern is it of yours?" Abdel said in an angry voice that carried up to Magada. He approached the officer, standing inches from his face.

"I'm waiting for my parents."

The police officer shoved him. "Watch how you talk. You'd better know who you're talking to," he said. Abdel cursed him. His one mistake, Magada thinks. The police officer grabbed Abdel. The other officer got out of the van, and together they opened the back doors and forced Abdel inside. By the time Magada ran downstairs, they were gone.

She asked for him at the police station but was told he was not there. She described the arresting officers: not very tall, stocky, black hair. One had a mustache. Both looked to be in their thirties. The desk clerk shrugged. He did not know anyone of either description. Magada left the station and described her son to a street vendor selling oranges and bananas. "Did you see him brought in?" she asked. He said he did see Abdel-Hamid walk into the police station with officers on either side of him gripping his arms. "Don't worry," the vendor said. "Your son is probably in the fridge."

Magada panicked. She thought he meant Abdel was in the morgue, but the vendor corrected her. The fridge was an interrogation room on the third floor of the police station.

Magada and her husband hired a lawyer and met with Abdel-Hamid a week later. His head was shaved and his clothes torn, as if he had been dragged across a floor. His face was swollen on one side. He said he had been tortured until he agreed to sign a paper confessing to drug dealing. "OK, I'll write what you want," he told his captors.

Remembering this, Magada begins to cry. A young man with a white-and-black scarf wrapped around his neck stops and asks if she is all right.

"Yes," she says.

"Why do you hold that sign?" the man asks her.

"This is my grandson. His father was falsely accused of dealing drugs and is now in jail."

"I am sorry," the man says. "Hopefully he will get out."

Friday, April 8, 2011, 1 p.m. | In east Cairo, miles from Tahrir Square, Naher Asser al-Sonousi, a twenty-seven-year-old Libyan rebel fighter, tells me that he knows all about imprisonment. As a boy he had seen Libyan police snatch people off the street without explanation, including one time his father.

Now he lies in a bed at Cairo Specialized Hospital watching television coverage of the protest. His face has been scorched a dark tan. Pink skin shows along the edges, as if he wears a mask. A cast encloses his right leg. Metal screws jut out of the cast and keep his nearly severed ankle bound together. Two of his right toes have been amputated. His big toe may be removed as well.

A static-filled cheer rises out of the TV. Flags wave frantically on screen. The static interferes with the voice of the broadcaster, making it difficult for Naher to understand him. Gadhafi called the revolution in Egypt the work of thugs. Naher knew he was lying. Naher's thoughts are always with Libya and the struggle there. At least Mubarak treated people as human beings and stepped down. Gadhafi attacks them with planes and maintains his grip on power.

The day Naher was wounded marked the highlight of his life. It was the biggest honor he could get. He had sensed an uprising in Libya as far back as 2008. Maybe he desired it more than sensed it. He had hoped to die a martyr. He imagined himself in battle. He thought it would be in Gaza, fighting the Israelis. But then war broke out in Libya. What the hell, a battle is a battle.

Fighting produced in him the best feeling in the world. It was like a wedding. Men fire guns at weddings as part of the festivity. Naher heard the sounds of the battlefield and exulted as if he were part of a celebration.

He was injured in Las Renuf when a shell struck his car. It spun in mad circles, the noise sealing his ears until all he heard was a muffled silence before the car stopped abruptly in a sand dune. The heat from a fire roaring out of the dashboard seared his face and hands, and he threw himself from the car to put out the fire consuming his clothes. When he stopped rolling on the ground, he could not move his blood-soaked right leg. He felt a fierce pain consuming his face and leg. He screamed when he was strapped onto a stretcher by other rebels. Then he felt nothing.

Naher was taken to a hospital in Benghazi, stabilized, and then driven by his father to Cairo. The hospitals there were better. War had not reduced the number of doctors and medical supplies as it had in Libya. Now, four weeks later, Naher vows to return to the front in Libya when he can walk again.

Another cheer returns his attention to the television set. More flag waving.

Although Mubarak was toppled, Egypt is still ruled by the military. There must be further change. Watching the protesters, Naher hopes that when Gadhafi falls, the military does not rule Libya.

While Naher watches television, Magada notices thirteen Egyptian soldiers approach one of the makeshift podiums the protesters have arranged in the square for anyone to bound up and rally the crowd. She listens to the soldiers declare their allegiance to the protesters. They call for the reform of the army and the downfall of the military coalition controlling the country. They pass around their military identification tags. Protesters standing beside the soldiers look at the tags and shout their approval of the soldiers' defection, and the crowd soon joins them. Magada watches as dozens of fists pump the air. Music blares over some loudspeakers. The soldiers leave the stage and walk to the traffic circle, sit down, and drink tea.

"One time during the revolution, I wanted to buy some motherfucking vegetables for dinner. I was hungry. I got home from Tahrir Square about 2:45 P.M. Curfew started at 3 P.M. and lasted until 8 A.M. Like living in a motherfucking prison, man. An effort by Mubarak to crush the revolt. I wanted to cook chicken and rice and didn't have any onions or garlic," Rashad tells me. "I go over to a corner supermarket. A security detail from the Ministry of Interior walked in a short time later and started shooting their guns in the air. They told everyone in the store to put their hands up and get home before curfew. 'Look at us on your way out, and we'll shoot you in the fucking face.' That's what they said: 'fucking face,' man. I walked out, staring at the floor. The security detail fired in the air again. Just to make a point. They used pellet guns. You know, the kind where bullets spray all over the place. Motherfuckers."

FRIDAY NIGHT–SATURDAY MORNING, APRIL 8 AND 9, 8 P.M.–5 A.M. | The Tahrir Square protesters shout their increasingly hoarse slogans deep into the night.

Magada wanders the sidewalks with her sign in the fading light. She sits with some women on the traffic circle and shares their dinner of bread, rice, and chicken. About midnight the soldiers who defected earlier in the day return. They carry the Egyptian flag on their shoulders and shout they are ready to die. Magada and the women think they are just chanting with the rest of the protesters. Everyone says they are willing to die for the revolution. But the killing and dying happened in the days Mubarak clung to power. Magada does not expect more death. She finishes her chicken. "It is very safe to say you will die for the revolution now that Mubarak is gone," she tells the women.

At about 2 A.M. an armored military vehicle shows up. Six soldiers get out. Magada watches them walk around the square. They do not speak to anyone. Their boots crunch gravel. Magada sees the defectors sitting stock-still, looking at the ground, until the soldiers leave without a word. Then the protesters carry the deserters in celebration, chanting, "Down with Mubarak, down with the military," rejoicing that the army did not arrest them.

They are still singing and chanting when Magada leaves for the women's dormitory of Omar Makram mosque. She has not been asleep long when she hears gunfire. She assumes thugs are harassing the protesters. But the gunfire increases.

Magada peers outside. She sees soldiers with ski masks charging the crowd. She watches the deserters run. She ducks at the *pop-pop* of gunfire. Soldiers swing batons, and she hears the flat smack of wood against flesh, the crack of bones. Tear gas canisters whine in the air. Protesters throw rocks, break tiles off a fountain, and toss those, too. Bleeding people sprawled on the sidewalk get trampled beneath the feet of those fleeing. A woman clutches the hand of her three-year-old son, but he cannot keep up, and she lets him go and continues running without him. Using a bullhorn, an officer announces a curfew until 10 a.m. "Stay in the mosque, or the army will take you home," he shouts.

In her bed at the mosque Magada covers herself with a blanket and presses her hands against her ears to block out the screams trapped in her mind. Finally she falls asleep, but when she awakens at dawn, she hears the mother of the three-year-old boy calling for her lost son.

SATURDAY, APRIL 9, 9 A.M. | On the way to my hotel this morning, Rashad saw soldiers blocking roads to Tahrir Square. In the middle of the night I had heard what I thought was gunfire. Then it stopped, and I dismissed the noise as firecrackers. A party somewhere.

"I don't think it was firecrackers, dude," Rashad says.

10:20 A.M. | The charred windswept remains of a bus smolder in the square. White smoke rises from the twisted steel. Singed paint peels off, curls into fists like shedding snakeskin. The roof caves inward, as if it were flattening beneath the unbearable weight of the still-static air. Gawkers stare, whispering among themselves, while vendors take positions around the bus and sell plastic bottles of water that sweat in white buckets of melting ice. Boys blackened from ash play in the driver's seat. They raise their hands and spread their fingers in victory signs. Over everything is an aura of stagnant alarm, as if somehow the mayhem was interrupted, left incomplete.

A group of women snap pictures and cluster together and compare photos.

"I'm digging the contrasts, man," Rashad says. "Burning buses and tight-ass jeans."

"They didn't warn us," a man shouts. He waves a jagged square piece of blood-smeared cardboard. In his other hand he holds six shell casings.

"They beat the shit out of us," he says. "They didn't tell us to leave. We threw rocks. We torched buses. We tried to put up barricades. Then we got out."

Other men gathering around him interrupt to relate what they saw just hours before. Some Egyptian soldiers had joined the protesters. The army killed one soldier on the spot. At least four were arrested. The other soldiers fled with the protesters. No one knows what happened to them.

"I don't believe any of you," a woman says, raising her cell phone to snap a picture. "Egypt is safe. We are not Libya."

"This is depressing," a man says.

"The army was not attacking protesters," another man insists. "They were going after the defectors. They see what's happening in Libya, what happens when soldiers defect."

A distant rumbling grows louder and louder until chanting protesters converge on the square from a side street and vow to reoccupy it. The small groups of people already there run toward them, cheering. A man in a red-and-white top hat selling T-shirts and peanuts watches as the rush of bodies flips his table.

Rashad recognizes two friends among the protesters, Torek Nour and Gamal Abd El-Hamid.

About fifteen minutes before the sweep, Gamal says, he ran into an army officer near the KFC. The officer was telling people to leave. "I know what's going to happen here," the officer told them. "You don't want to see it." Gamal freaked and split.

"I stayed all night," Torek tells us. "This defector I saw shot was in a tent. We told him to take off his uniform and put on normal clothes. He said, 'I'm not leaving. They can kill me first.' After the army came, an officer approached him and told him to get on the ground. He refused. The officer shot him in the heart on the spot. I was beside the tent, hiding. I was afraid, crying. I was shitting in my pants. The officer ignored me. He came in for a specific purpose—to get defectors."

"What the defector did was suicide," Rashad says.

"Definitely," Torek says. "He showed the bravery of Egyptian men."

"Let's forget the emotional bullshit," Rashad says.

6 P.M. | From his hospital bed Naher Asser al-Sonousi listens to a television news anchor describe the army's sweep of Tahrir Square. He says the army has promised to investigate allegations of civilian casualties. Naher shakes his head. The army will admit nothing. It should be protecting people. Why can't it just leave them alone?

He thinks of Gadhafi and of the people he has killed. He must be punished—if for nothing else, for taking Naher's father from him.

In 1993 his father, an army major, participated in a failed coup against the dictator. He was arrested and served ten years in jail, three of them in solitary confinement. Naher was ten years old at the time of his father's arrest. He was with his father when he was detained, two months after the coup attempt. They were leaving their house when an army general and six soldiers stopped Naher's father at the edge of their driveway. "Come with us," the general told him without offering an explanation.

"You are the son of a hero," neighbors whispered to Naher.

During his father's imprisonment Naher and his mother moved in with a cousin. Naher worked on a farm and fell behind in school. Keeping up with his classes was difficult when he was harvesting corn and feeding cows instead of studying. Years had passed since his father was imprisoned, and Naher did not know where his father was or if he was alive. Naher was unable to get the necessary security clearance to apply for jobs. He was denied entry into any university.

Naher won't say how he reacted when his father was released in 2000, and he saw him again for the first time in seven years, walking down the dirt road toward the house. "His hair was black when he went in, white when he came out," Naher says. He wore the same tan pants he had on when he was arrested.

As he's pushed to say more, Naher's eyes dampen. He smiles sadly and asks that the conversation focus on happier times. His father sacrificed for Libya, as the people in Tahrir Square are doing for Egypt. It doesn't matter what nationality people are if they love their country. They are doing as much as they can.

Leave them alone.

9 P.M. | Rashad and I stop in a tea shop in downtown Cairo for some dinner. Men sit in shadows on wobbly wooden chairs and sip tea from steaming glasses, pausing long enough to smoke tobacco from waist-high *shisha* pipes. Across the street a woman hangs laundry from her apartment balcony above a camera and cell phone shop. Boys run past us, their sandals flapping against the pavement. Rashad gives his shoes to a shoeshine man, who slides a piece of green cardboard beneath Rashad's feet so he does not dirty his socks against the pavement. I hear the snap of a whip against a horse drawing a wagon.

On television General Ismail Othman, the public relations director for the Supreme Council of the Armed Forces, insists that the Egyptian army did not discharge "a single live round" in the square. Soldiers fired only blanks to disperse the crowd. Forty-two people were arrested. There were no deserters. Othman said the military had detained several uniformed men "posing as soldiers to create unrest."

"There were no deserters," he says again.

"I was there on The Friday of Anger. January 28, man. Three days after the protests started. That's when the motherfucking police did their first crackdown on us. No, that was not the day the guys rode in on camels. That was later," Rashad says. "The camel riders may have been people pissed off that the revolution was hurting tourism. I'm happy they're fucked. The tourist industry distorts the image of the country. They rip off tourists. There's no set price. One guy charges someone $50 to see some motherfucking pyramids. They come back to their hotel and tell another guest, and the guest goes, 'What? I was only charged $10!' They got ripped off. Screws the whole trip.

"No, what I'm talking about was on the twenty-eighth. I was stuck in a friend's apartment near the Ministry of Interior. I'm talking random shooting, man. Tear gas blew into the apartment. I had the pleasure of smelling it for hours. It was fucked up, man. The shit sticks to your clothes. It's a smell like exhaust and chili mixed together. Burns your nose and eyes. You put water and lemon in your eyes. Stings like shit, but it's better than tear gas. All night long tear gas canisters going off. Fucking noisy. Kids came in and went into this one building and then jumped from building to building along the rooftops. They'd throw Molotov cocktails at armored vehicles. The soldiers shot all over the place. They'd run into one building, and the kids would jump rooftops to another building. I heard the sound of bottles shattering on cars. One soldier got hit right in the back of his fucking head. He was on fire, man. Soldiers jumped on him to put it out.

"They caught one kid and beat the shit out of him. His screams, man, echoed until I covered my ears. Three a.m. Just beat the motherfucking shit out of him. Then threw him in a car. I don't know where they took him. I'm pretty sure this kid is fucking dead by now."

SUNDAY–MONDAY, APRIL 10 AND 11 | Magada resumes her spot near the KFC and holds her sign. Protesters mill around the square but not nearly as many as on Friday. They try to rally one another with slogans, but the repetition of the chants soon flattens and fades.

"I will not leave until a judgment is passed on Mubarak," says a man with his face painted the colors of the Egyptian flag.

Magada ignores him. Her son's case has just become more complicated. The district attorney will have bigger problems to consider now. "I will be neglected further," she says.

10 P.M. | Lawyer Ahmad Alli sits at the Lawyers Club in the Cairo neighborhood of Giza and contemplates the Nile as it flows below him.

He knows that the sweep of Tahrir Square will double his caseload. He already represents dozens of clients detained since the military council took power after Mubarak stepped down. Now this latest roundup of protesters. His cell phone has not stopped ringing. He recognizes the number of one repeat caller: Magada. She leaves messages telling him not to be distracted by the crackdown. "Don't forget about my son."

He does not know what to do with her. She thinks sleeping outside and holding signs will make the district attorney sympathetic. "Egypt," Alli says, "does not work that way." She has to let him knock on doors, get an official to reconsider the case. Instead she listens to her friends, who tell her, "Lawyer So-and-So can get your son out." So she drops Alli, wastes months and money with a new attorney who does nothing, and then finally returns to Alli and asks his forgiveness.

Alli believes the police fabricated a case against her son, Abdel-Hamid, to solve a crime. Very common tactic in Egypt. He was arrested in November. End-of-the-year evaluations are administered in December. The evaluation comes with a bonus, providing an incentive to solve cases. The evaluation does not ask whether a suspect was found guilty and sentenced, only whether the case was solved, whether someone was accused and jailed. The police have so many unsolved cases. They round up parolees or just anyone. Young men on the street call this time "police wrapping-up season."

Alli has lived in the same neighborhood as Magada all his life. He has sources and connections in police stations and their investigation units. He knows everyone. Someone would have told him if Magada's son was a drug dealer. To get him out of jail, Magada must let Alli do his job. And now he will have little time to do even that much.

Tuesday, April 12, 5:30 p.m. | Rashad receives a call from Torek. Gangs of Mubarak supporters are swarming the square, picking fights with protesters. The fear is the army will use this as an excuse to clear the square for the final time.

Whether that is the motivation or not, it happens. By the time Rashad and I reach the square, military armored vehicles have commandeered roads leading into the square. Lines of soldiers corral protesters on the sidewalk, where fights break out between protesters and supporters of the army.

A garbage truck moves at a grindingly slow pace, allowing soldiers to throw banners, sleeping bags, tents, and vendor stalls into the back. Tow trucks haul away the charred remains of the burned buses. Behind the truck, cabs and buses progress slowly, as traffic begins moving through the square again. Protesters pace the sidewalk, many of them weeping.

"What is happening now is another form of abuse," one of them shouts.

"The army better punish Mubarak soon," another man yells. "The people will not take this harassment."

But the soldiers don't listen. Instead they hurry past us, hustling handcuffed protesters down the street. Rashad takes my arm and steers me in another direction. "Keep moving," he says. "They are arresting people randomly. You can never speculate, man, about what the military will do. It can show up out of nowhere in huge numbers like motherfucking X-Men."

FRIDAY, APRIL 15, 10 A.M. | On my last day in Cairo I stop by Cairo Specialized Hospital to say good-bye to Naher Asser al-Sonousi. He feels himself improving every day and is eager to return to the front, he says. He misses the sounds of guns, the sounds of celebration.

I return for a final visit to Tahrir Square. The military has eliminated all evidence that demonstrations took place here only days before. Every scrap of trash, every loose banner and leaflet, has been cleared. I can still make out the faded swirls of scrubbed revolutionary slogans on some buildings. Fresh sod covers areas where protesters once camped. Amid all the beeping and maneuvering, cars and buses flow in fits and starts around the traffic circle. Police chase away loiterers.

Mubarak and his sons were placed in custody the day after the military cleared the square. As a consequence some protesters, like Rashad's friend Torek, have decided the governing military council is finally responding to their demands.

"We have other things to do now than tie up the square and piss people off," Torek says. "We need to arrange rallies in support of the Libyan rebels."

I tell Rashad I don't share Torek's optimism. After all, Mubarak may be out, but the military still rules.

"Yes, the military still rules," Rashad agrees, "but now they have listened to the people. Maybe they are trying to calm us, and we will have to demonstrate again. Maybe they will be fine. Maybe the military will flip out. You never know."

As we leave the square, I notice Magada alone near the KFC. A tourist pauses, asks about her sign.

"This is a picture of my grandson," Magada says.

"Stay still," the tourist says, raising a camera.

"His father was falsely accused of dealing drugs and is now in jail."

"Stay still."

Magada hesitates, sighs. Her mouth settles into a determined line. Without another word she looks directly into the camera and waits.

12

War Wounds

Kabul, Afghanistan: July–August 2012

We stand by the bed of Mohamad Doad. Aziz translates.

Doad says he hates American soldiers.

He was shot by the Taliban and is a patient in the paraplegic ward of Kabul's Orthopedic Center. Across the hall is an examination and exercise room for amputees with new prosthetic limbs. Most of these patients lost a hand or leg to land mines and rocket-propelled grenades, some as long ago as the 1980 Russian invasion.

Why does he hate the United States? I ask. He's a police officer. The United States trained him. He says he saw three families killed by coalition forces. If he gets better, he says he will kill American forces himself.

"But he's willing to speak with me?"

"So he can remember your face and kill you when he is well."

I wedge my pen between the pages of my notepad and consider Doad. I arrived in early July. I had hoped to come earlier, but my Afghan colleague Aziz Ahmad had warned me in an e-mail that I would not be safe. In January, just six months before my arrival, a video surfaced showing U.S. Marines urinating on the bodies of Taliban fighters. A month later U.S. troops burned dozens of copies of the Koran, sparking days of deadly riots across the country and attacks on American troops. Then, in March, a U.S. soldier was charged with killing sixteen civilians and wounding five after entering their homes in Kandahar Province. U.S. officials apologized, but they failed to control protests and attacks that killed at least thirty people, including six U.S. troops. And in the weeks before I arrived, the Pentagon reported increasing numbers of American-trained Afghan police recruits turning their guns on U.S. soldiers.

"This is not a good time for you to visit," Aziz said when he picked me up at Kabul International Airport. "Everyone is very angry with America."

Twenty-three-year-old Doad looks no more than fourteen. His brown unblemished face seems almost waxen beneath the pale glow of the ceiling lights hanging above us from loose wires. His wide blue eyes consider me with more curiosity than hate. Plastic leg braces with Velcro straps straighten legs so thin I wonder if he had polio, a disease still prevalent in Afghanistan. Soiled Mickey Mouse socks donated by some humanitarian group and much too big for his feet droop over his toes.

Most patients in the paraplegic ward are paralyzed from the waist down. A few, like Doad, can walk short distances but only with the aid of leg braces and heavy iron walkers they call walking frames. Doad's cousin stands beside Doad's walking frame and offers him some juice. The center does not have the staff to feed patients, help them use the toilet, and bathe and dress themselves. A friend or relative must fill in; otherwise the patient will be discharged.

The Taliban ambushed Doad's car outside Kandahar in May. He had been destroying poppies, from which opium and heroin are made. Profits from drug trafficking help fuel the Taliban insurgency. Doad was shot in the back and the bullet exited the left side of his chest. He collapsed against his car, unable to move. Another police officer found him ten minutes later and drove him to the U.S. military base in Kandahar, from where he was helicoptered to Kabul Army Hospital. He stayed there five days. On the sixth day he was transferred to the Orthopedic Center.

"Remind him Americans saved his life," I tell Aziz. "What does he think of that?"

"He says it is not about his life but about Western armies' being in his country," Aziz says.

"Why did he become a police officer?"

"Because he needed a job. He liked it, but then he was shot."

As a police officer Doad earned about $66 every other month, Aziz says. Doad's commander has not called or visited him. I nod, take notes.

The patients around us stare at both Aziz and me as Aziz translates. They lie on brown plastic mats too large for the metal bed frames supporting them and shift one way and then the other, irritated by the July heat and the unrelenting cyclone of flies above their heads. I listen to the sound their skin makes peeling off the plastic, and I smell the raw funk of their bodies when they roll over and their sheets fall away. Large bedsores have eaten through the flesh of several men so that gaping holes the color of spoiled avocados consume their thighs and buttocks. They look as if they have been mauled.

"Oh, Jesus," I say and cover my nose and mouth.

Doad sneers.

"Fuck America," he says.

I tell Aziz I feel sick. He takes me by the elbow and hurries me into the amputee ward, where open doors let in a warm breeze. My head clears, and the tightness in my throat subsides. Framed sketches of prosthetic legs and hands and arms hang on the bright white walls. Patients sit on benches waiting to be seen. Some have removed their prosthetic legs, and the legs stand against the wall, lined up one after the other, worn sandals and shoes fitted onto the stiff plastic feet.

We listen to a therapist working with a boy. The boy's *salwar kameez*—a long tunic over pants—hangs loosely where his left leg had been. Kneeling, the therapist examines his stump, rubbing his thumb over the scars. He wears a white lab coat. He has bright blue eyes and a substantial gray beard. Deep lines divide his sunken face.

"What's the problem?" the therapist asks the boy.

"I can't bend it well at the knee," the boy says. He hands the therapist his prosthetic leg.

"What is your name and how old are you?"

"Zabiullah. Twelve."

The therapist writes this on a clipboard.

"How did this happen?"

"U.S. shelling, Colonel."

The patients call the therapist "Colonel" because he had been a colonel in the Afghan army during the time of President Mohammad Najibullah, who ruled Afghanistan from 1987 to 1992, when the mujahideen, or rebel fighters, ousted him from power. The colonel lost his right leg in 1991 after the mujahideen fired a rocket into his armored vehicle near the city of Ghazni. The explosion knocked him out. When he came to, he crawled out of his vehicle to a burning truck. Wind kept the flames from him as he hid. He inspected his body. His right leg appeared shredded into strips. He could not feel it. He tied it off with strips of his uniform to stop the bleeding. Then he passed out.

"I think the prosthetic needs some adjustments, that is all," the colonel says.

"Generally, I don't have a problem," Zabiullah says. "Sometimes my stump itches and I have pain."

"How were you injured?"

"Last year, in Wardak Province, I was in the mountains with our donkey collecting firewood. Two kilometers away was a coalition base. Coalition forces fired a mortar, and shrapnel hit my left foot. I was just thrown like somebody had picked me up. My cousin put me on the donkey and took me to the hospital."

The colonel makes a face and shakes his head, removes the prosthetic leg from the boy, and loosens a screw. Every day patients like Zabiullah remind the colonel of his own injury. When he woke up beside the burning truck, he did not know what had happened, where he was. Charred trucks and jeeps from his convoy blocked the road, and then he remembered. Shadows pooled around him and then began to shrink with the sun as noon approached. The colonel saw a car approaching and waved, but the driver did not stop. Two men on bicycles pedaled up to him. "If we pick you up, the opposition will kill us," one of the men told him, and they left. A small boy brought the colonel water in a dish. The dish had a hole in it, and the water drained out before the colonel could drink it, and he licked the damp plate dry. He did not know where the boy had come from. He heard two men cry for help. He did not recognize their voices but assumed they were injured soldiers. "Please, please help us." Their voices weakened. Then they stopped calling.

A truck driver saw him, and the colonel pleaded with him to pick him up, but the driver worried that should the mujahideen search his truck and find the colonel, they would kill him. "No problem, just tell them to kill me," the colonel said. The truck driver carried him into his truck and told him to sit up. He covered the colonel with a blanket so the mujahideen would think he was traveling with a woman.

"How is that?"

"It fits better," Zabiullah says.

"The U.S. soldier is blind," the boy's father says. "They see boys, why would they shell? Every day fifteen to twenty people die in Wardak. Just yesterday there was a lot of fighting. Three people were hurt and one man died. They were all civilian people. When the Russians were here, there was just fighting between the Russian soldiers, the mujahideen, and the government. Now there is fighting between the coalition soldiers and the government and the Taliban and civilians."

The colonel says nothing to this. He gives the boy ointment for red sores on his stump. The colonel remembers how the truck driver left him at a military checkpoint. Soldiers crowded around him, and he felt safe, and as soon as this safe feeling came over him, he felt a searing pain in his leg. He was rushed to a hospital. He asked a doctor if he had been shot in his right leg but does not remember the doctor's answer. First his foot was amputated, but then he developed an infection, and then his leg was amputated. There were not enough antibiotics. Amputation was common. Every day while the colonel was hospitalized, three or four patients had an arm or a leg amputated. The colonel was glad to be alive and did not miss his leg until he was discharged. He thought, "How can I go on?" A doctor told him he would use a prosthetic leg.

"Walk."

Zabiullah walks outside, testing his prosthetic leg. He turns around and walks back.

"Good?" the colonel asks.

Zabiullah nods.

"Are you happy?"

"If he is happy or angry, it doesn't matter," Zabiullah's father says. "He has no power."

The Orthopedic Center closes at two o'clock. The colonel walks us to the front gate, and Aziz and I cross the street to Aziz's car. My throat is raw and dry from the dusty air. An unnerving summer heat rushes out of the car when Aziz opens the doors. We wait for it to cool and then get in. I lean back against the headrest as Aziz starts the car and drives to my hotel.

Military checkpoints block even the smallest of streets. Camera-equipped blimps hover in the air, recording everything below to discourage terrorists. I notice a group of young men wearing T-shirts that read in English, "Christianity Is Not a Religion." Aziz tells me how Kabul has changed since I was here last summer. I close my eyes, hear the rush of air through the open windows, Aziz's disjointed voice shouting above the noise as he drives and talks.

"Security has been very tight since the burning of our holy book. Everyone knows America is leaving. You will see no Westerner sitting alone with his Afghan driver like we are now. No, Westerners now drive in convoys with security guards. Kidnapping is a problem. You should not wander off on your own. If you must go out, go a different way each time," Aziz warns me. "Kidnappers now take the Westerner and his Afghan translator. They release the translator to convey their demands. Even within families, people kidnap one another. One man's brother was very rich. This man kidnapped his brother and left a ransom note."

Aziz parks outside the Park Hotel. It's near downtown, about fifteen miles from the center. Concrete blast walls and a solid iron gate conceal the hotel. Aziz continues talking as guards with AK-47s escort us inside. A walk leads into an expansive courtyard. Peacocks strut on the green lawn. Two stone fountains bubble with water. White picnic tables reflect the sun, and a man waters the grass and potted geraniums along the walk. A British man jogs on the walk, counting each lap aloud.

"I don't know what will happen when the U.S. leaves Afghanistan. If corruption gets under control, then things will work out. But I don't have much hope for this. After the U.S. leaves, there will be fighting in all the neighborhoods because people will be looting. I will buy a gun to protect my house," Aziz continues. "No, not a Kalashnikov, only a pistol. I know a man whose son has a job with the U.S. Embassy. His supervisor said if things go to shit in 2014 when the Americans leave, he will make sure my friend's son and his family leave, too. Afghans known to work with the Americans will be a target."

In four corners above the hotel courtyard, guards in blue uniforms sit behind sandbag bunkers, cradling their AK-47s. Barbed wire stretches unevenly between each bunker. "Five!" the jogger shouts.

"The U.S. Embassy has already issued my friend's son a visa and green card," Aziz informs me.

At night I look out my room at the courtyard and the dark shapes of the peacocks and the security guards above them pacing along the roof. I feed a stray gray cat crying outside my door. I think of checking in with Aziz but decide not to. I suspect that each day after he drops me off, he drains his car's gas tank. It's always about half full when we return from a day's work to the hotel, but the needle is always on empty the following morning. Every morning he asks for money to fill the tank. Every morning I give him $10 and tell him he needs to inspect the car for a gas leak. Every morning he agrees to do so. I have worked with Aziz long enough to believe he would not want anything to happen to me. He would never turn me over to kidnappers. But he'll take more than his share of gas money from me.

At night a police officer telephones Aziz and asks if he has received an anonymous flyer distributed by Taliban sympathizers. It warns that anyone working with Americans will be killed. Aziz has not received the flier. When he gets off the phone, he tells his sons to stay inside. He locks the front door and all the windows.

At night the colonel remembers the day a rocket exploded in the middle of Kabul. He was eating bread and sipping tea in a park. He had just stood up to stretch in the sun, and the explosion threw him to the ground. People screamed and ran, and he remembers the blood and the shattered bodies. The severed head of a man rolling beside the headless body of a woman. Within hours fire trucks had hosed the streets of blood, and those vendors not killed returned to their stalls. All these years later the colonel sees patients injured on that day. He tells them he was in the park in 1995 too, when they lost their legs and arms. They talk and reminisce. In those days, the colonel says, the front line was in a specific place. Today with suicide bombers, the front line is everywhere, his patients say.

At night in bed Zabiullah feels where his left leg should be.

At night in the Orthopedic Center's dormitory, Doad reads from the Koran. Another patient listens to a radio. One man stares at the ceiling and hardly blinks. The twenty-two other paraplegic patients sleep. Dim lights cast broken shadows on the brown walls. A dripping faucet splashes the black floor, and water rolls across it in oily lines.

A thirteen-year-old boy, Wasim, sits beside his father and listens to the drip. Wasim wears a purple salwar kameez he has not changed in days. He slumps in his chair, listens to his father, Abdul Sabur, snore. Sabur is a large man with a mop of black hair. His body fills the bed. It sags under his weight.

Sabur fought for the mujahideen against Najibullah. In 1991 he was shot in the back near Pulicharki. He spent a year in a hospital. He has been in and out of the Orthopedic Center for years because of infected bedsores. He was admitted again in June. He feels nothing below the middle of his chest. Sometimes his legs shake and bounce like flopping fish, and Sabur watches his legs as if they are not part of his body but exist separately. Wasim holds his father's legs down until the spasms pass.

When his father wakes up, Wasim will help him eat, help him to the bathroom, help clean his bedsores using iodine diluted with water. Sometimes the physical therapists send Wasim on errands and ask him to tend to other patients. Wasim rolls his eyes at all their requests, as if he already carries too many burdens. Then he runs off, sandals snapping against the floor, happy to complete the task. Wasim doesn't like to just sit.

Wasim and his father and mother live with his uncle, Mohammad Nasim. Nasim works as a money changer. Some days Nasim earns $60, and on those nights they eat lamb and rice and beans. Other days Nasim earns half that much, and then he and his wife and three boys, and Wasim and his mother, eat only garlic and tomatoes and spinach. Wasim's father discourages his brother from visiting him in the hospital because bus fare costs a dollar.

"Save the money to feed the children," Sabur tells Nasim.

"Don't worry about me, Father," Wasim says.

"Look at me," Sabur says. "The jihad is over. What good came of it?"

"When America leaves, Afghanistan will enter another jihad and be destroyed," Nasim says. "All the people know this."

Sabur agrees. Wasim frowns, frightened by the serious silence settling between his father and uncle. He hurries away, looks for a fun task to occupy him, the noise of his loose sandals against the floor signaling his retreat.

In the morning I feed the cat. It rubs against my legs. I open my door. It looks outside, sniffs at the air, and then crawls beneath my bed. I let it stay.

Aziz waits for me in his car on the ruined road outside the hotel. The road is less a road than a wide rutted path with broken chunks of asphalt. The money for roads, Aziz tells me, is given to one contractor, who keeps a percentage for himself and then hires another contractor to do the work. This second contractor also keeps a percentage of the contract for himself. He then hires another contractor. What little money reaches the final contractor allows for only a negligible amount of roadway repair.

"There is no plan," Aziz says. Instead of surveying the road and then paving it, they pave the road and then survey it. The surveyor says, "Oh, it is bad. We need two million dollars to repair it." And then they tear up the road again. It is a kind of a game going on here. After ten years the United States doesn't understand this and keeps giving the government money for roads.

He starts the engine.

"I will need gas money."

Doad sits on the edge of his bed, gripping his walking frame. His cousin attaches the leg braces. He wraps a Velcro strap around a urine bag so it does not bounce when Doad walks. Doad sees Aziz and they embrace.

"Salaam," Aziz says.

"Salaam," Doad says.

He tells Aziz to press his hand against his foot. "Press hard. Harder." Aziz squeezes his foot, but Doad shakes his head.

"I feel nothing," he scolds Aziz. "Only when my foot is squeezed hard do I feel it."

Doad grips the walking frame and pushes himself off the edge of his bed to a standing position. He moves forward a few inches, rests the walking frame on the floor, arches his back, and swings his right leg forward. Then he brings his left foot forward. His cousin steps beside him.

"Try to walk," his cousin says.

"I am trying."

"Right and then left."

"I don't have power."

"Try."

Doad's arms shake.

"I'm dizzy," he says.

Zabel Ullah, a physical therapist, watches Doad. Ullah lost his left leg to a mine. Only a slight limp to his walk suggests that he wears a prosthetic leg. In 1996 he was weeding the garden of his father's house and planting pink geraniums. His father worked in the Ministry of Agriculture. Ullah stood up to stretch, stepped forward. When he put his left foot down, the ground exploded.

Ullah and the other physical therapists tell the paraplegic patients that their recovery may take a long time. But some patients grow impatient. They insist on traveling to India or Pakistan or some other place abroad for treatment. Then Ullah tells them the truth. "Look," he says, "this other doctor you want to see, he will tell you what I am going to tell you now. Don't waste your money. You won't walk again. You have your life. Praise God you have that much."

In the amputee ward the colonel examines a boy's prosthetic leg. The boy's name is Raholla. His clothes hang on his narrow frame, no better than that of a scarecrow. Baz-Mohammad, his stern-looking father, stands beside him.

The colonel: Walk back and forth. You're a little lopsided. Your leg is short. You're growing. You've outgrown your prosthetic. We will fit you with a new leg. How old are you?

Raholla: Fifteen.

In 2007 I was with my brother, taking six sheep to pasture. As the sheep grazed, my brother Juma found some metal. The metal was round, with two holes on either side. I told him not to touch it. It might be bad. He said, "It's just metal," and hit it with a stone. I tried to stop him with my hands but was too late. He was lifted into the air and pieces of him hit me. He died. I lost my right leg and the fingers of both hands. Four sheep died. The grass burned. The air and the ground shook. I lay on the ground, afraid my father would beat me because Juma played with a mine. I shook him, but he didn't move. I crawled on the ground, my leg stayed behind me. A bus driver saw the explosion. He stopped and took me to the army hospital in Kabul.

The colonel: Let's try this new prosthetic. Put this sock over your stump. Now fit your stump into the socket of the prosthetic. Stand up. Stand straight. Okay, sit. Take it off. It's a little high, a little long. Where do you live?

Baz-Mohammad: Hyat Khan Village in Logar Province. We came by bus.

I was in Kandahar. My uncle called and told me Raholla was injured from a mine. He didn't tell me Juma had died. When I saw Raholla, he was in a coma. He woke up two days later. He said, "It wasn't my fault. Please don't beat me, Father. Juma hit it." I was crying. If you saw your son bleeding and lying in a bed, would you not be crying? I think the mine was left from the Russian time. A Russian checkpoint was near our house. There may be other mines, I don't know. Sadly, one found Juma and killed him. I am afraid to even touch a stone now.

The colonel: Face me. How does your prosthetic feel? Are you balanced? Is your foot touching the ground flat, not bent at the knee? Keep your head up. Walk. How does that feel?

Raholla: Good.

Last night there was fighting between the Taliban and the coalition. There was bombing close to our village. I heard three explosions. I fell asleep and dreamed of the mine.

Aziz and I step outside, and Aziz lights a cigarette in the shade of a tree dusted with the diesel fumes of passing trucks. The sight of so many war-wounded men reminds him of the time he worked as a police statistician in Parwan Province, not far from Kabul, at the height of the war between Najibullah and the mujahideen.

One day Aziz's commander said the HQ had too many officers working behind desks. He ordered Aziz and fifteen other officers to meet him in an adjoining room. The commander then asked who would volunteer to fight on the front line. No one moved. After a long uncomfortable silence, two men said they were ready to fight if they had no choice. The commander sent them back to their desks. Aziz and the remaining twelve men were driven to a barracks and told they would be sent to the front the following day.

At two in the morning Aziz asked permission to leave the barracks. He told the guard a fellow police officer was asleep in his car. Aziz said he wanted to wake him so the officer would not miss the convoy to the front. Permission granted. Aziz left the barracks and caught a taxi to his parents' house in Kabul.

Five days later Aziz called the commander. "I can't fight," he said. "I can't shoot other Afghans. My job is in the office. Kill me now. I'll never go to the front." "No," the commander said, "we need you. You are Pashtun. I am Pashtun. All the other officers are Tajik and Hazarra. You are the only one I trust. Come back. You can stay in the office."

In this way, Aziz says, he survived the fighting.

Aziz stubs out his cigarette, and we get in the car and begin the drive back to the hotel. We have not gone far before we get stuck in traffic at a roundabout. Drivers honk their horns and jockey for what little space exists between the stalled cars. I crane my head out the window. A police officer storms back and forth in the roundabout, waving a Kalashnikov. Other police officers approach him, but he waves them away with his weapon. He screams, "America!" but the rest of what he says is drowned out by all the honking. He points the Kalashnikov at the stopped cars and sweeps left to right. Aziz and I drop down in our seats.

"America! America!"

I tell Aziz we should get out of the car and lie face down on the road, but Aziz thinks the car offers more protection.

"On the ground we'd be low and mobile," I say.

"Too many stray bullets may hit us," he says.

"We could roll under cars for protection," I say.

Aziz and I argue, sinking further in our seats, our eyes just level with the dashboard.

"America! America!"

The police officer lowers his Kalashnikov, gives one long angry look, and storms off. The other police watch him go. After a moment they start waving traffic through.

At night I feed the cat and think about Aziz and how, just hours before, he and I had a calm rational disagreement about how best not to get shot. Unable to sleep, I listen to BBC Radio. A new police recruit shot and killed two Americans in western Afghanistan. He had just been assigned a gun to begin training. Hours later in Kandahar Province, an Afghan army soldier fired on international troops, wounding two.

At night the colonel recalls a patient from Ghazni he no longer sees. They had become close friends. The man had lost both his legs in Helmand in 2011. He was a translator for the coalition and was worried about his job. He practiced walking on his prosthetic legs at the Orthopedic Center for twenty days. When it was no longer necessary for him to come to the center, the colonel would call him, but after a while the patient stopped answering his phone. Did he return to the coalition? Did he get killed in the fighting? Did he leave Afghanistan? The colonel wonders.

At night in the paraplegic ward Doad says: "I was shot by the Taliban. I can't feel my legs."

Wasim's father says: "I was shot by Najibullah's forces. For twenty-one years I just lie in my bed."

The next morning Doad asks Aziz if I fast.

"Yes," Aziz says. "As a Christian he fasts forty days every year in the spring."

"Does he pray?"

"Yes."

"How does he pray?"

"On his knees. And he prays only on Sunday."

"Jesus Christ is his prophet?"

"Yes."

"What does he call his God?"

"His God has no special name. Sometimes they call Jesus Savior."

"Jesus was sent by their God?"

"Yes."

"And he believes this?"

"Yes."

"At least he believes in God," Doad says.

In the amputee ward Mansoor Kohistani, a soldier in the Afghan National Army, stands by his friend Moor al Haq, another soldier. An ambulance from Kabul Army Hospital brought Haq to the center. He lost both his legs in May, when he stepped on a mine in Helmand Province. He lies on a gurney, the lower half of his body covered with a sheet. He wears the green tunic of his uniform. The colonel raises the sheet to inspect Haq's stumps.

"How is it in Helmand?" the colonel asks.

"Some places fighting, some places are quiet," Haq says. "There are mine explosions every two or three days. It is usually mules and civilians who are injured."

Kohistani stands off to one side. He joined the army in 2011 when he graduated high school. He trained for six months and was commissioned a first lieutenant. He has fought mostly in the mountains. Usually the Taliban fires rocket-propelled grenades directly into their base. In the eastern province of Nuristan, Kohistani saw two Afghan soldiers blown to pieces by an IED. Their families were given $1,000 each and enough food for three days of mourning.

"You have an infection," the colonel tells Haq. "Most of your right buttock is gone and has not healed. There is nothing we can do until the infection clears."

"Then I can stay here?"

"If we have room."

The colonel pushes Haq's gurney back to the ambulance. Kohistani follows, his face downcast. He can still see the rocket-propelled grenade that struck a Humvee and cut an Afghan driver in half. Then there was the Taliban boy, maybe fourteen years old. He was alone and shooting at them. Kohistani told him to surrender. He kept shooting, and Kohistani called up a sniper. Afterward he considered the boy, sprawled on his back behind a rock, so young and dead, and Kohistani knew he would remember him, too.

My last morning in Kabul I pack my duffel bag and feed the cat one final time. It doesn't want to leave my room, and I nudge it outside with my foot. It sits by my door as I walk down the stairs. Aziz meets me outside, and I tell him I feel a little guilty about leaving the cat. I probably should not have fed it and given it false expectations. Aziz waves a hand. He can't be bothered. He compares the cat to Afghanistan: It was surviving before I came. It will survive after I leave.

We stop by the Orthopedic Center on our way to the airport. The colonel speaks to a man on crutches. The man has had a prosthetic leg since 1998, when he stepped on a mine near the Iranian border. Last night he was cold and had no fuel. So he burned his prosthetic leg to warm his room.

In the paraplegic ward Doad lies on his bed and tells Aziz that an uncle died and his cousin left him late last night to be with the family. Because he has no one to help him, Doad has been discharged.

"What about my bedsores?" he asks.

"Clean them every day," the physical therapist Zabel Ullah tells him. "Don't sit on them. Use your walking frame."

"On the road, if I have problems, there will be no one to help me. The road is very long."

"Take the number 303 bus. It goes straight to Helmand."

"There'll be no one to feed me," Doad says.

"If you find someone to stay with you here, you can come back to the center."

Doad sits up and reaches for his walking frame. I can't imagine how useful it will be to him on the pitted, uneven roads.

"Will you visit me in Helmand as you have here?" Doad asks Aziz.

"Inshallah," Aziz says. God willing.

"You can bring your American journalist," Doad says. "I will invite him into my house. His face does not say, 'I will shoot you.' He doesn't carry a gun. He's an American but not a fighting man."

Aziz translates and I shake Doad's hand. The look in his eyes betrays his fear and sadness. All that he is, he is at this moment: a young man alone, paralyzed from the waist down, who hates the United States and has no future.

Aziz hugs Doad and then shouts for Wasim and tells him to help Doad with his leg braces. I follow Aziz outside, and we cross the street to his car, open the doors, and lean on the roof to let it cool. Aziz reaches into his pocket for a pack of cigarettes.

"Do you think he meant it?" I ask.

"Doad? About you?"

"Yes."

Aziz thinks for a moment, taps out a smoke, and shrugs.

"He meant it here."

13

Maybe the Children Will Forget

Antakya, Turkey: February 2013

Classmates Moutasem and Sarah watch their breath steam in the frigid February air. We are in the principal's office of Muhammad al-Fatih, a secondary school for teenage children of Syrian refugees in Antakya, Turkey. The school has no heat. Still, it is better to freeze here than to be in Syria right now, my Syrian translator, Hazim, tells me. In Syria the army patrols villages and cities, killing suspected activists. Men, women, children. No one is safe. If the army could arrest the air it would. Hazim is a Sunni Muslim, as are the students here, as are the rebel fighters in the Free Syrian Army, which has been battling the troops of President Bashar al-Assad since March 2011.

Syria's Alawite minority and Sunni majority have been at odds for hundreds of years. The minority Alawites, of which Assad is one, dominate Syria's government, hold key military positions, and enjoy a disproportionate share of the country's wealth, much to the bitterness of the majority Sunni.

Moutasem and Sarah and other children whom I will meet in the coming days have had their lives upended by a war made more complicated by centuries of ethnic rivalry. Moutasem is fifteen. He wears black shoes, pressed blue jeans, a red wool sweater. He slouches in his chair, has an easy relaxed way about him. His eyes stare intently. When he sees me shiver in the cold, he offers me his coat.

His father, Wahob, was a member of the Muslim Brotherhood and opposed the regime of Assad's father, Hafez al-Assad. The regime tried to kill Wahob in the 1980s, and he fled Syria with his family to Jordan.

When Moutasem was seven, he went to Syria with his mother and two brothers to renew their passports. A Syrian border guard arrested them. When they entered the jail, they were stripped of their clothes, given gray prison garb, and put in the same cell. On a table Moutasem saw electric cords, stakes, ropes, hooks. At night he heard screaming. After the screaming stopped, his mother warned him, "Don't say anything about Assad, or we won't get out." They were released without explanation after twenty-eight days and returned to Jordan.

When Moutasem's father heard about the revolt against Assad, he said the regime must fall. He moved his family to Antakya.

"The Alawites hate the Sunni," Moutasem says. "My father tells me the Alawites think Sunni are worse than Jews. They love to kill Sunni more than they do the Israelis. But, my father says, we will kill them now."

"You understand," he says to Hazim.

"Of course," Hazim says.

He watches Moutasem leave.

"Fuck this war," Hazim whispers under his breath so Sarah doesn't hear him.

I had met Hazim a few days earlier by chance. I was walking in downtown Antakya, trying to find a store where I could replace my broken cell phone. I had just returned to Turkey from a reporting assignment in Syria. No one I spoke to understood even the slightest English and I knew no Turkish. Then I saw a thin young man in a leather coat cleaning his glasses at a bus stop. On a whim I asked if he spoke English.

"Of course, why wouldn't I?" he said. He was Syrian, he explained, and had learned English in school. He spoke Arabic but was studying Turkish in the hope of finding a job. I told him I was a reporter and about to begin work on a story about the children of Syrian refugees. I not only needed a phone, I needed a translator too and offered him a job.

Hazim told me he had fled to Antakya in December 2012. He was a twenty-five-year-old medical student in Taybet al-Emam, a village near Hamma, Syria, when the revolution started. He did not participate in the demonstrations. He never felt oppressed by Assad. To him the government was like the mafia. If a Sunni man didn't get a job, he said, "Oh, it must have gone to an Alawite," and that was that. No big deal. And everyone knew not to discuss politics. Since he was a child, Hazim's family told him, "Don't talk politics."

He thought the rebels should not have resorted to arms. The regime was too strong. Assad had thousands of soldiers, tanks. No way will he fall. If they wanted change, the rebels should have stayed in school. Start with yourself, that's what Gandhi said. The only thing guns will do is start a civil war.

Hazim blames the rebellion for his arrest last year when the security forces held him because his name was the same as that of an FSA fighter. An officer forced Hazim to stand in a field under the sun for six hours. Then he beat him. He asked no questions. When he stopped hitting Hazim, the officer took him by the shirt and looked at the names on his cell phone but recognized none of them. He let go of Hazim's shirt. "It seems to me you did not do anything," the officer told him. "Go home."

When the Free Syrian Army descended upon Hazim's village, people pleaded with the FSA to leave. It was not a strategic place, they said, but the FSA didn't listen. It was not his wish to be there, an FSA commander said, but he had his orders. Soon the government began shelling the village. People fled to their basements and were buried alive by collapsed buildings. There was no place to hide, no place to go but Turkey.

Leaving Syria was the worst day of Hazim's life. He felt paralyzed. He had a girlfriend he wanted to marry. But he is the only son in a family of seven daughters, and his father refused to let him stay behind. Hazim had a responsibility to live, find a wife, and perpetuate the family name. His father would not leave him to die in the revolution.

The truck they shared with other refugees had no room for luggage or possessions of any kind. Hazim and his family brought only the clothes they wore and their cell phones. He thought the FSA would soon leave his village and he would be able to return. How could they match Assad's forces? But the FSA stayed and the shelling continues.

"The rebels say they are fighting for freedom," Hazim told me. "Freedom? Really? Our house is destroyed and people are being killed. We are refugees and I have no job. Fuck this freedom."

After Moutasem leaves, Sarah pulls her chair closer to Hazim and me. She has on jeans, a cream-colored sweater, and a white hijab. Her smile will break hearts one day.

Sarah is thirteen. She was born in the Syrian city of Homs. She enjoyed playing in public gardens with her friends. They drew lines in the dirt and jumped rope, skipping over the lines. They told each other secrets: about a boy who said he loved a girl and about another boy who always stared at a girl none of the other girls liked. A whisper in the ear meant it was a secret, although it was just normal talk between girls.

Politics didn't exist in her home. Her parents never spoke about it. They warned her not to get close to Alawite girls. Their parents may have a relative in the army or in the security forces. They might make trouble for us if you have a problem with her. Sarah had heard stories about Sunni people being arrested by the security forces. They cut off the ear of an old woman, they beat a man to death. Sarah stopped talking to Alawite girls.

Although her parents did not participate in the anti-Assad demonstrations, seven security officers barged into their house one morning at six o'clock to search it. They broke down the door and overturned furniture and swore at the family. After they left, Sarah's parents righted the furniture and told her not to speak to her friends about what had happened.

When the demonstrations turned violent, Sarah heard shooting outside her house almost every day. She couldn't eat because she saw people killed. One time a government sniper shot an old man. Another time a sniper shot at two boys walking down the street. He missed. The taller boy embraced the smaller boy and knelt on the ground and the sniper fired again. The boys died holding each other. The next day Sarah saw a woman shot in the shoulder. She lived.

When they left Homs, Sarah's family took a bus to Damascus to apply for passports and visas. A week later they took another bus to Antakya. They stayed with friends who helped them find an apartment. The apartment did not have a refrigerator or washing machine. Thieves broke in one afternoon and stole coal, blankets, and clothes. Now, a year and a half later, the family has some furniture. A sofa, table and chairs. They sleep on mattresses on the floor.

Sarah no longer thinks about her home in Homs. It was destroyed in the fighting. It's gone. It no longer matters.

The Almaz Yilmaz Market, in an Alawite neighborhood, stands a few blocks from the school. Hazim and I stop there for lunch after we speak with Sarah. The shopkeeper asks Hazim where I am from. Hazim explains I am an American reporter writing a story about the students at the school. The shopkeeper then asks Hazim his nationality. "Lebanese," Hazim lies. "My parents emigrated to the United States, where I now live."

The shopkeeper nods. "I thought you were Syrian," he said, "because you speak Arabic. Syrians make trouble in Turkey. They eat at restaurants and don't pay. They say they are in the care of the government, and the prime minister pays their bills. Hospitals give Syrians priority. If a Turk is sick, too bad. The hospitals have no room for them. Some Sunni say, 'We are fighting the Alawites in Syria, and when we defeat them, we will fight them in Turkey.' Everyone knows this. They are a big problem."

"I know how it is," Hazim says. "It's like the Mexicans. They are coming into the United States all the time."

When we finish our lunch, Hazim and I walk across town to al-Bashaer Elementary School. It serves Syrian refugee children aged six to twelve. The school resembles a series of square blocks piled one atop another and painted bright colors that have long since faded. A muddy road leads to a broken front gate. We let ourselves in and follow a cracked stairway to the principal's office. Hazim explains our purpose, and she tells us of a boy, Abd-alrahman, who lost his father in the war. We ask to meet him.

After a few minutes Abd-alrahman walks into the principal's office and sits in a chair. His feet barely touch the floor. His jeans puddle around his ankles, and his worn brown sweater sags about his chest. Abd-alrahman tells Hazim he is twelve years old. The principal gives him a look. He stares at the floor and admits he is ten. But, he hastily adds, he feels as old as twelve. He lives in Antakya with his mother, older brother, and three sisters. His father was an FSA soldier. He died a martyr.

Abd-alrahman grew up in Idlib, Syria. He played soccer with friends and liked to hang around shops in the bazaar. On holidays he studied the Koran. His father was an imam, a prayer leader. He had a wonderful voice.

In school, Abd-alrahman knew boys with no fathers. He asked them, "Where is your father?" "He was in the Muslim Brotherhood and killed by Assad," they told him. What is this brotherhood? Who is Assad? From these conversations, he learned to hate Assad. He wrote Assad's name on paper and put it inside his shoe so he would step on him throughout the day. He took the paper out only when he entered a mosque so he would not insult God.

One afternoon Abd-alrahman jumped on the back of a pickup driven by security forces. He wanted to show he was not afraid of Assad. He wanted to be a martyr. The pickup moved very fast. "In the name of God!" he yelled and jumped off. He brushed the dust from his clothes. Only a few scratches on his hands. He survived. He would lead his family into paradise another day. His mother nearly fainted when he told her what he had done.

Abd-alrahman learned about the revolution on the same day his father had promised to give him a bicycle. He pestered his father for it throughout the day until his father snapped, "Go away!"

"But you promised!"

"Don't bother me! A man was killed today by the security forces for demonstrating."

As the revolution grew increasingly violent, Abd-alrahman saw lots of men carrying guns and shooting them. He collected shell casings to sell for scrap. He would give the money to the FSA. At one demonstration he opened his arms and screamed, "Kill me! God is great!" He heard bullets whistle past him. He did not run and he did not die.

A concrete wall encloses a courtyard used by the elementary school as a playground for the children. Trash fills cracks in the ruined walls and open sewers. Water gathers in pools beneath limp vines clinging to the walls.

Samer Mohammad apologizes for the condition of the playground. "We are so poor this is the best we can do," he says. "We have nothing but a dirt road to the school and garbage for the children to play in." He moves in rushed little jerks and jolts like someone in a maze unsure where to turn next. His face drains into his narrow chin, his eyes bloodshot from too little sleep.

Mohammad was a merchant in Damascus when the revolution started. He saw government planes bombing villages outside the city. Tanks rumbled through downtown and he felt the ground quake. The tanks fired and buildings fell. He heard gunfire but never knew what direction it was coming from.

Every day he hurried his wife and children out of their apartment when it felt too dangerous to stay inside, but he had no idea where to take them next. No place in Damascus seemed safe. When his six-year-old daughter began to vomit daily, he carried her to a hospital. She was not sick, the doctor told him, just terrified. Fear controlled him, and he fled with his family to Antakya.

Sometimes when he walks among the students, Mohammad weeps. They have been through so much. They play war games. Two boys take on the role of the government-backed militias. The other boys try to capture them. "Stop killing, stop killing," they shout.

The students often talk about Assad, repeating the words of their parents. "He kills people," they say. "The Alawites hate us." They tell each other, "My house was destroyed and I saw a man killed by a bullet." Another will respond, "My brother was killed in the shelling. We couldn't save him."

Now the children see their parents distracted by the struggle to find work and food. They learn their parents can no longer help them.

Adults understand it's a war. Children, however, understand only that they feel sad. Their souls remain attached to their country, their homes. "Their bodies are in Turkey but without their souls," Mohammad says.

In the afternoon a bus carries Sarah and the other girls home from school. Her family lives in an Alawite neighborhood. They are the only Sunni family in the area. They appreciate the generosity of their Alawite neighbors for permitting them to rent an apartment. However, they seldom go out.

When they do, passersby see them and ask, "How are you, Sunni Syrians? Good morning, Sunni Syrians. Have a nice day, Sunni Syrians." The greetings make Sarah feel weird, especially because the people acknowledging them are Alawite. Are they making fun of us? she wonders. Mocking us? Making jokes about us?

Her father found a job as a driver for a doctor who lives in Reyhandli, a Turkish town almost on the border with Syria. One afternoon, driving home, he got into an accident and broke his right leg and some ribs. The police and an ambulance soon arrived. He was lifted out of the truck and laid on the ground and left there. He called some Sunni friends on his cell phone to take him to the hospital.

At home Moutasem's family teases him for eating too fast. He smiles, shovels food into his mouth. In jail he and his mother and two brothers were given one plate of rice and bread for the day. The guard would open the door and throw the plate in. The food scattered on the floor, but Moutasem ate it anyway. He was very hungry.

Hazim, his parents, and seven sisters share an apartment with another Syrian family not far from where Sarah lives. Eighteen adults, including three of Hazim's married sisters and their husbands, and many children squeezed together. The two families sleep in one large room. Hazim has a small room to himself because he is not married. Some nights he walks outside and screams, "I don't want to be here!"

His father hopes to return to Syria soon. A science teacher, he does not look for work in Antakya. Instead he just waits for the war to end. In the morning he buys bread for the family but does little else the rest of the day. A woman in their building told him it was the destiny of Syrian refugees to be like the Palestinians and live without a country of their own.

Hazim does not want to be like the Palestinians. When he feels desperate, he calls his girlfriend. He cannot describe her beauty. Everything around her, the trees, the river, the singing of birds, even the sunlight, enhances her good looks. Syrians appreciate love. If two guys saw them sitting together, they would leave them alone without a word. Hazim and his girlfriend held hands when they could but not often. Some of her friends were conservative. People might talk, assume they were having sex. It would be bad news for her and her family if a rumor like that started. Instead they would touch each other's hands and then withdraw their fingers quickly. If no one was around, Hazim's girlfriend would remove her headscarf and reveal her long black hair. "Don't cut your hair," Hazim always tells her.

Hazim tries to speak with his girlfriend on the phone, but the coverage is poor, and they are often cut off. So they wait. They agree they can't wait forever. They have to make a decision about their lives and whether they have a future together.

"I miss you," she tells him.

"I wish I could see you," Hazim says, "but I can't."

Abd-alrahman's mother, Taj al-deen Barhoom, feels as trapped as Hazim does. At night she struggles against the cold. She can't afford fuel to heat the apartment. When her children complain of the cold, they gather in one room and huddle to warm themselves. If her husband were here, he'd move them to another building where the heat was not so expensive. If he were here, she would say to Abd-alrahman when he misbehaved, "I'll tell your father." Now, when she says, "Don't go to the park, you're a Syrian in a foreign country surrounded by Alawites," he doesn't listen.

Barhoom and her husband, Walad Said Eissa, had raised their family in Idlib before the war. They hated the Assad regime long before the revolution. Her uncle and a brother were executed by Hafez al-Assad in 1982. Her husband tore photographs of Assad from his children's textbooks and spit on them.

Eissa used to teach the Koran. The security forces wanted to know how many students he had, what kind of work they did, and what they spoke about. Eissa told them, "I won't be a spy for you. I just want to teach the Koran."

He was arrested and held for three to four hours. His hatred for Assad grew deeper and deeper. His children knew this but he told them, "Don't tell any of your friends we hate him."

When the revolution started, Barhoom and Eissa joined in the demonstrations. She was so enthusiastic, she marched while pregnant with their youngest daughter. "If anything happens to us," she told her husband, "it is God's wish." Her faith did not prevent her from worrying, however. Eissa told her death would be more merciful than arrest. She kept an eye on her children, especially the boys. When Abd-alrahman jumped onto the pickup, she thought he had lost his mind. She told him to stay away from the demonstrations, but he was stubborn. He would stand on the balcony of their house and shout, "I'll jump if you don't let me out. I hate Assad!"

When they heard the Syrian army was converging on Idlib, the family decided to leave town. They knew they would be arrested as activists. They stayed in Aleppo with Barhoom's sister-in-law. Then news came that the army had entered Idlib and destroyed their home. They fled to Turkey and stayed in a refugee camp, where she gave birth to her daughter. They remained in the camp for sixteen weeks before they moved to Antakya and moved in with members of her family who had left Syria months earlier.

"Live with your family so I can go back and fight with the FSA," Eissa told her. "I hope our triumph is fast so I can come back with a big car and we can all return to Syria."

They called one another every day. A week after he left, Eissa told Barhoom that he was about to go into a big battle and asked for her prayers. The next day the army surrounded his FSA platoon, but with God's help they survived. That night Eissa suggested to the other FSA fighters that they not sleep together as a group to avoid being wiped out if the regime started firing rockets. Each fighter picked a different olive tree to lie under. Eissa propped up on a bedroll and read the Koran by moonlight. At some point in the night the regime began shelling. Eissa was struck in the stomach. He died immediately, a rebel commander told Barhoom.

On this afternoon Hazim and I sit in on a political science class taught by twenty-two-year-old Nuboog Barakat at the secondary school.

Barakat: What are the reasons behind the revolution?
Students (shouting): To seek freedom and justice.
To spread Islam everywhere.
To stop torture, imprisonment.

Barakat looks little older than her students. But she can be stern, tells them to speak one at a time, no exceptions. Like an auctioneer, she points at their upraised hands. She started teaching at nineteen in Aleppo. She lived in a classy neighborhood of public parks and gardens and tall apartment buildings with courtyards and fountains. When the fighting started, many families fled. Abandoned, the neighborhood reminded Barakat of a flea market after the merchants had gone for the day and only empty vendor stalls and swirling scraps of trash remained.

At the secondary school she teaches seventh through tenth grade. History, science, math, English, political science. Sometimes one or two of her students will act depressed and won't participate in class. Then she is more mother and psychiatrist than teacher. The students tell her about their flight from Syria. They miss every piece of their home. They miss their own beds and even their pillows.

Barakat: What is going to happen in Syria?
Students (shouting): The revolution is going ahead to victory.
We have hope Assad falls soon.
We'll triumph. The order from God is coming to spread Islam.

Moutasem sits among Barakat's students. She will never forget his story. That his first memory of Syria was going to jail. What is Syria to him? That is not Syria. That is the regime. Once she asked her students to make drawings of how they felt. They chose dark colors, red and black. One boy told her, "I lost my father to the regime." What could she say? Your father is in paradise now, be happy? Be pleased he's no longer being tortured?

Barakat: What will happen when the revolution is victorious?
Students (shouting): The hands of Alawites and those with the regime will be red with blood.
We will find and punish supporters of Assad.
Everyone with the Syrian army must appear in an Islamic court.
No, we just want them to leave.
Our religion teaches us killers should be killed.

Sometimes Barakat and her students sing simple songs about Syria to ease their pain. But the memories remain. Perhaps what her students are experiencing is all part of the sacrifice for freedom. Barakat can accept this if in the end something worthy develops from the struggle. What is the price that should be paid for freedom? How much of it should be borne by children? What is the will of God?

During breaks between classes Sarah and her friends run through the halls. "Down with the regime!" they shout, "God bless the FSA!" Out of breath, they stop and tell one another stories. How they snuck into Turkey illegally. How the security forces broke into their homes and destroyed everything and arrested everyone they saw. They sit in a group. Girl after girl speaks. Then it's sixteen-year old Farah's turn.

Farah grew up in Latakia, Syria, a gorgeous city, she tells the girls. So lovely she cannot describe it. She remembers the balcony in her grandmother's apartment. From it she saw a vast area of neighborhoods, parks, and skyscrapers. She felt as if she were looking upon the entire world.

Her father became an activist when the revolution started. He often had to leave the house and hide from the security forces in a friend's home. The family stayed in touch through Skype. One time, when they thought he was still hiding, he came to the house. "I miss you," he said. "I'll stay with you tonight."

The next morning, March 23, 2012, two busloads of security forces, followed by three cars and three pickups, descended on the neighborhood. The soldiers spread out on the street and on rooftops. They aimed their guns at Farah's house. Her father ran from room to room looking for a place to hide. He dashed upstairs to a second floor as the security forces kicked in the front door. "There are only women here, what do you want?" her mother shouted at them.

Farah stayed upstairs with her father. Her heart beat so hard she had difficulty breathing. She helped hide him in a bedroom closet behind a rack of clothes. Her uncle argued with the soldiers outside the room in the hall. "It is just myself and women," he told them. "You are only here to steal from us." They ignored him and knocked on the bedroom door. "Let us in!"

Farah shouted, "Wait! I am putting on my hijab." She waited until the clothes around her father stopped moving and then she opened the door. Her uncle followed a soldier inside. The soldier searched the room with a gun. Farah tried to slow her breathing. But her heart beat so hard she thought she would choke. The soldier opened the closet door, closed it. "Nothing here, sir!" Farah let out a long breath as quietly as she could. The soldier smiled at her and left, but another soldier came in. He paused and stared at the closet. Farah's mouth went dry. The soldier reached inside the closet and threw clothes on the floor until he saw Farah's father and pulled him out by the hair.

"Let my father go!" Farah screamed. "Leave him, leave him!"

The soldier hit her in the face and she fell. Her uncle reached for her, and the soldier struck him with the butt of his rifle. Her father resisted, and the other soldiers crowded into the room and handcuffed him and began to beat him. Farah's mother screamed at her husband, "Let them arrest you! They are just beating you up, and blood has covered your face in front of your daughter! What is the point? They are killing you in front of the children! You cannot defend yourself!"

He was dragged outside shoeless. Farah's mother and Farah continued screaming, "Leave him, leave him! He has done nothing!" Neighbors gathered around and shouted, "Thank you for this martyr. God is great." The soldiers swore at the neighbors and pointed their guns at them. "We will shoot you if you don't stop!" the commander said. Farah's father struggled to his feet. His shirt had risen up and his back and neck were red. He looked around, and Farah thought his eyes seemed to be saying good-bye to everything he saw. He didn't speak. Then a soldier pushed down on his head and shoved him into the backseat of a car. Farah's ten-year old sister collapsed on the ground. "Father, Father, Father," she said. The entire family wept.

Farah has not seen her father since he was taken away. The family fled to Turkey to avoid further arrests. Today, when Farah hears children in the neighborhood call for their father, she cries because she cannot call her own. She has a three-year-old brother. He tells friends that the security forces tortured his father and took him to jail. But then his father escaped to fight with the FSA.

The boy, Farah tells the girls, has convinced himself of this story. Farah is happy for him. He's too young to understand. Let him have his story.

Teacher Amina Osman Kosa stands in the hall and listens to the girls tell their stories. God willing, her students will forget the horrible things they've seen. God willing, the regime won't continue and Syria will rebuild itself. Maybe that's how the children will forget.

She and her husband anticipated the revolution after watching on TV the demonstrations in Tunisia and Egypt. When the protests started in Latakia where they lived, her forty-nine-year-old husband and eighteen-year-old son joined them. Kosa stayed home and cried and prayed to God to keep them safe.

Her husband and son joined the FSA in August 2012. She moved to Antakya to avoid arrest. She tried to convince her son to leave the FSA and come with her, but he refused. "If the revolution is triumphant and I'm in Turkey, I will be seen as a coward," he told her. She felt a burning in her heart when she left Syria without her husband and son.

When Kosa arrived in Antakya, some landlords told her they didn't rent to Syrians. Then she found a Syrian woman married to a Turk, and he agreed to rent an apartment to her. At first she didn't go outside. She lost track of time, didn't know what day of the week it was. She looked out the window and prayed, "May God help me."

Her husband and son visit her separately every few weeks. They travel through mountain passes and sneak across the Turkish border. Their filthy clothes hang from their bodies and smell of the mules that carry them, and their beards reach down to their chests. They change into civilian clothes to avoid detection by Kosa's Alawite neighbors.

During his visits her husband tells her about the difficulties of living in the field. The FSA gets close to the enemy when it fights. The fighters from both sides hear one another shouting and swearing. After one battle her husband buried his cousin. He dug the grave with his hands.

Another time a Syrian soldier called out to the FSA that he wanted to defect. He began to cross over but stepped on a mine. His body was shorn in half. "Come help me," he called. "I've been hurt." He did not realize he was already dead. When her husband and other FSA soldiers reached him, they saw his legs had been blasted back to the government side. They buried the part of him that remained on the FSA side.

Days later her husband caught two Syrian soldiers. They were Sunni. "Why didn't you defect?" he asked them. It was too difficult, they told him. "Stop lying," he said. "You are not that far from us. You could have walked and reached us." He hit them again and again until they could no longer stand.

"Did you not want to kill them with a knife like sheep?" Kosa asked.

"No, I could not," her husband said.

Her son left the FSA after two of his friends were killed near him during a battle. Their blood covered his shirt. He kept the shirt. He didn't sleep for three days. He began volunteering at a hospital. At first he didn't like it. He was angry and complained that the work was too slow. Then the hospital began sending him to battlefields to pick up the wounded. The exposure to danger, the noise of gunfire and shelling, calmed him. He thanked God for this new opportunity.

In the elementary school Abd-alrahman stares out a classroom window at an olive tree. His geography teacher asks him, "What are you doing?" "I'm just looking at tree. It reminds me of my father." He shows her photos of his father on his cell phone. In one he wears a Yankees baseball cap. In another he carries a gun. In still another he lies dead on the ground, eyes closed, a thick gray beard around his face.

"OK," the teacher says. "Try to pay attention."

Abd-alrahman does not like her. She is too nervous. She shouts all the time. When he asks to leave class to pray, she refuses. He does not fear her, but he does not want to make her so angry that he gets kicked out of school. That would sadden his mother too much. He likes his other teachers, especially the ones who teach biology, Islamic studies, and math. He loves math. He just learned how to multiply. Ten times ten equals one hundred. He knows that now. He enjoys biology and learning what organs are inside his body. Like the liver. He read about it the other day. He never knew it existed. Now he does.

Everything changed when his father died. The world spun in circles and had no shape. Nothing seemed as it was. There were no people around. No buildings. No ground. Only his family, and they no longer behaved like his family.

His mother still cries all the time and gets angry. It's not true he doesn't listen to her. He listens to her all the time because she is so angry. She hits him before he has time to do what she wants. He grabs her hand and kisses her fingers. "I forgive you," he says. "God bless you," she says and begins crying again.

On my last day in Antakya, Hazim tells me that he met a young woman on a bus who asked him to teach her English. He enjoyed her company and promised to call. He also applied to be a translator with an international aid organization.

His father, on the other hand, has decided to return to Syria. He refuses to wait any longer for the war to end. He wants to teach again, resume his life. If he finds that he can travel safely, he will come back to Antakya for his wife and daughters. Hazim may decide for himself whether to stay or leave.

Hazim worries his father will be arrested. His father had a cousin who was involved with the FSA. The security forces killed this cousin's father, and the cousin said he would not stop resisting the government until Assad brought his father back. "Assad can't bring you this," Hazim's father told the cousin, "only God." "Then I'll continue with the resistance until I die," this cousin said. And he did. He died fighting with the FSA.

Moutasem looks forward to living in Syria. What does it look like? The ground, the buildings? He saw only the inside of a police truck and a jail before. He wants to see this place, the country of his family, his country. "You will," his father tells him. "You will see the Sunni raise the Islamic flag. When it is raised, then we'll have justice. It will be a sweet feeling."

Sarah never thinks of leaving Antakya. She sees Syria in her dreams, but she does not see herself there.

Her friend Farah, however, dreams herself into Syria almost every night. She stands on her grandmother's balcony and looks out at the entire country. There are no people, except one man, her father. He faces her from a distant hill. He appears no bigger than a wavering dot against the skyline. "I'm free," he shouts. "I'm free. I'm coming home."

In his dreams Abd-alrahman runs from the security forces. They chase him, and his father sees them chasing him, but he can do nothing, because in the dreams he is only a street sweeper.

"Stick with your broom or we will kill you and your son, old man," the security forces tell him.

"I will come back for you, Father!" Abd-alrahman says.

He runs into a tall building and closes the door. The security forces surround the building and break down the door. Abd-alrahman bounds up a flight of stairs. He jumps out a window.

"God protect me!" he shouts.

He lands on the street beside his father.

"Father," he says, "run with me and escape!"

"I can't," his father says. "They will kill me and you."

"Just go!" Abd-alrahman says.

They run together. They reach their home. They shut the door behind them. They survive.

PART 3

Home Bound

14

Unpaid Leave

Kabul, Afghanistan: Summer 2011

The reporter scooped a spoonful of canned tuna onto the plastic bag used to line his hotel wastebasket and left it outside his door for the cat. A gardener watering potted red geraniums in the courtyard from a hose nodded at him.

"Salaam alaikum," the reporter said.

The gardener placed a hand over his heart, bowed, and turned away. The reporter licked the fish oil off his fingers and squinted at the scorched sky. Seven o'clock and an oppressive summer heat had already penetrated this, his last morning in Kabul. Glancing around the courtyard, the reporter did not see the cat and doubted it would come by. The cat was an old gray tom that had made the hotel its home. It had eaten the tuna the reporter had left for it two days before, and it had slept at his feet while he typed at his desk, but yesterday the cat refused to eat and instead wandered off to the room of an Ohio contractor who had put out something the cat apparently preferred. The reporter was embarrassed by the envy he felt for the contractor. The reporter knew no one in Kabul other than his translator, Aziz Ahmad. For a brief moment the cat had provided him with quiet company.

The reporter sipped his coffee, stared out his open door, and listened to a woman from the World Food Programme talking on her cell phone above his room. She was inquiring about the cost of a jeep. The reporter smiled. He had shared a table with her at breakfast the other day. She had talked and talked about how she needed to spend $50,000 by the end of the week because her budget was coming up for review. If her supervisor saw she was in the black by fifty grand, he would likely cut her budget for next year. She thought she would buy a pickup or a jeep and list it as a transportation expense. How much did a pickup or jeep cost? Before the reporter could answer, the woman quickly explained that she had been thinking aloud and did not expect him to know anything about jeeps and pickups.

Looking at his watch, the reporter calculated that in about four hours he would start his flight back to the States. Aziz would take him to the airport, and the reporter would have stops in Dubai and Washington, D.C., before he reached his Chicago home. He and Aziz had not worked together for the past ten days while the reporter wrote a series of stories about his recently completed two-week stint embedded with the U.S. Army. But Aziz would expect to be paid for those days. The reporter paid Aziz $50 a day. That would be $500 for days not worked. The reporter thought hard about that.

He rubbed his stiff neck. He had been in Afghanistan for two months and was eager to go home, but he did not look forward to the twenty-seven-hour flight. In the past he'd landed at Dulles International Airport with the odd sense that he was still in Kabul, as if the airport were a memory he had brought with him to Afghanistan and not at all real. It would take him days to wake up in his apartment and not feel a sudden panic. Then he would recognize his bedroom and understand he was no longer in Afghanistan—it would be days before he felt he was back, but he would be home.

The reporter let out a long breath and looked in his passport to see how much Afghan money he had left. Then he counted the remaining U.S. dollars that he had hidden in a pocket of his duffel bag: a daily ritual to assure himself he had enough cash if he was delayed and had to stay a day or two longer than expected. With so much time to kill before his flight, he decided to drink one more cup of coffee, then take a walk. He sat down and heard the buzzing of flies swarming the tuna. He got up again and threw the fish into some bushes, came back inside, wiped his hands on a towel, and sat down once more.

Fucking cat, the reporter said to himself, tossing the towel on the floor. *Fucking contractor. Fucking Aziz.*

One night shortly after the reporter arrived in Kabul, and as a courtesy to a guest, Aziz invited the reporter to his house for dinner. Aziz led him into a small square red-carpeted room. Aziz's four sons joined them. The reporter heard Aziz's wife and two daughters talking in the kitchen. The women cooked, and when the food was ready, Aziz's oldest son carried it out on platters and arranged the platters on a rubber mat on the floor. The women stayed in the kitchen. With their fingers Aziz, his sons, and the reporter ate bread and *qabli,* steamed rice with raisins, carrot, and lamb, and *mantu,* steamed dumplings, and did not speak.

When they finished eating, the two men entertained the sons with stories of their work together. Like the time Aziz and the reporter met with the governor of Jalalabad. The governor offered them watermelon and what the reporter thought was a bowl of sugar. Much to the consternation of the governor, the reporter coated a piece of watermelon with the sugar, only to realize that it was not sugar at all, but salt. He ate it anyway, too embarrassed to admit his mistake. Aziz imitated the altering expressions of anguish on the reporter's face as he forced down the watermelon, and his sons laughed. The reporter laughed with them. They talked and talked, and laughed and laughed, until midnight. Then Aziz drove the reporter to his hotel about ten minutes away. When he dropped him off, Aziz asked him for money to fill his gas tank.

The reporter and Aziz had begun working together in 2004. At the time the reporter paid Aziz for his days off. He considered those payments an investment. Most journalists paid $100 a day for a translator. At $50 a day Aziz was a bargain. Paying him for those days guaranteed he would not work for someone else. And until this trip Aziz had never been off for more than a day or two.

Then, in 2008, the American economy crashed, and the reporter lost his newspaper job and began freelancing. He financed his trips out of pocket, gambling he would be able to sell stories from Kabul, earn back his expenses, and make a little profit. The gambles had paid off, but the margin for error grew slimmer each year. He could no longer afford to pay Aziz for days he didn't work.

The reporter had explained all this to Aziz when he arrived in Kabul two months earlier. Aziz said nothing. The reporter wondered if the man thought that, by explaining, he was bartering, as he had seen Aziz do with merchants in the downtown bazaar. One time Aziz had persuaded a vendor to lower his price on a bag of grapes from the equivalent of 25 cents to 20 cents, for no other reason than the game of making a deal.

How could the reporter explain to Aziz that this was not a game? How could he explain that he needed to earn at least $3,000 a month to meet his expenses and have a little left over to put into his savings, when Aziz and his family got by on so much less? How could he explain that in the United States, a monthly income of $3,000 was not much for a middle-aged, college-educated man?

He tried, but he couldn't. And Aziz behaved as if the reporter had said nothing. On this trip Aziz expected not only to be paid for days he had not worked but for the reporter to fill Aziz's gas tank every time they went out, even if they drove only a few miles. Rather than eat lunch with the reporter, Aziz asked for money so he could eat later. The reporter suspected he pocketed it. Aziz asked him to buy phone cards for his cell phone so he could call the reporter at night and check in. But he never called.

"No problem, my friend," Aziz said when the reporter questioned these expenses. "No problem, Malcolm." However, fearful that there would be a problem, the reporter continued to buy him phone cards and to fill his car with gas and to give him lunch money and to pay him for days he didn't work. The reporter was captive to an unspoken blackmail of his own creation. He was angry with himself, and over the past few days, as he thought more and more about it, his anger had turned into increasing resentment of Aziz.

When he finished his coffee, the reporter went outside and locked his door. Geraniums dripped water on the stone walk, and steam rose from the walk and carried with it the smell of wet grass. He stepped over the gardener's hose and followed the walk to the front of the hotel, pausing to be let out by four security guards.

A rise in insurgent attacks in and around Kabul had prompted the hotel manager to hire the guards. Weeks ago the robbery of a bank security truck downtown had netted its attackers four million dollars. According to news reports, the police watched the robbery but did nothing other than collect some money the robbers threw to them.

The reporter smiled at the guards. "Salaam alaikum," he said. The guards offered him the bread they were eating. According to the Koran, whoever believes in Allah and the Last Day (also called the Day of Judgment) should be generous with guests and provide them with food and drink. The reporter shook his head, declining the guards' offer. One guard stood to unbolt the metal door that opened to the street. The other guards watched. Although his back was turned, the reporter felt them watching him.

"Some people look at you weird," a U.S. soldier told the reporter when he was embedded at Fort Salerno in Khost Province near the Pakistan border. "That kind of stare you get from people because they know you got more than them."

The reporter stepped from the cool dark lobby into the broiling sun. A guard slammed the bolt shut and locked the door behind the reporter, making him jump. He shuddered, and an unreasonable rage seized him. He yelled, "Jesus!" Then exhaustion overtook him, as if he were already worn out from the long flight home. He breathed deeply and regained his composure. He knew he had to make a decision. So make it, he told himself. He would not pay Aziz for the ten days he had not worked.

Shielding his face until his eyes adjusted to the glare outside, the reporter walked from the hotel to Shar-e-Naw, a main thoroughfare that led into downtown.

Blue-glass office buildings of international banks reflected the sun, and the blinding light bounced off the buildings and speared the glossy black Hummers of aid organizations and private contractors racing across the rutted roads. The light bounced again and washed through the dust and car exhaust that congested traffic spewed into the air with the steadiness of a cement mixer.

Drivers honked at men hauling wagons of scrap, at boys selling candy, at begging war widows ghostly and witch-like in their worn burqas, arms outstretched, pale and trembling. Schoolchildren in blue uniforms and white socks walked past the reporter. "Hello, thank you, how are you, good night," they shouted in one long disassociated stream of the few English phrases they knew but did not understand.

Four Afghan soldiers stopped him at an intersection and asked for his passport. Cars jostled for position in the stalled traffic, turning at odd angles to squeeze through, and a pressing layer of heat turned everyone's face into a squinting grimace. The reporter tried to turn away from the noise, the glare, and the grit. He felt pulled apart by the commotion, dissolving atom by atom, so that he barely noticed the soldiers handing his passport back and forth between them, searching its pages for his visa stamp.

One soldier found ten 50-Afghani bills, about five dollars, the reporter had clipped inside his passport. "Baksheesh," the soldier said. Tip. He took one 50-Afghani bill, closed the passport with the rest of the money inside it, and slapped it against the reporter's chest.

"Go," the soldier told him, and pushed him into the tumult of the intersection.

Kabul was not at all like being embedded in Fort Salerno, where he was always among U.S. soldiers.

The fort had been the size of a small gated community. Paved roads ran between rows of square tan huts and square tan storefronts housing restaurants, coffee, and DVD shops. Off-duty soldiers jogged or lingered beneath trees, talking.

From the press barracks the reporter could see a block-long bazaar not far from the trash pit where garbage was burned. A public information officer told him the bazaar was a way to expose the soldiers to the local culture without the fear of being attacked. Outside the base the soldiers never interacted with Afghans—other than in armed patrols.

The reporter had dreaded accompanying the soldiers when they searched villages for weapons caches. Traveling anywhere required riding in armored vehicles on ruined roads and creeping behind slow-moving minesweepers. Barred windows limited visibility outside, and the cramped claustrophobic quarters inside made the reporter squirm.

After hours of driving the patrol would arrive at a village that resembled an illustration from a children's Bible. The mud-brick homes reminded the reporter of Aziz's house. Five rooms, three generations of one family living together. Goats tethered to trees in courtyards amid heaps of hay. Small children running barefoot among squawking chickens. Women covered head to toe in body-length veils revealing the barest glimpse of their darting eyes.

A sense of guilt would overcome the reporter, as if his presence with the soldiers were a betrayal of the hospitality Aziz had offered him that one night when they had laughed together and had enjoyed one another's company, when there was complete trust between them and the reporter had not thought of money or of Aziz's asking for it.

"I'll talk and then you talk," said the lieutenant to an army translator in the first village they had stopped in on that day's afternoon patrol. "Try to build trust, so they come to you and tell us what's going on."

The translator said a few words to an elderly man with a thick white beard. He was the elder of the large family assembled before the lieutenant. The reporter watched a soldier behind the old man hold the butt of his rifle above a wooden trunk. The soldier yelled at an uncomprehending boy that he would break the trunk unless the boy found the key to open it.

"How're things?" the lieutenant asked the old man through the translator.

"Good."

"Insurgents using your home?"

"God damn it—I'll bust it wide fucking open!"

"The Taliban have never been here."

"Six hundred meters from your house, we found an IED," the lieutenant said. "Do you ever talk about the IED problem?"

"I'll break it!"

"People don't talk about it," the old man said.

"Got an intel report that someone riding a red bike is placing IEDs on this route."

"I don't know," the old man said.

"Get your momma and find the fucking key!"

"Motorcycle coming up, sir," a soldier interrupted.

"Anything on them?" the lieutenant asked, referring to the people on the motorcycle.

"I'll break it!"

"A bag in back."

"Check it out," the lieutenant said and turned back to the old man. "People here ever talk about IEDs?"

"People don't talk about it," the old man said.

"They talk about it. You know where the IEDs are or you would be killed. Instead it's us that get killed. Why's that?"

"I don't know," the old man said. "I was a police officer. I lost my job in all the fighting. How do I get my job back?"

"I'll break it!"

"You can work for us as a source," the lieutenant said.

"I'll work. I am tired of having my house searched. What will you pay me?"

"We'll work that out later. Anything going on here?"

"No IEDs here," the old man insisted.

The sharp crack of wood splintering

"Anything?" the lieutenant shouted.

"Clothes," said the soldier who broke open the trunk.

"Why's that kid crying?"

"I don't know, sir. He couldn't find the fucking key, I guess."

Turning back to the old man, the lieutenant stared at him for a long moment.

"No baksheesh unless you give us information," the lieutenant said.

"There're no IEDs here," the old man said. "How do I get my job back?"

The lieutenant ignored him and turned around.

"I'm not paying this guy," he said. "Let's go."

The soldiers and the reporter followed him out, and the old man watched them go, and it wasn't too long before the reporter no longer felt him staring after them or heard the boy crying.

The reporter followed Shar-e-Naw to Chicken Street, Kabul's equivalent of a tourist trap, where carpet merchants dominated. Clogged sidewalks forced people to walk on the street, but fruit vendors jammed the narrow road, and mules hauling wood stood motionless while their drivers shouted at the vendors to move. But the vendors could not move because of the cars backed up behind them, and the shouting and the beeping consumed whatever space existed between people, mules, and cars, and a carpet shop owner waved at the reporter and held his door open for him.

The reporter ducked through a curtain into a cool room filled with the damp musty smells of wool. A bare lightbulb hanging from the ceiling flickered weakly beside a strip of greased paper thick with stuck flies. Folded stacks of multihued red, brown, green, and blue hand-stitched carpets stood in tall piles against the walls. Some fringed tan carpets with tightly woven green triangular patterns caught his attention.

The shop owner offered the reporter a cup of tea, and the reporter sipped the hot tea and felt the steam dampen his face. The shop owner asked about his family. "Everyone is fine?" "Everyone's fine," the reporter said. "Yours?" "Very fine, thank you," the shop owner said. The reporter nodded. Small talk. The merchant was waiting for the reporter to offer him a price for a carpet.

"I'm not going to buy anything," the reporter said.

"No problem, my friend," the merchant said. "Just look."

An hour later, back in his room, the reporter stood over his bed as he stuffed a red carpet into his duffel bag.

Carrying the duffel bag from his room to the courtyard, he sat down in the limited shade offered by a torn table umbrella and ordered a Coke. The gardener's hose lay coiled on the ground. Petals from the geraniums had fallen on the walk and curled from the heat. He did not see the tomcat. He faintly heard someone speaking English but could not determine from where. The day's burdensome heat flattened the slightest sound, until what noise he heard was disembodied from everyone and everything.

The Ohio contractor, sitting at one of the plastic tables across the courtyard, saw the reporter and raised a hand, and the reporter picked up his bag and walked over and sat with him.

"Leaving?"

"Yeah," the reporter said.

"Wish I could," the contractor said.

His salary as an electrician moving from one U.S. Army combat outpost to another was more than 200 grand a year. His mother had cancer, and he wanted to get home, but "the money, man, the money was too good." He had two kids in their twenties out of work. They lived in his house but didn't help with the mortgage. "Spoiled is what they are," he said. He was dating a gal who flashed him when they talked on Skype. She expected him to send her money. "I'm paying for her, believe me," the contractor said.

A waiter brought the reporter his can of Coke and the reporter snapped it open. As he tipped the can to his mouth, he saw Aziz coming up the walk in a white *salwar kameez,* a long tunic over pants, and leather sandals. His black hair was combed back and looked wet. He gave the reporter a broad smile. They embraced, kissing one another on each cheek.

"How are you, my friend?" Aziz said. "Good to see you, Malcolm."

"And you," the reporter said.

"I'm sorry I didn't call you."

"You were busy with your family, I'm sure."

"Yes," Aziz said.

The reporter introduced him to the contractor, who excused himself and walked to his room. Aziz watched him go, then turned back to the reporter, who offered to get him something to drink, but Aziz refused.

Aziz smiled as the reporter sipped his Coke. They sat together without talking. The unspoken issue of money lingered between them. It would be discourteous for Aziz to ask a guest about his salary. The reporter knew Aziz would wait to be paid at the airport.

Finishing his Coke, the reporter stood and picked up his bag, but Aziz took it from him.

"Are we ready?" Aziz said.

"Yes," the reporter said.

They followed the walk into the hotel lobby. The reporter left his key on the front desk. He listened to it click against the counter in the vacancy of the empty lobby. A half-filled aquarium chortled on a shelf, and two goldfish floated motionless behind a scrim of algae. A vague sort of loneliness filled the reporter as he anticipated telling Aziz that he was not going to pay him for the days he had not worked.

They left the lobby, walking together past the guards to Aziz's car, and the reporter watched him open the trunk and heft his duffel bag inside. He got in the passenger seat. Aziz slammed the trunk shut, rocking the car.

Aziz followed Shar-e-Naw to Airport Road just east of Chicken Street and city center, passing billboards advertising "Armoured Vehicles to Buy or Lease." Aziz slowed for a military checkpoint. A soldier leaned in Aziz's open window. Aziz gave him loose coins collected in an ashtray. The soldier closed his hand around the coins and waved Aziz through without looking at him.

"Any time now an explosion can happen," Aziz said. "Two, four, six in the morning. Sometimes ten o'clock at night. Our government is very stupid. After an explosion, it secures the road, but it is too late. The bad people have gotten away."

The reporter made no comment. Traffic was much lighter than he had expected and they reached the airport in fifteen minutes instead of the more typical half hour. Security guards stopped them at the entrance. Aziz and the reporter got out so the guards could pat them down.

Then Aziz popped the trunk with a lever by his seat, and the guards asked the reporter to open his duffel bag. Aziz watched him pull back the zipper and looked with the guards at the contents of the bag. The reporter's clothes covered his carpet. The guards patted the clothes, felt the sides of the bag. They motioned to the reporter to close his bag, and he and Aziz got back into the car.

Driving about a half-block farther, they stopped again, opposite a luggage-screening office. The reporter opened his door. After he got his bag Aziz would park and meet him inside the airport.

Aziz leaned over and stopped the reporter before he got out of the car and reached to shake his hand. His look told the reporter that he wanted to be paid here instead of inside the airport around a lot of people. The reporter took Aziz's hand. He knew Aziz expected him to have his money hidden in his palm, concealing it from possible onlookers.

Withdrawing his hand, Aziz shoved it in his pocket out of habit before he took it out and looked at his empty palm.

"My salary?" he said.

"We didn't work the past ten days, Aziz."

"I picked you up at Bagram after your embed," Aziz said, referring to the U.S. airbase sixty miles outside Kabul.

"That took no more than an hour. And I filled your gas tank."

"My salary," Aziz said again.

"We didn't work," the reporter said, his voice rising, the sound reminding him of when he was a boy standing up to a bully.

Aziz stared over the steering wheel.

"I can't," the reporter said. "Not this time. I explained this to you before."

"Some of my salary, then," Aziz said. "You can pay me the rest on your next trip."

"No," the reporter said. "There's no salary for days you didn't work."

Aziz sat motionless. Then he got out of the car without another word.

The reporter walked around to the trunk and hoisted out his bag. Aziz did not offer to help. "We'll meet inside," the reporter said, but Aziz said no. He did not want to pay for parking. The reporter offered to pay, but Aziz had already begun getting back inside the car. He shut his door and turned the ignition. The reporter closed the trunk. He lifted the duffel bag over a shoulder and walked toward the screening office. He heard Aziz drive away.

A security guard told him to put his bag on a conveyor belt. Together they watched it roll through a curtain and inside a square metal contraption. The conveyor belt stopped, and another security guard stared intently through a window that showed the oblong shape of the duffel bag and the outlines of the reporter's folded clothes and carpet. A third security guard asked the reporter for his passport.

When he handed it back, the conveyor belt started again and the reporter's bag rolled through and fell to the floor. An old man the reporter had not seen earlier picked it up. The reporter thanked him and took it from his hand, and the old man followed him outside toward the terminal.

"Baksheesh," the old man said.

The reporter faced him. He smelled tobacco on the man's breath and the hot odor of his sweat beneath his soiled clothes and said no and continued walking. "Baksheesh!" the old man called. The reporter continued walking. Running up behind him, the old man balled up his fist and punched the back of his head. Stumbling forward, the reporter weaved drunkenly, dropped his bag, and fell to one knee. The old man shouted something and spit, then stomped off.

Glancing toward the parking lot, the reporter hoped Aziz had changed his mind. Taxis shimmered in the heat. A few luggage porters and some cigarette vendors wandered about, and children begged by the parking lost entrance, but the reporter did not see Aziz.

He picked up his bag and followed a walk inside the airport. The lobby was empty except for one security guard. The reporter paused to rub the back of his head. He wondered how angry Aziz really was. He remembered seeing him shout at a merchant and call him a thief when the merchant refused to lower his price for a bag of rice. Then days later he hugged the same merchant, kissing him on both cheeks. Bartering was a sport, the reporter had concluded then, the outrage part of the strategy.

He tried to assure himself that Aziz would e-mail him in a few days as if nothing had happened and ask about his flight. The reporter would come back to Afghanistan, and they would work together again. Aziz would know the reporter was no longer a naive Westerner who could be taken advantage of endlessly. They would move on. They would have an understanding.

As the reporter prided himself on his new assertiveness, the airport security guard stopped him and held out his hand. The reporter showed him his passport and ticket. The guard barely considered either one.

"Baksheesh?" he asked.

The reporter stared at the guard and then at the grimy crooked floor tiles beneath his feet. Looking up, he reached into his pocket and gave the guard fifty Afghanis and kept moving.

15

City of the Dead

Cairo: April 2011

Her crimped fingers uncoil one by one against the gnarled restraints of her arthritis. With what little flexibility remains in the nearly petrified muscles, the fingers crab walk across the rumpled sheets of her bed; they probe forward, as would a spider on ruined legs, toward a brown bottle of medicine she takes for ailments whose names she has long since forgotten.

As I look at her claw the bottle to her chest, I can hardly believe that Thoray Hamdan is just sixty years old. Her eyes are cloudy from cataracts; her polio-afflicted legs, thin as loose ribbon, lie folded beneath her wasted body. Face jowly, voice thick and rough. She turns in my direction, eyes unseeing. I tell her I will leave her some money before I go. Thoray mutters a verse from the Koran that bestows blessings I don't understand.

She reminds me of my mother. At ninety-four and bound by arthritis herself, and blind in her left eye, my mother sits marooned in one spot on the living room sofa during the day and reads the newspaper, a slew of prescribed medications for her heart, blood pressure, and stomach in a frayed plastic shopping bag by her side. A glass of water stands on a coaster on the end table near her cane. Sometimes my mother looks up from the newspaper and asks, "What is green energy?" "What is Google?" "What is an iPhone?"

Outside Thoray's door chickens strut around the tomb of Basha Mohammad Retab, a towering stone castle-shaped edifice in the middle of a sooty walled-in courtyard. Thoray has lived beside the tomb for thirty years but has no idea how old it is. Two hundred ten years, maybe 150 years. She cannot say.

Thoray grew up in Cairo but never married. She had lived with her brother downtown when she was younger. When he died, another brother told her about this place, City of the Dead, at the edge of downtown. He worked here cleaning graves, including the Retab tomb. No squatters at the time had claimed the burial site, he told Thoray. "Come and live here for a while," he said. "Please, make it your home. It will cost you nothing."

Thoray's brother convinced her, and along with a widowed sister and a niece she moved into the Retab mausoleum. In those days, she recalls, there was a garden in the courtyard. Back then the descendants of the Retab family owned one hundred acres of farmland outside Cairo. They sold crops and used some of the money to maintain the tomb. Then, in the 1950s, President Gamal Abdel Nasser nationalized private property, and the Retab family lost most of their property and could no longer afford to care for the tomb. They removed a glass chandelier that had hung above it and donated it to a mosque, leaving a hole in the ceiling now filled by bats. As far as Thoray knows, the Retab family has not been back since. Their distant relative lies in his grave, forgotten.

The four-mile-long City of the Dead stands below the Mokattam Hills in southeastern Cairo in an area known as al-Arafa. The earliest graves date to 642 B.C. The thick network of bald domes of many of the mausoleums slopes above the four walls enclosing the cemetery and gives the impression of a small neighborhood, which indeed it has become. Here poor families unable to afford Cairo's high rents have turned house-like tombs into homes. The narrow alleys twisting through the cemetery have no names other than those of the people who live on them. "I will meet you in the place where the Shafi family lives," someone might say. "No, let us meet in the place of the Pasha family."

Thoray lives on the street of the Gabaly family in a room that would have belonged to one of the servants responsible for the upkeep of the Retab tomb. A short narrow hall wrapped in dampness and shadow leads into the crumbling room where she sits on her bed. Off to one side, a space in the wall provides enough room for a bucket beneath the wood frame of a chair: her toilet. One of her nieces carries her to the chair when the need arises. Thoray would much rather have someone lift her out of this place, but most of her family is deceased, including her widowed sister, and she suspects that whoever might still remember her outside the City of the Dead no longer asks about her.

By her bed on the floor I notice some newspapers with photographs of demonstrators and a radio held together by thin rubber bands. I ask Thoray if she had followed the eighteen-day protest in Cairo's Tahrir Square earlier in the year that led to the ouster of President Hosni Mubarak.

"No," she says. "I would be the last person the revolution would have thought about."

Next door, in the larger of the two servants' quarters, lives Ramadan Sueiman, Thoray's niece. When I emerge from Thoray's door, Ramadan scowls and grips a broom in both hands. I apologize for intruding, explain I'm a journalist. She nods, tells me thugs from neighborhoods far from the City of the Dead race through on motorcycles and scare her. Strangers arouse suspicion. She does not go out alone.

Ramadan's husband works in Saudi Arabia as a plumber and earns about $300 a month. They met in the City of the Dead, where he also grew up. He sends what money he can home to his family. "Good for nothing," Ramadan says of his earnings. The money does not cover living expenses anywhere but in the City of the Dead.

Ramadan has lived in these servants' quarters since she was three months old. She knew she was living among dead people even as a small girl. She felt their spirits hover around her, propelling her to clean the courtyard of fallen leaves and bird droppings; when she finished sweeping, the presence of the spirits abated for a time, but a sense of past lives remained.

As she got older, Ramadan grew used to the spirits and no longer felt compelled to do their bidding. She came to understand that the dead could do nothing about the deteriorating tomb, no matter how they hectored her, anymore than she could change the circumstances of her family.

On occasion but not often, men hired by the government stop by and rake the grounds and trim dead vines snaking downward from low-slung tree branches. Sometimes a government man in a suit and tie will stop by and give Ramadan two dollars to clean the tomb herself. But he does so only rarely.

Ramadan wonders whether the sweeping she still does on and around the tomb is the same kind of work the servant who lived here did. Probably. The servant remains unknown to her, enigmatic. No clues have ever surfaced to suggest who he or she was. The servant must have had a family, however. Three rooms surround a large living room Ramadan has filled with rugs and plump pillows. A television set stands in one corner with a hanger for an antenna. Despite its being a tomb, Ramadan's home, I tell her, resembles a small apartment.

"Yes," she agrees, "this place does looks like an apartment." The same but different. In an apartment she would not be afraid at night. After the sun sets here, she does not allow her three daughters outside, even in the courtyard. No one is around. It is too silent, too dark. There is little light even when the moon comes out. Although she no longer listens to spirits, she does not trust them.

I tell Ramadan that I grew up in a Christian family that was a big believer in spirits, although we called them saints. My mother still prays to St. Christopher to keep my brother and me safe and to St. Anthony whenever she can't find her glasses. She says she believes in heaven and hell. Yet lately she has begun wondering aloud about the existence of a hereafter. Perhaps because she has lived longer than she ever expected. At ninety-four she appreciates that she won't last forever. That indeed the end can't be that far off.

"Where do you think we go when we die, if at all?" my mother asked me one night.

"What did you tell her?" Ramadan asks me.

"That I had doubts we go anywhere."

"You are like my daughter who doubts everything," Ramadan says.

The daughter in question, eighteen-year-old Amisi, participated in the protests at Tahrir Square against her mother's wishes. Ramadan blames her husband for their daughter's activism. When he is home, she says, he always talks about poor people, asking rhetorically how can Egypt be so harsh to its sons and daughters and allow only a few to have so much. He admired Nasser and what he called the dictator's socialist acts on behalf of labor.

But Ramadan concedes that it was not just her husband who has influenced their daughter. Amisi had experiences of her own at an early age that politicized her. When she was about thirteen, a police officer stopped a bus she was taking to visit a friend. He beat the bus driver and took his money. Amisi began shouting at him and then ran off the bus. Amisi told her mother she could not concentrate for the rest of the day.

At the time of the protests Ramadan locked Amisi in her room to prevent her from participating. Amisi screamed through the shut door that her mother was a typical stay-at-home Egyptian wife who knew nothing of the world. She went on a hunger strike for two days until Ramadan relented and released her.

"What if you go down there and die?" Ramadan asked Amisi.

"Someone will tell you I died a martyr," her daughter said.

Amisi stayed in the square until the night President Mubarak resigned. Then she came home. "Everything has changed in Egypt," she told her mother.

"Nothing has changed here," Ramadan said.

Amisi helps her mother cook and wash laundry. She sweeps the courtyard, raising clouds of dirt. She does not want to stay in the City of the Dead, Ramadan knows, but Mubarak or no Mubarak, it is still all the family can afford.

"My husband and I were so excited when he got the job in Saudi Arabia," Ramadan says. "We were young. We had just one daughter. At that time—" She shrugs and stops talking, and I am left standing in her home, smiling stupidly without a clue as to what I should say.

I consider giving Ramadan some money, as I had Thoray. But doling out change too easily becomes a trap. Who do I not give it to? How much am I helping? Years ago I challenged myself about giving and left a fourteen-year social work career when I concluded I was doing little more than applying Band-Aids to urban problems beyond my comprehension. I had stopped believing my work would change anyone's life.

Now, as my brother and I look after our mother, I deal with matters that have no grand social vision but that do allow for concrete results. I make sure my mother's bills are paid, that the home health-care giver is prompt and reliable, that my mother takes her pills and gets to her doctor appointments.

After dinner I dial the phone for her so she can call one of her few remaining childhood friends. "Hello, Anita, how are you feeling?" she shouts. The conversation always begins with questions about Anita's health. Anita suffered a stroke last year and no longer walks. "I'm the same," Anita says. Then my mother segues into "Do you remember?" and launches into a memory of their childhood together in New York City.

I feel lost listening to just my mother's end of the conversation. I want to hear how Anita fills gaps in the story and learn something I may not know about my mother. I hear the crack and wheeze of Anita's voice through the receiver, the strain in it, and then my mother interrupts, "What did you say, Anita?" and the tortuous process for her to push past her near deafness and understand Anita and reclaim the past begins anew. After a while I quit my eavesdropping and leave the room, my mother's small voice raised once more behind me: "What did you say, Anita?"

Ramadan watches me as these thoughts of my mother distract me. I notice her puzzled expression and shake my head loose of my mother and apologize. "It is nothing," she says. Despite my rationale against handing out money, Ramadan's hardship moves me. I leave her a few dollars, which she accepts with a bow of her head. She follows me to the gate of the tomb, and I walk out onto a dusty street in the stark heat of midday. A man a few feet ahead hears me and turns around. He introduces himself as Fathy Mohammad. He is short and stocky and has on torn jeans and a worn T-shirt. He has a crushing grip when he shakes my hand. He tells me he grew up in the City of the Dead on the street of the Abdelazim family. His father was paid to bury people here, but he never earned enough to live outside the cemetery.

When Fathy was still a boy, his relatives told him ghosts wafted out of the tombs like steam from a kettle. Fathy snuck into the Retab tomb next door to see for himself if this was true. He did not see any steam. He felt a heavy silence and the manifestation of unseen things.

Now he believes that no one sees spirits or ghosts. You feel them instead, just as he did that night as a boy. Years later, when he was about thirty, he was walking through one of the alleys of the City of the Dead when he felt invisible hands grip his ankles and hold him to the ground. He panicked and did his best to run, but the hands held firmly, and he ran as if he had lead in his shoes, until finally the hands let go and he jerked forward and sprinted away. He believes he passed the tomb of someone who must have died a horrifying death, and the person's spirit was seeking vengeance on the living. Nothing like that ever happened to him again.

Every morning about five o'clock, Fathy sits beneath an overpass near the City of the Dead. There he waits with other day laborers for someone to pull alongside him in a truck and offer him work. A mallet with twelve steel spikes bound to it by a thick ring of rubber lies at his feet. For twenty years he has worked on construction sites.

Since the revolution it has taken about a week for Fathy to get one job, and it lasts no more than seven days. Contractors are not hiring. Egypt is too insecure. Everyone hoards money. Construction is all fucked up. If Fathy had some land, he would work it like a farmer. He accepts any job. Carrying bags of cement, carrying sacks of gravel, carrying steel rods. Anything. The new government needs to provide the unemployed with compensation or land to farm, Fathy complains.

By midmorning, if no one offers him work, he walks to the City of the Dead and spends the rest of the morning in the tomb that was his childhood home. Maybe an old employer will contact him on his cell phone. If not, Fathy will return to the underpass after lunch.

A lord, Basha Rashad, is buried in the tomb. The tomb has slowly sunk into the bare ground. Gold lettering glints in the sun from the top of the tomb. Fathy can't read and does not know what it says. Empty birds' nests take up corners in the cracked dome ceiling. Fathy knows of better tombs to use as a resting place, but this is where his family lived. He left the City of the Dead in 2010 when he met his wife. Her family had money and helped them rent an apartment they can no longer afford.

As Fathy rests, he takes a radio from beneath a cot and listens to the latest news of the Supreme Council of the Armed Forces, which now rules Egypt. The council has arrested Mubarak. "What about jobs?" Fathy says aloud.

He followed the revolution from the start. He argued with his wife, who opposed it. "If something bad happens to the country because of the revolution, I'll call the police and tell them you supported it," she told Fathy. He ignored her and watched the protesters on Al Jazeera. He told his wife the revolution would provide for guys living in graveyards and working day-labor jobs. At the time he truly believed that.

In the afternoon, his cell phone silent, Fathy picks up his tools and prepares to leave the tomb and walk back to the overpass. Across the street Fatima Ahmad stands in the front door of the tomb where she lives and watches Fathy and me leave. He compliments her garden of cactus, guava, and jasmine. Fatima smiles, throws a bowl of soapy dishwater onto the street, and turns to go inside. I ask her if I can see her home. She hesitates and then nods, and I fall in behind her, the cool stone floor of the tomb absorbing her bare wet footsteps.

Fatima's father and mother moved to the City of the Dead in 1941 when he lost his job and could no longer afford his apartment. As a girl Fatima used the three graves that fill the interior of the tomb, where she now hangs buckets, for hide-and-seek. These days a stove, a sewing machine, and an ironing board cluttered with lettuce and cucumbers take up one corner of the tomb; in another corner connected to a generator stand a refrigerator and washing machine. Dishes fill a listing metal cabinet. The largest of the three graves supports two mops dripping with the rainwater that came through the broken tiles of the roof earlier in the day. Laundry lines stretch behind the tombs, sagging with rain-dampened sheets. Behind the sheets a narrow hall leads to what was a servant's room and is now Fatima's bedroom.

Fatima knows nothing about the three dead people who share her living quarters: El Hag el Fouzy, Yousef Pasha Fakher, and Tafida el Basry. Their graves rise toward the ceiling and are almost like small castles with spires and narrow columns. A long time ago Fatima knew a little about them, but she doesn't remember anything at this point. She does recall that family members of the deceased would visit from time to time. They did not seem to mind the rags and bottles of laundry soap wedged into nooks and crannies of the graves. She doesn't remember the last time they came. Years and years ago.

Yousef Pasha Fakher is buried beneath the largest grave. He was an officer in the Egyptian army. Fatima knows this because of the royal stamp and two crossed swords chiseled beneath his name. What moment of history did he live through? What wars did he fight? Fatima shrugs, embarrassed.

Her ignorance reminds me of how unaware I am of my own family. Sometimes my mother will ask me, "Do you remember so-and-so?" and I don't. So-and-so might be one of my mother's cousins or a great-uncle long since dead. Maybe I met them as a boy, maybe I didn't. The memory of so-and-so might prompt my mother to talk about "the war." Halfway into the conversation I realize she means World War II, not Afghanistan and Iraq.

Like my mother, Fatima did not leave home until she married. My mother's marriage lasted sixty-two years, until my father's death in 2009. Fatima's husband died early in their marriage. She returned to the City of the Dead and her parents' home with two baby daughters. Today the daughters are twenty-two and twenty-five, married, and live in northern Cairo. They both work as receptionists, and Fatima can only hope their husbands do not die. It would be difficult for them to move back to the City of the Dead, as it was for her, but Fatima had no choice. By herself she could not afford the apartment she had shared with her husband.

The other day Fatima participated in a City of the Dead wedding. After the celebration the newlyweds entered the tomb they would share as a couple and that had been decorated with flowers by their families and other guests like Fatima. She hopes this couple will be like a few other families who save money and leave the City of the Dead. Two years ago a medical student, an engineer, and their wives and children moved out. During the revolution someone torched the tomb they had lived in.

Fatima does not know why someone would do that. Maybe the people who burned the tomb were celebrating Mubarak's resignation. Maybe they liked Mubarak and were angry he was overthrown. Maybe they didn't know how to stop protesting.

This last possibility makes sense to me. I can only imagine that the adrenalin rush of toppling a government would be hard to control. The unrestrained energy could all too easily be released in destructive ways. I remember my own reactions just watching the first days of the Tahrir Square demonstrations on television thousands of miles away in Chicago. My heart pounded as I saw the crowds grow day after day; pounded at the idea of so many young people standing up to a police state, while at the same time in the United States ideological posturing among politicians increasingly struck me as tired, manipulative, and so beyond the point of anything having to do with anything. I wanted to be in Cairo. To be part of something inspiring not just to Egypt but the entire world.

Every night as I watched the news from Tahrir Square, my mother remained in her spot on the sofa reading the newspaper. One evening she asked me, "What in God's name is a tweet?" Before I could answer, she glanced at the television and said, "What is this you're watching?" I explained the uprising in Cairo as best I could. She responded by telling me that her family had visited Egypt in 1925 when she was eight years old. In those days you traveled aboard ships, she said. There were no passenger planes. She remembered her brother sitting on a camel, his arms crossed over his chest, while she and her mother rode donkeys, because they were afraid of heights. About the Tahrir Square demonstrations taking place nearly ninety years later, she had no comment.

Fatima first heard about the protests on the radio while she was gardening. She went inside and prayed for the martyrs. These many months later she does not know what will be next for Egypt. Like the dead buried around her, her life is done, Fatima says. Egypt's future lies with the next generation. She will remain in the tomb of El Hag el Fouzy, Yousef Pasha Fakher, and Tafida el Basry without heed to the mystery of their lives and will worry instead about the hole in the roof.

I reach into my pocket and withdraw a $5 bill. To help with the roof, I tell Fatima, but she shakes her head no. I shake the bill in my hand, insistent. Please, I say. No, Fatima says with another more emphatic shake of her head.

An ache runs up my outstretched arm, and I shove the money back in my pocket and look at my watch. It's getting late, but it will be early afternoon in Chicago. When I return to my hotel, I'll call my brother and ask about our mother. I imagine her sitting in self-imposed exile in her spot on the sofa reading the newspaper but really just waiting. Waiting out her life, disturbed by the mystery of so much that transpires beyond her understanding.

For myself I have years ahead to seek achievable ideals.

Credits

These stories first appeared, some in different versions, in *Ascent Magazine* ("The Dead Lieutenant," December 2011; the introduction, first published as "How It Begins," December 2012); *Guernica: A Magazine of Art & Politics* ("Missing," October 2010; "Bed 18," January 2011; "Pyramid Schemes," June 2011; "Revolution Download," April 2013; "Maybe the Children Will Forget," first published as "Assad's Castaways," May 2013); *McSweeney's* ("Who Is in the Power?" December 2009); *New Letters* ("City of the Dead," fall 2012); *Southampton Review* ("Unpaid Leave," spring 2012); *Superstition Review* ("Securing District Four," spring 2012); *Vice Magazine* ("War Wounds," first published as "Broken Hearts, Lost Minds, and Missing Limbs," December 2012); *Virginia Quarterly Review* ("Beneath Us the Ground Still Moves," summer 2006; "African Promise," winter 2007; "You Cannot Tell from the Expressions on Our Faces What We Are Feeling," summer 2009; "Here Everything Is Poison," fall 2010).

About the Author

Photo by Dave Anderson

J. Malcolm Garcia's latest books include *Most Dangerous, Most Unmerciful: Stories from Afghanistan* (2022) and *A Different Kind of War: Uneasy Encounters in Mexico and Central America* (2021). His stories have been featured in *Best American Travel Writing* and *Best American Nonrequired Reading*.